From 'Foreign Natives' to 'Native Foreigners'

From 'Foreign Natives' to 'Native Foreigners'

Explaining Xenophobia in Post-apartheid South Africa

Citizenship and Nationalism, Identity and Politics

Michael Neocosmos

CODESRIA

Council for the Development of Social Science Research in Africa

First published under the CODESRIA Monograph Series, 2006
© CODESRIA 2010
Council for the Development of Social Science Research in Africa,
Avenue Cheikh Anta Diop, Angle Canal IV
BP 3304 Dakar, 18524, Senegal
Website: www.codesria.org

ISBN: 978-2-86978-307-2

Layout: Hadijatou Sy
Cover Design: Ibrahima Fofana
Printed by: Graphi plus, Dakar, Senegal

Distributed in Africa by CODESRIA
Distributed elsewhere by the African Books Collective, Oxford, UK.
Website: www.africanbookscollective.com

The Council for the Development of Social Science Research in Africa (CODESRIA)
is an independent organisation whose principal objectives are to facilitate research,
promote research-based publishing and create multiple forums geared towards the
exchange of views and information among African researchers. All these are aimed at
reducing the fragmentation of research in the continent through the creation of thematic
research networks that cut across linguistic and regional boundaries.

CODESRIA publishes a quarterly journal, *Africa Development*, the longest standing
Africabased social science journal; *Afrika Zamani*, a journal of history; the *African Sociological
Review*, the *African Journal of International Affairs*; *Africa Review of Books* and the *Journal of
Higher Education in Africa*. The Council also co-publishes the *Africa Media Review*, *Identity,
Culture and Politics: An Afro-Asian Dialogue*; *The African Anthropologist* and the *Afro-Arab
Selections for Social Sciences*. The results of its research and other activities are also
disseminated through its Working Paper Series, Green Book Series, Monograph Series,
Book Series, Policy Briefs and the *CODESRIA Bulletin*. Select CODESRIA publications
are also accessible online at www.codesria.org.

CODESRIA would like to express its gratitude to the Swedish International Development
Cooperation Agency (SIDA/SAREC), the International Development Research Centre
(IDRC), the Ford Foundation, the MacArthur Foundation, the Carnegie Corporation,
the Norwegian Agency for Development Cooperation (NORAD), the Danish Agency
for International Development (DANIDA), the French Ministry of Cooperation, the
United Nations Development Programme (UNDP), the Netherlands Ministry of
Foreign Affairs, the Rockefeller Foundation, FINIDA, the Canadian International
Development Agency (CIDA), IIEP/ADEA, OECD, IFS, OXFAM America, UN/
UNICEF, the African Capacity Building Foundation (ACBF) and the Government of
Senegal for supporting its research, training and publication programme.

The right of man to liberty ceases to be a right as soon as it comes into conflict with political life, whereas in theory political life is only the guarantee of human rights...

(Marx, *On the Jewish Question*, 1844, MECW3: 165)

Contents

Preface to the First Edition

As this work progressed, it became apparent that what was required in a study of xenophobia in South Africa today was not an empirical assessment of its extent, which by all accounts is indubitably (although contradictorily) widely prevalent in society as well as within state institutions, neither a description of its characteristics, as there are plenty of these already, but rather an explanation for its existence. Empirical studies of xenophobia in the country are in fact extensive and detailed. On the other hand, existing explanatory accounts are deficient as they are primarily asocial and apolitical, and hence are unable to suggest ways of overcoming the problem. Therefore, overwhelmingly, they tend to metaphorically throw their arms up in explanatory impotence. The core of this particular account must be explanatory if it is to make a contribution to our understanding. Fieldwork in the form of interviews with (mainly West) African immigrants to South Africa was undertaken in both Johannesburg and Pretoria in 2003, but this provided qualitative data which generally corroborated that of other studies, while at the same time providing greater ethnographic detail to popular experience. There was nothing particularly original or novel here. Much more important was to attempt an account of xenophobia which could combine theoretical sophistication with historical sensitivity. It is this which has been attempted in this work.

Some comments regarding the title may be appropriate at this stage. Archbishop Desmond Tutu ('the Arch') used to make speeches in the 1980s wherein, in his customary manner, he would chuckle at jokes and encourage his audience to do the same. One of his favourites was the point that apartheid referred to Black South Africans as 'foreign natives' as it maintained that they were not South Africans but 'Transkeians', 'Bophutatswanans', 'Vendans' or whatever. How could such a thing be? Was not this a contradiction in terms, an indication of absurd logic? Tutu would note. This logic was indeed absurd, but not much more absurd than any other state politics which, while adhering to a conception of citizenship as equivalent to indigeneity, attempts simultaneously to draw distinctions between different sections of the population living and working within the country. On the other hand, I use the term 'native foreigners' to refer to those Black South Africans in our new South Africa who, because they conform to the stereotypes which the police and home affairs officials have of 'illegal foreigners' today (their skin may be 'too dark' or whatever), arrested along with more genuine foreigners. The epithet is also applicable to South Africans of Asian descent who are often told that they do not belong in the country by xenophobic politicians in Natal. This shows that the absurdity continues. These expressions suggest not only that citizenship and xenophobia are manufactured by the state, both under apartheid and post-apartheid forms of rule, but also indicate a transition between two different forms of xenophobia, simultaneously with a continuity between state practices. These expressions imply the centrality of citizenship in understanding the phenomenon of xenophobia.

The main argument of this work, has been influenced by the philosophy of Alain Badiou for whom politics must be understood fundamentally to be a militant emancipatory practice, a prescriptive universality vis-à-vis the necessarily particularistic political prescriptions of the state which is always that of a dominant minority. The argument here is fundamentally that xenophobia in South Africa is a direct effect of a particular kind of politics, a particular kind of state politics in fact, one which is associated with a specific discourse of citizenship which was forged in opposition to the manner in which the apartheid state interpellated its subjects. This statist notion of citizenship has been buttressed by a 'Human Rights Discourse' for which the politics of agency are substituted by appeals to the state for redress. It follows then that the solution to xenophobia cannot be found in state policies and hidden state prescriptions nor indeed can it be addressed by appeals to a mythical 'Human Rights Culture'. It can only be overcome through political prescriptions of a truly universal kind.

This book is divided into three chapters and a conclusion. The first which also serves as an introduction, outlines abstractly and in some detail, the theoretical perspective to be followed. The second, which is mainly historical is concerned to trace the origins in detail of the different perspectives of citizenship as they arose around the struggle for and against the apartheid state. The third chapter discusses xenophobic discourse today, as a direct outcome of state practices as structured both by the practices of the apartheid state, as well as by the discourses developed by the nationalist movement, and systematically reproduced by the legislative and daily practices of the post-apartheid state. The bulk of empirical evidence on xenophobia today is included in this third chapter. Finally, in the conclusion, I return to a discussion of the centrality of politics for any serious understanding of xenophobia in South Africa and indeed elsewhere.

I am grateful to CODESRIA for funding the research on which this book was based, to Francis Nyamnjoh for encouraging me to undertake this research project, to Jude Fokwang for undertaking excellent qualitative interviews with West African migrants in Pretoria and Johannesburg, to Jonathan Mafukidze for surfing the web, and to the CODESRIA leadership for showing patience when the constraints of bread and butter work and the exigencies of intellectual endeavour threatened to derail my meeting of deadlines.

Preface to the Second Edition

The fundamental reasons for a second edition of this book were the events of May 2008, which could only be described as systematic pogroms against 'foreigners' in many South African townships. These violent events left 62 people dead at least, and displaced thousands more, leading to introspection in the press regarding the violent re-assertion of social differences which the country, it was felt, had been able to overcome through its reconciliation process 14 years previously. The surprise expressed at the violent expression of xenophobia was nevertheless a clear result of ignorance of the evidence over the past 15 years or more, some of which had already been outlined in many reports by NGOs and state agencies included in this book and elsewhere. As a result, it was thought opportune to include a new chapter in the form of an epilogue which has been devoted entirely to explaining these specific events.

Yet, this book had not really addressed the violent expression of xenophobic sentiments because at the time of its writing (end 2005), this had only occurred in isolated incidents. What the book sought to explain then was the pervasive and predominant xenophobic attitudes within South Africa. It did so in terms of the development of a dominant political subjectivity over time. The organiser so to speak of this political subjectivity was to be the state and its various institutions, and it was also noted that while state discourse and practice was overwhelmingly xenophobic, the attitudes of South Africans were much more contradictory as there also existed evidence for a certain amount of 'xenophilia' among a minority of the population.

The core of the book argues that xenophobia should be understood as a political discourse and practice. As such, its historical development as well as the conditions of its existence must be elucidated in terms of the practices and prescriptions which structure the field of politics. In South Africa, its history is intimately connected to the manner in which citizenship has been conceived and fought over during the past fifty years at least. Migrant labour was 'de-nationalised' by the apartheid state, while African nationalism saw the same migrant labour as the foundation of that oppressive system. However, only those who could show a family connection with the colonial/apartheid formation of South Africa could claim citizenship at liberation. Others were excluded and seen as unjustified claimants to national resources. Xenophobia's conditions of existence, the book argues, are to be found in the politics of post-apartheid nationalism where state prescriptions, founded on indigeneity, have been allowed to dominate uncontested in conditions of an overwhelmingly passive conception of citizenship. The de-politicization of an urban population which had been able to assert its agency during the 1980s, through a discourse of 'human rights' in particular, contributed to this passivity, it is argued. State liberal politics have remained largely unchallenged. As in other cases of post-colonial transition in Africa, the hegemony of xenophobic discourse, according to the book, is to be sought in the character of the state consensus. The core argument of the book ends by asserting that only a rethinking of citizenship as an active political identity could begin to re-institute political agency, and hence, begin to provide alternative prescriptions to the political consensus of state-induced exclusion.

It would appear then that the events of May 2008 could possibly be seen to undermine the argument above, as here were the poor seemingly exercising their agency albeit in a manner contrary to the main argument of the book. Can the pogroms of May then be described as the exercise of popular agency? According to one author at least, 'the xenophobic discourse current in South Africa today represents the authentic effort of the subaltern classes to make sense of their conditions: nor is their reading irrational'. Not only is it not a 'false consciousness' inculcated by right-wing elites mobilising ethnic sentiment for their own political interests, it is 'profoundly democratic, albeit in the majoritarian sense ... the truth is that popular democracy in action is not a pretty sight'. The vulgarity of these assertions is simply quite staggering. The poor are authentically xenophobic, we are told. Reading on, the idea seems to be not only to make us grateful for our liberal democracy which 'provides institutional protection from the immediate expression of popular passions', we should also be thankful for not living in an African 'basket case' where leading politicians have been manipulating national sentiment (Glazer, 2008: 54-6). It is difficult to think of a more crass supposedly intellectual 'reflection' on the pogroms. Of course, none of these statements are backed up by any evidence whatsoever. Most are simply false. At the same time the author can conveniently use the occasion to take a swipe at supposedly cherished 'leftist' accounts and their extolling of the virtues of the masses. Thank God for sensible liberalism, the people (read the middle-class in the suburbs) can feel safe in its embrace and sleep quietly at night, knowing that the state is looking after their interests and protecting them from the mob. It is difficult to think of a cruder journalistic opinion piece.

What beggars the imagination is the poverty of thought for which if there is no evidence of crude manipulation by elites, then the crypto-fascism (a severe term perhaps but I can think of no other one) to be found among subaltern classes must be somehow 'authentic' and essential to the life of the poor. Are we to believe that this is because nativist exclusion is also authentic? That it is primordial and thereby inherent in African society, even though all the evidence from tradition ('invented' or not) shows that African cultures had sophisticated mechanisms for integrating strangers? In actual fact there can be no such thing as an authentic politics. To state as much is to advance the crudest reductionism which the author wishes to point to in others. What is interesting about these otherwise vacuous statements is that they are precisely located within the exceptionalist view of South Africa which I show below constitutes one of the conditions of existence of xenophobia, not least among the middle classes. The pogroms, it seems, were an expression of a rational popular agency, even though it may not have been a morally defensible one. We need not look any further, the political choices of the poor mean that ultimately this is a problem of the poor who should be kept in their place; afterall the middle classes, however xenophobic they may be, are far too civilised to do their own killing.

Can the poor then be seen as exercising their agency when they killed their fellow poor and thus contributed to their own exclusion and oppression? What I argue in this book is that this was indeed a political choice, but if we are to speak of agency, then it must be considered as the 'agency of zombies' as Francis Nyamnjoh would put it. After all, choices are made in relation to the limits of existing hegemonic political subjectivities, and in the absence of clearly formulated alternatives, it is the state which is the main creator and organiser of these. As Mamdani (2001) has pointed out in his analysis of the genocide in Rwanda, ethnic and national identities and differences can become institutionalised. The systematic differential treatment of citizens and foreigners in South Africa for many years, some having the right to rights and others not (*de facto* if not always *de jure*) has had similar effects. The various political actors in this country have allowed its political culture to provide the foundation for xenophobic and inter-ethnic violence. A choice exercised within such parameters is in fact a simulacrum of agency, a pseudo-choice; in reality it is no choice at all for it requires no thought, but the mechanical reiteration of the logic and statements of those in power. This is borne out empirically in the book which follows.

Thus, if such subjectivities have become so hegemonic, so consensual that the majority of South Africans of all classes, racial groups and genders maintain similar xenophobic attitudes as attitude surveys show, then it would indeed be surprising if the majority of the poor (like the majority of the rich) were not bound by the same assumptions, the same questions and the same solutions. This no more implies a 'subaltern authenticity' than the apparent favouring of the death penalty by the majority of South Africans also implies authenticity. The fact of the matter is that many among the poor, as I show in some detail, resisted the dominance of hegemonic xenophobic discourse and provided political alternatives in practice, and even in one case, in theory. To do so, they had often to challenge the state consensus itself. The politics of xenophobia are therefore the outcome of struggles in society and to simply go along with state propagated ideologies – and hence to assert the authenticity and naturalness of nativism - is to fail to exercise a choice beyond the limits of these ideologies when such a choice is indeed possible. It is a failure to understand that what we are told is impossible can indeed be possible. At the intellectual level, it amounts to evacuating the possibility of thought beyond determination by state, class, race or ethnicity. It is to fall headlong into the ideology of given essentialisms for which nothing outside the obviously extant can be done. The intellectual is particularly guilty herself when, knowing precisely that society is generally oppressive of the other, she chooses to do nothing and simply waits for a disaster to occur before expressing her humanitarian concerns. As one of the characters in Marcel Pagnol's brilliant novels *Jean de Florette* and *Manon des Sources* states: 'those who knew and did nothing are equally guilty'. It would be difficult for many middle class South Africans to wriggle out of this, despite their subsequent expression of solidarity with the thousands of displaced in the period following the pogroms.

Apart from a few minor corrections, the original text of the first edition remains unaltered. The epilogue to the book constitutes an attempt to extend and develop the arguments of the main text, to put political subjectivity explicitly at the core of the explanatory framework. In addition to those mentioned in the preface, I wish to express a deep debt of gratitude to Ernest Wamba-dia-Wamba for helping me to form my political thinking around the work of Alain Badiou and Sylvain Lazarus in particular, to Richard Pithouse for constant encouragement, and to Never Lungu for helping me understand a little of some of the terrible experiences which a Zimbabwean refugee has to confront in South Africa. I also wish to thank, from the bottom of my heart, KS and KN for always being there.

Michael Neocosmos

CHAPTER ONE

Introduction:
Accounting for Xenophobia
in Post-apartheid South Africa

> Between resounding assertions of the unity of the continent and this xenophobic–
> behaviour of the masses which has its inspiration in their leaders, many different
> attitudes may be traced. We observe a permanent see-saw between African unity
> which fades quicker and quicker into the mists of oblivion, and a heart-breaking
> return to chauvinism in its most bitter and detestable form (Fanon 1990: 126).

Xenophobia: Absence of Theory, Absence of Politics

By all accounts, the South African society has experienced a massive problem of
xenophobia since its liberation in 1994, a problem which is particularly shocking
given the massive international support for the struggle against apartheid, particularly during the 1980s. This xenophobia is directed overwhelmingly at Africans from
all over the continent while some nationalities, for example Nigerians and
Mozambicans, are singled out, particularly in the press, as being associated with
illegal activities (drugs and illegal immigration respectively). An increase in xenophobic hostility directed at those who are deemed to be non-citizens amounts to a denial
of rights and entitlements, expressed through prejudice and stereotypes. It manifests
itself through incitement to and actions of obvious exclusion, hostility and violence
against people just because of what is deemed to be in the specific context, their
'foreign' status. The fact that this exclusion and discrimination impacts on South
African citizens also, simply because 'foreign' status is declared on the basis of the
crudest of racist stereotypes, suggests that the issue is not only one applicable to
'foreigners' as defined by legal discourse (*Mail and Guardian*, 3-9 March 2000). Rather
it is a form of discrimination closely related to racism and liable to affect anyone or
any group which for whatever reason is considered non-indigenous or non-autoch-
thonous. Migrants who come to the country for political or economic reasons (the
two are often indistinguishable) are regularly associated, particularly in the state
discourse emanating from the press, with crime and criminal activities, while their

attempts to secure economic survival is also criminalised. The use of the term 'illegal' is often employed in conjunction with 'immigrant' to intensify their de-humanisation. This discriminatory treatment is time and again justified on the basis of the economic and social crises facing South Africa where around half of the population is said to live in poverty. This has been said to have resulted in the deepening social exclusion of and violence towards 'foreigners'. As under apartheid, 'foreignness' is apparently recognisable by physical characteristics, and the police force in particular is notorious for exercising its power so as to extort funds from the politically vulnerable and powerless 'foreigners'. A Human Rights Watch (HRW) report from 1998 identified the problem precisely:

> South Africa's public culture has become increasingly xenophobic, and politicians often make inflammatory statements that the 'deluge' of migrants is responsible for the current crime wave, rising unemployment, or even the spread of diseases. As the unfounded perception that migrants are responsible for a variety of social ills grows, migrants have increasingly become the targets of abuse at the hands of the police, the army, and the Department of Home Affairs. Refugees and asylum seekers with distinctive features from far-away countries are especially targeted for abuse (HRW 1998: 4).

We should note here the stress on the role of politicians and state institutions in the making of a culture of xenophobia, a point to which I shall return in detail in a later chapter. However this 'public culture' has filtered down to the whole of society. In fact, xenophobia seems to have become so prevalent among all sections of the population in post-apartheid South Africa that it has led one recent analyst to comment:

> Negative attitudes [...] are so pervasive and widespread that it is actually impossible to identify any kind of 'xenophobe profile'. In other words, the poor and the rich, the employed and the unemployed, the male and the female, the black and the white, the conservative and the radical, all express remarkably similar attitudes. This poses a significant problem of explanation because it runs counter to the more general belief that certain groups in a population (usually those who are or who perceive themselves to be threatened by outsiders) are more prone to xenophobic attitudes than others. It also provides a massive public education challenge not only of knowing where to begin but also in deciding who to target (Crush and Pendleton 2004: 2).

Interestingly this comment was made with reference to a survey of a representative sample of urban residents in five Southern African Development Community (SADC) countries undertaken in 2001-2, and is intended to apply not only to South Africa, but to Botswana and Namibia as well. These three countries are the receiving ones for migrants from the region, as they have expanding economies and are contiguous to countries which are in deep crisis or have a history of emigration (for example, Zimbabwe, Mozambique, and Lesotho). South Africa, Botswana and Namibia also have large percentages of their populations living in poverty, which may account for some of the perceived threat from immigrants, an inaccurate perception which is regularly used as a factor for explaining xenophobia. At the same time the results of the survey also noted that across the region, citizens were prepared 'to accept and welcome non-citizens if their economic impact is demonstrably positive' (Crush and Pendleton 2004). In other words populations are less prejudiced than is sometimes thought. However, all three countries are also mentioned in a positive light in the literature as the three shining examples of liberal democracy in the region if not on the continent, although rarely in this context of overt discrimination. It is therefore not impossible that some connection could exist between liberal democracy and the prevalence of xenophobia, and that the latter is not solely to be associated with obviously authoritarian regimes, although this question has rarely been asked.

The connection between liberal democratic politics and xenophobic attitudes is one which I shall have occasion to return to in the course of this work, but at this stage I only wish to note that the last quotation stressed the inability of a demographic or statistical perspective to account for such widespread prejudice among these populations. Moreover it assumed that the problem of xenophobia can be resolved through state-run public education programmes. Such opinions are widespread in the literature, yet what if it was state institutions themselves and the subjectivity which they propound which were at the fundamental root of the problem? What if state discourse itself was fundamentally xenophobic because of a specific political history and practice? Perhaps then, in order to understand and indeed to resolve the question, we would have to look elsewhere than in statistical evidence. If the aetiology of the problem is connected to the politics of state power, then it seems unlikely that a state-led education programme could hope to provide a cure, at least not on its own; what may be required is a different form of politics.

In fact, the difficulties faced by existing attempts to explain xenophobia are accurately expressed by the extract above although much of the empirical work having been undertaken by NGOs is not so much concerned with intellectual understanding, but more with ensuring that foreigners in South Africa can access their 'human rights', something which is seen as the responsibility of the state under pressure from these same NGOs (HRW 1998, Harris 2001, SAHRC 1999, LHR 2004, Reitzes 1997b).[1] A Human Rights perspective militates against explanation and understanding for it appears to provides a ready-made 'solution' which requires little intellectual effort. The dominant assumption is that, irrespective of what the causes of the prevalence of xenophobia may be, the existence of a Bill of Rights in the South African Constitution means that such rights should be applicable to all, even though the constitution itself is far from universal as we shall see. Rigorous explanations are not so much what matters, rather it is a question of the application of the law by the appropriate state organs, although it is regularly stated in the same breath that 'contemporary legislation regarding foreigners is underpinned by racism and prejudice' (Harris 2001: 49). In hegemonic discourse then, the question ends up being conceived as a matter of law and its enforcement by power, but not one of politics, of power relations themselves, and this even though it is agreed, as Human Rights Watch stresses above, that it is mainly state institutions, legislation and personnel which are the most obviously guilty of xenophobic practices.

When some explanations have been attempted, these have been woefully inadequate. For example, having usually asserted that xenophobia is a new phenomenon linked to the transition to liberal democracy in South Africa, it is often speculated that the frustrations expressed in the form of xenophobia result from some form of 'relative deprivation', a gap between people's aspirations of what they feel entitled to, and what they are in fact getting (Morris 1998; Tshitereke 1999). Another favourite account is to refer to South Africa's history of exclusion from the rest of Africa, so that foreigners represent the 'unknown'. The creation of a brutal culture of hostility towards strangers by apartheid means that South Africans are unable to tolerate difference (Morris 1998). Finally the old favourite of racism is adduced to account for xenophobic discrimination as Africans from beyond South Africa's borders are easily identified as the 'Other' given their accents, physical features and their apparently idiosyncratic clothing styles (ibid). The general problem with all these attempted accounts is their methodological individualism and their fundamentally speculative nature. Why we may ask if people feel economically deprived should they scapegoat foreigners? Surely this must have something to do with both the political weakness of 'foreigners' and with the failure to blame others such as whites, the bourgeoisie, politicians or even capital (domestic or foreign). In other words it should tell us something regarding the presence or absence and character of people's political identities which are influenced not only by 'transition', whatever that may mean precisely, but fundamentally formed by state discourse and interpellation, including statements of numerous organisations such as trade unions, political parties or churches inter alia within the 'public sphere'.

Moreover such accounts tell us absolutely nothing regarding the xenophobic practices of state institutions and their employees vis-à-vis others whom they define as 'foreigners' in specific circumstances. There is no denying the fact that racist exclusion as well as economic and political crises prevail in South Africa. However these do not get to the root of any explanation as reference to them does not help us to understand why these prejudices are directed towards African foreigners as opposed to, say, European foreigners. There is of course a dominant arrogant political discourse held by many South Africans of all racial groups regarding the apparent exceptionalism of the country on the African continent, a discourse which forms part of South African nationalism. According to this perception, South Africa is somehow more akin to a Southern European or Latin American country given its relative levels of industrialisation, and now increasingly of liberal democracy (Mamdani 1996).[2] In this view, Africa is some kind of strange backward continent characterised by primitivism, corruption, authoritarianism, poverty and 'failed states', so that its inhabitants wish only to partake of South African resources and wealth at the expense of its citizens (Harris 2001). There is little doubt that this is one characteristic among many of a South African nationalism propagated by state discourse, but it is not always clear why this may be so, or indeed why such a discourse would become hegemonic. This is particularly so as it used to be maintained by the liberation organisations in the 1980s that foreigners, especially in the form of migrant labourers from the region, were instrumental in building South African industry – especially its mining industry – in the first place. The point remains, why should South African nationalism take a form which is exclusive of those living beyond its colonially established boundaries, rather than a more inclusive form? It is sometimes forgotten that miners citizens of Lesotho were given citizenship voting rights in South Africa in 1994, in other words it is forgotten that the post-apartheid state could indeed adapt legislation regarding citizenship to make it more inclusive when it wished to do so. An exclusionary conception of the nation and citizenship was not an inevitable outcome in post-apartheid South Africa.

Another feature of South African post-apartheid political culture, which combines with exceptionalist ideologies, is its complete out of hand rejection of any notion of 'group rights' because of the development of a nationalism which in many ways is the simple mirror image of apartheid nationalism. Because apartheid oppressed the people via a notion of group rights, it is maintained that only an individualistic notion of rights can be 'democratic'; anything else is seen as a sop to apartheid ethno-culturalism. It is not understood that rights depend on context, and that a rights discourse can be used to maintain privilege as well as to undermine it, depending on context. What this has meant is a complete capitulation to hegemonic neo-classical notions of individual freedom although these sit ill at ease with collective positive discrimination policies such as 'Black Economic Empowerment' and 'Affirmative Action'. For the present argument, this stress on individualism has meant that South African nationalism has exhibited a visceral antagonism to 'group rights' as a threat to the nation, much as in post-colonial Africa after independence. This antagonism is not unrelated to a perceived threat from 'foreigners' as both are seen as threatening the unity of the nation, the former through division, the latter through invasion. At the same time Affirmative Action and Black Economic Empowerment discourses, both understood as processes of individual accumulation, contribute to a culture of entitlement among the new middle-classes, much as Fanon had observed. The outcome is a contradictory mix of nationalist and individual arrogance and entitlement at the expense of the rest of the world, particularly Africa.

There is little doubt that nationalism is an important component of xenophobia, but the reasons for nationalism exhibiting such a particular form need to be explained as this form is neither obvious or natural, particularly as many foreigners were directly involved in the liberation of the country; and also given the integration of the Southern African region many South Africans, including many of those in leadership positions, are of 'foreign' origin. Clearly exclusion is not simply directed against 'foreigners' but against those who seem to correspond to stereotypes of the stranger in specific situations, especially that from Africa. This pre-supposes a conception of citizenship founded on indigeneity or autochthony which, given the long history of migration in the region, is not evidently the case. In order to understand the politics of indigeneity in South Africa it is not particularly useful to begin from state conceptions of the 'nation', or of 'migrant', or of 'immigrant' which are taken for granted or 'obvious' in most analyses. These conceptions have been usually

created for specific purposes, say for those of legislation. Thus the distinction between 'economic migrant' and 'political migrant' or 'refugee' is a legal distinction
which was developed in Europe relatively recently for the purposes of restricting
access to Western economies by job seekers. The fact that the South African state
has emulated this distinction does not mean that it is a real one for migrants who
may lose their jobs at home because of political reasons. One needs to critique and
transcend such state categories if one wishes to provide a coherent explanation of a
xenophobic discourse which by most accounts originates from the state itself. This
means providing a theoretical explanation which is firmly located within the field of
politics. This suggests that a distinction needs to be drawn between state discourse,
state politics, state categories, and popular ones, the former consisting of rigid categories – typically legal ones – and the latter being more fluid and much more
evidently the objects of contestation.

Xenophobia: Bringing Theory and Politics Back in

The link between the nation state, post-coloniality, autochtonous notions of 'belonging' and political identity is stressed in a recent article by the Comaroffs (2001).
Here they comment on what they claim to be three key features of post-colonial
polities in the era of globalisation, namely the 'reconfiguration of the subject-citi-
zen', the 'crisis of sovereign borders' and the 'depoliticisation of politics'. The authors draw a parallel between the moral panic surrounding the cause of bush fires
around Cape Town in January 2000 which was put down in the local press to the
pervasiveness of alien plant species which burned more fiercely than local ones, and
the fear of strangers. While this parallel is indeed mildly amusing and informative,
the authors stretch it to draw conclusions regarding the construction of a 'public
discourse' for which anxieties surrounding 'foreign' plants are extended to 'foreignness' in general. They ask: 'to what anxieties, interests, historical conditions does the
allegory of alien-nature, the allegory fed by fire and flood, finally speak?' (ibid: 644).
The answer they give is that a 'cluster of implicit associations and organic intuitions
that, as they surfaced into the public sphere, gave insight into the infrastructure of
popular consciousness-under-construction' (ibid: 645). Analogies are excitedly made
between fear and blaming of alien plants by the press in Cape Town, and xenophobia throughout the country. The idea then is that the demonisation of plants can
provide 'insights' into a discourse which demonises migrants as both are being 'othered'.
What insights may these be, and how may they increase our understanding?

There is little doubt that the Comaroffs' observations are so wide-reaching that
they often hit the mark. It is indeed the case as they observe, not only that the
allusions regarding aliens in the public sphere 'flow from the naturalisation of xenophobia' (ibid: 645), but also that state institutions adhere to a contradictory discourse, on the one hand upholding volubly 'the standards of liberal universalism,
insisting on the uncompromising protection of human rights', on the other contributing 'to the mood of xenophobia' (ibid: 647). The thrust of their argument then is
to draw out the construction of national 'meanings' by 'public institutions' such as

the press and the government (they rely overwhelmingly on extracts from the press for their evidence). In doing so they attempt to draw some theoretical conclusions, 'whatever that may mean at this moment in the history of Western social thought' with regard to 'post-colonial polities' in general (ibid: 649). All these theoretical generalisations are put unsurprisingly down to a change from modernity (the first phase of post-coloniality) to post-modernity and globalisation at a world level (the second phase, from 1989 to the present), and to the contradictions endemic in the pursuit of decidedly 'modern policies' in such a fundamentally changed post-modern context.

These polities they argue exhibit 'three notable features'. The first is a move away from a 'homogeneously imagined community of rights-bearing individuals towards one in which difference is endemic and irreducible' (ibid: 649, emphasis in original). In other words according to them there has been at a global level in general and within post-colonial societies in particular, a recent change from a notion that attachment may be acquired in different ways (ascription, immigration, residence, naturalisation) 'toward the primacy of autochtony' (ibid). The second is a contradiction resulting from the globalised phase of modern capitalism which impinges on national sovereignty, between the need to keep borders open to allow the free flow of commodities and the need to 'serve the material interests of a national citizenry' as well as those of local capital and the state which require some border restrictions (ibid). A third and final feature is the now widely noted 'depoliticisation of politics, their displacement from the realm of the social and the cultural, the moral and the ideological, into the technical, apparently value-free dictates of the market - and its attendant forms of economic and legal "rationality"' (ibid).

While many of these observations are indeed apt and to the point, they remain fundamentally speculative. It is not evident precisely why a conception of citizenship reduced to autochtony or indigeneity is apparently so prevalent today. This is usually put down to globalisation and the more intense struggle for resources, the rights and entitlements to which are more successfully secured through such identities (Geschiere and Nyamnjoh 2000). But this fundamentally takes the existing balance of power relations as given, as if there are no competing experiences either within or outside the 'public sphere' to such identities and politics. Clearly there is no doubt that states find it difficult to pursue what they often deem to be the national interest within a globalised economy, but the apparently overwhelming power of globalisation is simply repeated like a mantra, rather than serious attempts being made to confront this external imposition, either through regional cooperation and/ or through greater reliance on popular power for example. In any case, why should the 'national interest' of the South African citizenry be to uphold chauvinism? A strong argument could be made that it is not so, as chauvinism and racism weaken popular struggles. To simply understand the popular interest as given by the 'interests' of the market as the Comaroffs do is fundamentally false (not to say frankly reactionary), and to simply re-iterate the contradiction between modern policies and a post-modern context does not enable us to ask questions regarding alternative truly democratic politics. What would 'post-modern policies' look like anyway?

The last comment regarding the technicisation or indeed 'naturalisation' of politics today is an important one, but it is scarcely a feature of the post-modern period. What was the whole idea behind state-planning in the early post-colonial period if not the technicisation of politics? Although most developed in India, development planning was prevalent throughout the post-colonial world (not to say in the whole social democratic post-Second World War world) and central to the ideology and functioning of the 'developmental state'. In fact, it can be argued that the de-politicisation of politics has a much longer history apparent in what Foucault (2000) called 'governmentality' and which Chatterjee (2004) has recently used as a way of understanding popular politics beyond the 'public sphere' and civil society in the post-colonial world precisely. Considerations of space preclude a detailed discussion of these concepts here and I have undertaken such a discussion elsewhere (Neocosmos 2005). Briefly, it can be usefully noted that Chatterjee (2004) draws on Foucault's distinction between sovereignty and governmentality to specify two distinct modes of rule. Under sovereignty, the legitimacy of state rule is secured through a certain amount of participation by citizens in the affairs of state. Indeed classical liberal theorists of the state (in particular Rousseau and J. S. Mill but others also) stressed the importance of participation by citizens, as did the French Revolution of course. Under governmentality on the other hand, it is the provision of resources to the population which becomes the dominant mode of securing state legitimacy. This form of rule becomes dominant in the twentieth century for Chatterjee, although Foucault stresses its appearance much earlier. The provision of resources to sections of the population is what gives rise to the disciplines of demography and statistics (stat(e)-istics).

This latter mode of rule, it could be said, becomes crucial under colonialism in Africa which, like development itself, was as Cowen and Shenton (1996) show, dominated/justified by a notion of 'trusteeship'. The state becomes a trustee of the welfare of its colonial (as well as of its metropolitan) charges. Similar notions are of course evident in T. H. Marshall (1964) and his three forms of citizenship, which provide the main theorisation for British social democracy. The social democratic state now legitimises itself through the provision of social services, in particular social rights on top of the civil and political rights central to all liberal democratic states. In the conditions of the post-colonial state, this notion became clearly reflected in the 'developmental state' whereby the latter secured its rule through the provision/delivery of 'development'. This argument also suggests the technicisation of politics by the state, as governmentality gives rise to and is congruent with such technicisation of politics, and it also shows how politics is expelled from the sate by technique, especially managerial technique (Neocosmos 1995).

It is worth noting that the Comaroffs' argument largely operates through analogy and juxtaposition of statements, and tends to substitute the use of language for intellectual rigour. No distinction is made between say debates in the press in Cape

Town and the rest of the country (why should the moral panic in Cape Town over alien weeds have an impact on the 'national psyche' anyway?), an important fact in South Africa where 'public spheres' and cultures are quite regionally demarcated. No distinction is made between state discourses and other discourses from say trade unions or churches, between popular experiences and state discourse, in sum between the various elements of a socially disaggregated country. The argument operates on the basis of a spurious homogeneity, to produce a mélange, or should I say 'pastiche', of images which is singularly unhelpful for thinking explanations of xenophobia through nation, state and politics in the country, let alone what this means for democracy. Despite its often perspicacious observations, the argument simply amounts to sophistry like much of the trendy post-modernism within which it situates itself.

The Comaroffs do indeed make one important point which is that xenophobia should be accounted for in the post-colony in a specific manner, different from any account of xenophobia in a European context, but they are mistaken when they put this phenomenon down to an effect of the condition of post-modernity. There is in actual fact evidence that xenophobia was prevalent in post-colonial Africa in the immediate post-colonial period of the 1960s, a fact which was extensively discussed by Fanon in *The Wretched of the Earth*, particularly in the chapter entitled 'The Pitfalls of National Consciousness'. I briefly wish to turn to this account in order to elucidate what could be learnt from it for the present study.

Xenophobia then is not so much a problem of post-modernity as such, but rather one of post-coloniality in particular, a phenomenon which Fanon squarely connects to the politics of the dominant groups in the period following independence. It is therefore for him a problem of political consciousness, a consciousness which is inimical to the majority of the African population even though they may partake in it. In *Studies in a Dying Colonialism*[3] Fanon provided a detailed study of different changes in social relations brought about by popular struggle. These included changes in the position of women in society, the effect of independent radio stations and changes in the family. Within this period, his comments on citizenship contrast radically with his later account of the same issue under post-colonial conditions. Writing in 1959, i.e. during the Algerian liberation struggle and before his work on *The Wretched of the Earth* he states:

> ... in the new society that is being built, there are only Algerians. From the outset, therefore, every individual living in Algeria is an Algerian. In tomorrow's independent Algeria it will be up to every Algerian to assume Algerian citizenship or to reject it in favour of another (Fanon 1989: 152, emphasis in the original).

In other words, the point made is that during the period of popular national upsurge, citizenship is a unifying, inclusive conception. No distinction whatsoever is made between people on the basis of indigeneity but only on the basis of their living in the country. By the time he writes *The Wretched of the Earth* and observes the effects of post-colonial state nationalism, Fanon's account of citizenship has shifted. Now the prevalent chauvinism and racism towards other Africans in the post-colony is seen as an effect of the politics of a particular form of nationalism, that of the middle-class or national bourgeoisie. He argues that this class is primarily interested in 'stepping into the shoes' of the departing European colonialists and occupying their positions, taking over their jobs and owning their companies. They have no interest in 'transforming the nation' but simply of 'being the transmission line between the nation and capitalism' (1990: 122). 'On the morrow of independence' the 'native bourgeoisie':

> violently attacks colonial personalities... It will fight to the bitter end against these people 'who insult our dignity as a nation'. It waves aloft the notion of the nation-alization and Africanization of the ruling classes. The fact is that such actions will become more and more tinged by racism, until the bourgeoisie bluntly puts the problem to the government by saying 'We must have these posts'... The working class of the towns, the masses of the unemployed, the small artisans and craftsmen for their part line up behind this nationalist attitude; but in all justice let it be said, they only follow in the steps of their bourgeoisie. If the national bourgeoisie goes into competition with the Europeans, the artisans and craftsmen start a fight against non-national Africans... From nationalism we have passed to ultra-nationalism, to chauvinism, and finally to racism. These foreigners are called on to leave; their shops are burned, their street stalls are wrecked, and in fact the government... commands them to go, thus giving their nationals satisfaction (ibid:125).

As a result, he states 'there arises a "permanent see-saw between African unity... and a heart-breaking return to chauvinism in its most bitter and detestable form"' (ibid: 126). For Fanon then, there had been a shift from citizenship as a unifying notion during the struggle for independence, a struggle which also possessed a strong eman-cipatory and pan-African component, to citizenship in the post-colony which is now founded on a notion of indigeneity and is essentially exclusive. In fact if we did not know better this could easily be a description of changes in South Africa between 1984 and 1990, and especially since 1994 and the establishment of post-colonial liberal democracy when, within the public sphere, the celebration of Africanism and an 'African Renaissance' has alternated with xenophobic statements and practices towards other Africans.

It would be facile to dismiss Fanon's arguments as 'class reductionist'. There is clearly a chauvinist effect of national class accumulation which plays itself out in post-colonial conditions. But there is much more to Fanon's arguments than that, as he is in fact describing a particular form of nationalist discourse, in other words an ideology, politics and practice which equates nationalism with access to economic resources for accumulation by an aspiring middle class. This is something which the newly independent state is expected to enable, as the basis of the claim for such resources is indigeneity, in relation to the outsiders/foreigners and not to the oppres-sors as such, for many nationals would also be oppressors. It is as a consequence of such politics then (a particular kind of nationalism of the bourgeoisie) that for Fanon, chauvinism and xenophobia grips the masses as they feel entitled to simply do the same – to claim the resources occupied by foreigners as their own. Of course, within the context of such politics, what provides you with the power to claim these resources is indigeneity, hence it is usually directed against those foreigners in positions of political weakness, the seemingly non-indigenous. To this kind of politics, Fanon counterposes Pan-Africanism of a popular kind in which the people participate directly in the management of the country 'for they do not slow the movement down but on the contrary they speed it up' (ibid: 152).

Precisely what this means is not developed as Fanon still operates within the confines of the ideas of his time, seeking salvation in 'the combined effort of the masses led by a party of intellectuals who are highly conscious and armed with revolutionary principles' (ibid: 140), although he also clearly understands how the party of nationalism after independence 'sinks into an extraordinary lethargy' (ibid:137) and gradually becomes bureaucratised melding with the state (ibid:146). This faith in political parties should however not been held against him, for Fanon shows not only the visionary capacity to analyse the characteristics of chauvinism and xenophobia after independence in Africa, but also the analytical depth to understand its fundamental character. This understanding is that it is about politics and particularly the politics of the powerful, of the ruling classes and the post-colonial state, so that it exhibits a fundamentally undemocratic character.

In more recent years, the centrality of a political explanation for political identity and citizenship has been stressed in the work of Mahmood Mamdani (especially 1996, 2001). Mamdani's work will be returned to in the next chapter but at this stage it is important to note one major point. This is that he stresses the need to analyse politics in political terms, not as a derivative of economics or culture for example, and that this perforce applies to the formation of political identities in general and to that of citizenship in particular. This I believe to be a major step forward in African studies both intellectually and politically. Where I differ as I shall presently make clear, is in Mamdani's understanding of what is political. In his first important book in this context (Mamdani 1996), he was concerned to explain how the 'mode of rule' during the colonial period ended up continuing in all fundamental respects in the post-colonial period, and to argue as I shall show in the next chapter, that apartheid can only be understood as a form of the colonial state. What is important for our present purposes is simply to note that for Mamdani, European settlers who had citizenship rights in colonial Africa and the African majority who were rurally based and ruled via tradition and customary law, experienced different forms of citizenship (rights-bearing citizens, ethnic subjects) as a result of legal engineering by the colonial state.

Thus, while moving beyond a liberal conception of citizenship at one level due to the fact that he recognises a concept of 'ethnic citizenship' beyond the individual rights-bearing subject, at another level, Mamdani ultimately remains the prisoner of the assumptions of this same liberalism in his reduction of citizenship exclusively to a state-defined identity. What I mean in particular is that while he is fundamentally correct not 'to see political identities as derivative of either market-based or cultural identities' (Mamdani 2001: 23), he sees such identities as 'a direct consequence of the history of state formation, and not of market or cultural formation' (ibid: 22). More precisely, he stresses, if we wish 'to understand how "tribe" and "race" and by extension "nation" got animated as political identities, we need to look at how the law breathed political life into them' (ibid: 20). This perspective is pursued at length in his more recent work where the colonial state is seen as constructing or making political identities through legal interpellation (Mamdani 2001: passim, 2002: 500).

The difficulty with this notion of creation of identities by the state (colonial or otherwise) is that it tends to equate popular identity with state interpellation. In other words it tends to be assumed, because of the absence of detailed analysis of politics beyond the state domain, that subjects simply respond (more or less) automatically to the manner in which they are addressed by the state. People in Rwanda accepted the characterisation of the colonial state as to whether they were an 'ethnic group' or a 'race'. The difficulty here is that this process of political interpellation by the state takes place in society and not just at the level of the law and other state institutions. The political process is also a social process. This means that it is mediated by cultural and political prescriptions (the two are/were intertwined in African tradition) in various forms, and also that it is the object of struggle; the state, in order to secure its dominance in society, usually requires certain groups in society (often even beyond civil society) which follow its 'line' or general perspective. The sociology of this process is absent from Mamdani's work, although he is regularly sensitive to the fact that not all members of political identities were comfortable with such ascription and challenged it (for example, minorities among both Hutu and Tutsi, Banyarwanda etc).

To put the point slightly differently, these identities for Mamdani result from the manner in which the colonial and post-colonial states have addressed people as ethnic or tribal subjects and have institutionalised such identities over time. These identities then provided the conditions for mass slaughter in Rwanda. Now, despite its undoubted originality in that it accounts for the genocide in that country in terms of political identities (as opposed to economic or psychological forces), what this argument seems unable to account for is the politics of those Hutu who protected and saved Tutsi from certain death (and vice versa), and there are many instances of this in the literature (see for example Gourevitch 1998; Cohen 2001). In other words, what remains unaccounted for is the possibility of an alternative politics in the specific situation of Rwanda in 1994 because Mamdani's overriding concern is state politics and state induced subjectivities. It therefore becomes difficult if not impossible to think an emancipatory politics from such a perspective. My point should not be understood as an argument for the replacing of state politics by say the politics of social movements in analysis, the former being labelled as negative and latter as positive; there is no a priori reason for the politics of social movements to be democratic. Rather the point is to emphasise the necessity to analyse all forms of politics emanating from state and society, from the perspective of an emancipatory politics (Neocosmos 2005).

It must be emphasised that the process of acquiring political identity is itself the result of struggle and that as I have noted, the state requires 'interests' within society to pursue its agenda of creating tradition, a point made at length by historians (for instance, Vail 1989a; see also Neocosmos 1995). First among such 'interests' was precisely the chieftaincy, which was not only a political institution as stressed by Mamdani, but also crucially a cultural one. This meant that culture was closely intertwined with politics in tradition, with the result that the colonial state's political interpellations had authoritative cultural support, and thus resonated much more effectively than if the chieftaincy had been exclusively political. Although Mamdani is methodologically correct to stress that political identities cannot simply be derived from cultural ones, so that a political analysis is required, the intertwining of culture and politics under tradition in Africa was a fundamental reason for the colonial state's prescriptions being so successfully accepted by colonised populations, and for why the same state insisted on identifying tribe with ethnicity, politics with culture. But this process was not one which went without contestation, as women, youth, the poor and other dominated groups within the particular identity challenged (often in hidden ways) its definition imposed by the state in alliance with chiefs, men, the wealthy and other dominant groups. The resistance of women in particular has been documented in the literature (see Schmidt 1990 inter alia).

The acquiring of political identities is often a long and complex process of struggle without an understanding of which it becomes difficult to see not only how alternatives to the state politics of essentialist interpellation (particularly as autochthony) can exist, but also how the different representative forms of this politics (religious, ethnic and other cultural forms) operate. The result is that they may become unrecognised as the politics they often are. Mamdani's theoretical position, despite the brilliant insights it produces, tends to be limited by the fact that it is a-sociological, with the result that politics outside state conceptions of what politics is, cannot be conceived – people are said to be politically what state institutions make them.

Citizenship and Political Identity: Four Theses

It is possible to outline the theoretical position taken here under four main headings or theses.

Thesis One: Xenophobia is a Discourse and Practice of Exclusion from Community

Xenophobia is a discourse concerned with a process of social and political exclusion of some groups of the population. This amounts to a process of social exclusion from community (usually but not exclusively the nation) and citizenship (its resources, privileges, duties, etc., or some of these) of such groups. This exclusion is regularly seen as necessary for the existence of the community/nation in that the 'Other' must be excluded for the 'We' to be. This means that citizenship is reduced to indigeneity while remaining in essence passive. This is because under such circumstances, citizenship is state-constructed and the state sees citizenship as being concerned with populations within a territory under its control, much as Foucault argues in relation to governmentality (Foucault op cit., Chatterjee op cit.). In its form of indigeneity, citizenship is given by territory and birth, not by political agency and is underlined by state power. Indigeneity implies an exclusive conception of nationality and citizenship, meaning that those conceived (in whatever way) to be outside territorial boundaries are excluded from rights and entitlements.

Thesis Two: This Process of Exclusion is a Political Process

This exclusion is a political process in that the state plays a central role in the process, however implicit or hidden, and only politically weak or marginalised groups (i.e. political minorities) can be socially excluded, although they may participate in state politics to various extents. The state in a relation with society defines who is a citizen and who is not, who is included in community and who is excluded. Collective ideologies struggle over conceptions of the nation or community more broadly. Political discourses demarcate boundaries. It is these discourses then, the parameters of which are forged in debate between state and society, which form a state domain of politics which in turn provides the conditions for the forming of political identities.

Thesis Three: Xenophobia is Concerned with Exclusion from Citizenship which Denotes a Specific Political Relationship Between State and Society

This combines theses one and two. Exclusion from community means exclusion from citizenship, its rights and duties, as it is the latter which defines community membership of the nation in particular. Xenophobia is thus intimately connected to citizenship, in other words to the fact of belonging or not belonging to a community, often but not exclusively to a nation. It is important to stress this given the pervasiveness of legalistic perspectives in studies of the phenomenon. Xenophobia is about the denial of social rights and entitlements to strangers, people considered to be strangers to the community (village, ethnic group as well as nation) not just to 'foreigners' as conceived by the law. It is thus about a certain conception of the community as founded on indigeneity/autochthony from which follows that this conception of community is necessarily essentialist and ahistorical and is visualised as unchanging. This 'belonging' must be understood in two senses: first politically so that it refers to access to rights, entitlements to various resources etc.; second subjectively in other words in terms of the identity of a group. This 'belonging', it must be emphasised, should be understood fundamentally as a political identity rather than simply as a personal one because it is acquired in some relationship to the state and power; it is the outcome of power relations between state and society. Finally, in hegemonic (state) discourse, citizenship is reduced to passive citizenship and nationhood is reduced to indigeneity as noted above.

If we approach the study of xenophobia in this manner, it follows that such 'belonging' is constructed by the state and the way it 'interpellates' groups as citizens or non-citizens on the one hand, and by the social experience and political agency of such groups on the other. Political agency here refers to a popular politics constructed in relation (and possibly in opposition) to the state's 'interpellation'. This implies a struggle around the content of citizenship, more or less distant from state conceptions, more or less the prisoner of state notions (passivity/indigeneity); the context is one where the state is concerned with establishing its control over populations within a territory (especially in Africa where that territory has been insecure) and thus its reliance on 'governmentality' in Foucault's sense as a form of rule. This governmentality is first established by the colonial state which becomes obsessed with classification of populations in different ethnic cultures with its most extreme form being apartheid itself (Mamdani 1996, 2000; Chatterjee 2004). Today, the discourse of Human Rights through which xenophobia is deemed to be overcome, points to a contradiction in the heart of liberalism: as Marx noted at the head of this book, the state is seen by liberalism as the main guarantor of human rights whereas it is, at the same time, the main threat to such rights. For Human Rights Discourse, as we shall see, it is state politics which are dominant over democratic popular forms of politics. Statism is, in actual fact, central to political liberalism (Neocosmos 2005).

Thesis Four: Xenophobia is the Outcome of a Relation Between Different Forms of Politics

In this sense, Xenophobia (its existence, character, and extent) can be said to be the outcome of a relation between two sets of politics: state politics and popular or subaltern politics, or to put the same point in another way, xenophobia exists at the interface between state and sociality, or state subjectivity and popular subjectivity. Although state nationalist politics in Africa have tended to be overwhelmingly 'exclusive' and territorialised in the form of indigeneity, there have been struggles at the level of popular politics (within society) between exclusive and inclusive citizenship (the latter tends to be popular-democratic in content and its orientation may be universal) particularly during periods of mass popular upsurge such as during the struggles for independence. In Africa such inclusive politics often took the form of Pan-Africanism (Neocosmos 2003). Clearly xenophobia is at its minimum when 'inclusivist' national politics dominate, and exists to various extents and in various forms when an 'exclusivist' politics of nationalism dominates. Fanon's comments are obviously central here.

In sum, xenophobia must be understood as of the domain of political identity or political consciousness and discourse. Not that it is itself such an identity, but because it is fundamentally about exclusion from citizenship rights. It is the other side of a particular kind of nationalism (state nationalism) which includes as well as excludes on the basis of indigeneity. It is a consequence of an understanding of politics which presupposes boundaries and territories the other side of which is populated by others who do not possess the rights which we enjoy. It is therefore historically linked to the rise of the territorial state in Africa as this develops primarily with colonialism/apartheid and which is then consolidated in the post-colonial period. Xenophobia was challenged during the struggle for independence/liberation in Africa (for example, in Ghana) including in South Africa in the 1980s (as we shall see in chapter two) usually by a popular form of Pan-Africanism. However Pan-Africanism floundered (and became statised) as the continent came to be seen by its leaders (but not always by its people) as an addition of independent states represented in the OAU (Neocosmos 2003). The post-colonial/apartheid state and its relations with society, provides the political context, through its practices and discourses of inclusion/exclusion surrounding 'nation building' of national chauvinist discourses and interpellations as Fanon has noted. In South Africa I will argue that the 'exclusionary' conception of the nation-state is a direct result of both the mode of rule of the apartheid state (vis-à-vis rural migrants in particular) and of the manner in which this rule was understood and fought against by the nationalist movement.

The Study of Xenophobia in South Africa

As I have argued, xenophobia, like political identity more generally, cannot exclusively be accounted for by state interpellation, or indeed solely by reference to competition over scarce resources, social change etc., but must also include some understanding of popular-democratic politics (even in its absence). Rather, the following schematic theoretical outline must provide the basis for understanding xenophobia in South(ern) Africa, and presupposes a number of theoretical steps or processes:

The division of labour: The point of departure must be a political economy within the context of imperialism and globalised capital (including market divisions, migration and globalisation with its political and cultural aspects) which provides the conditions for social divisions and fragmentation along certain social dimensions and lines/cleavages. These distinctions and divisions are state-sanctioned; they provide the material conditions for the moment of interpellation. The history of this political economy, especially of migrant labour in Southern Africa and its understanding provide the necessary background for a specific conception of 'the nation' associated with African nationalist discourse in South Africa. It is a notion of the nation which is a fundamentally urban one, centred on the cities. As a result it tends to exclude the rural in the 1980s, and eventually transfers this exclusion to the non-South African rural hinterland whence migrants had emanated and where current immigration originates; 'illegal immigrants' in South Africa are implicitly or explicitly seen as coming from the 'backward rural' areas of the continent, or from 'failed states', they are ultimately the same thing: the impoverished Other.

The moment of interpellation: The process of state interpellation takes place as ideology, power and institutions address people as citizens or subjects over time; this is the core of Mamdani's argument. People are interpellated by state discourse as belonging to specific groups, national, ethnic, tribal, gender, businessmen or otherwise (although rarely as working class for reasons we cannot go into here), which correspond to this division of labour. In fact this process of interpellation forms part of the process of the production of such divisions as the historians of the 'making of tradition' (see for instance Ranger 1985b, Vail op cit.) have noted. Of course the construction of citizenship by the state as indigeneity and as passive citizenship is also central here. Under apartheid all rural migrants to cities whether emanating from South African territory or not, were interpellated as foreign through the medium of tribal identification. Post-apartheid, only those emanating from beyond South Africa's borders are interpellated as foreign, as the Bantustans are simply struck off the map. It is no longer ethnic identity but national (and increasingly black African) identity which enables access to resources.

The mediation of politics: But this power of (state) interpellation is mediated by experience and politics, meaning that it is not necessarily apprehended/internalised mechanically or automatically. In particular, the levels of presence/absence (silence or voice) of politics in society and community (popular prescriptions), including the existence of critical intellectuals, affect the character of political identity or consciousness. Insofar as national political identity is concerned, an understanding of citizenship is also constructed from below, at times in opposition to the state, at times in conjunction with it. Indeed this struggle can be argued to operate within the confines of civil society and beyond. As we shall see, the anti-apartheid struggle in South Africa led by the United Democratic Front (UDF) in the 1980s although overwhelmingly urban based, stressed the development of the nation on the basis of political allegiances and agency (commitment to popular transformation) rather than to indigeneity. The urban-biassed character of its discourse however, meant that it tended to be exclusive of rural migrants.

The prevalence of xenophobia in post-apartheid South Africa I suggest, is an effect of the hegemony of a particular form of state politics; a politics which reduces citizenship to indigeneity and to a politically passive conception of citizenship. The hegemony of this mode of politics was secured as a result of a failure to sustain an alternative popular-democratic politics which had stressed the centrality of political agency and inclusiveness in the construction of South African citizenship. The securing of this hegemony of state politics was enabled it will be suggested, by the specific theoretical understanding of the apartheid state and the ethnic interpellation of its subjects, adhered to by African nationalism. This provided the parameters within which debates regarding citizenship and conceptions of the nation took place. The two chapters which follow are divided historically. Chapter two is concerned with understanding the manner the apartheid state addressed its subjects and the manner in which this was resisted. I also refer briefly to the struggle for independence in Zimbabwe in order to elucidate some characteristics of popular resistance politics which were also apparent in the South African context. Chapter three provides an account of the post-apartheid situation and why a liberal state discourse in the specific context of post-liberation thinking was able to secure the hegemony of state-structured xenophobia, despite the apparent celebration of human rights and Africanism.

In sum, an attempt will be made not so much to assess the extent and character of xenophobia in the country, but much more importantly to explain its existence (and absence) in terms of the changing configuration of politics from a period of popular national struggle ('national democratic revolution') lasting from 1984 to1989, to a state-led process of 'nation building' from 1990 to the present. The post-apartheid state dates from 1990 and not from 1994 as usually maintained. The point of difference is not so much the introduction of universal suffrage, but rather the unbanning of nationalist political parties in 1990 which were thenceforth allowed to operate within a state domain of politics – they were legitimised in the eyes of the state as was African nationalism as a whole. This process thereby engendered the collapse of popular prescriptive politics as popular organisations were gradually but clearly and irreversibly de-politicised through linkage to a state subjectivity. Different conceptions of the nation dominated nationalist politics during these two different periods along with differing notions of those outside it and different relations between state interpellation and popular prescriptions. The absence of popular prescriptions on politics today (their collapse since the end of the apartheid state in 1990) is what largely enables the existence of various forms of xenophobia as directed against both foreigners and ethnic minorities. Examples of state interpellation through state utterances and policies as well as the results of ethnographic and other research in the country will be outlined to provide evidence for the variations in form of xenophobia within differing contexts. I will thus attempt to use the case of South Africa to argue that xenophobia emanates in society as a direct outcome of the hegemony of a state discourse of nation-building and human rights – in other words of citizenship. I will suggest that xenophobia is a product of the parameters of this discourse and of the obscuring, subordination or defeat of an alternative popular-democratic political discourse which had stressed a different understanding of citizenship and the nation. The argument will show the specific ways in which a state discourse of post-liberation citizenship in South Africa developed in a systematic exclusionary (rather than inclusive) manner. In fact this discourse emanated from the nationalist critique of apartheid racial exclusivism, to which it counterposed a national exclusivism rather than a (Pan-African) democratic inclusivism which had been stressed during the liberation struggle inside the country in particular. The victorious and hegemonic dominance of nationalist exclusivism (also present during the anti-apartheid struggle) over popular nationalist inclusivism is explained, following Fanon, as a direct outcome of state conceptions of citizenship and a discourse of human rights on which such notions of citizenship are founded. Alternative conceptions of citizenship must be sought beyond state forms of politics.

CHAPTER TWO

The Apartheid State and Migration to South Africa: From Rural Migrant Labour to Urban Revolt

The living expression of the nation is the moving consciousness of the whole people; it is the coherent, enlightened action of men and women. The collective building up of a destiny is the assumption of responsibility on the historical scale (Fanon 1990:165).

In this chapter, the relationship between political economy and the apartheid state, in other words the character of structural relations historically dominant in the Southern African region, is established. This issue is important because social divisions developed around migrant labour on the one hand and the character of state interpellations on the other, provide the structural context for the formation of ethnic and national identities and their changed character during and after apartheid. The core idea behind the argument is to stress the centrally divisive character of apartheid oppression and to elucidate how it worked with regard to the political economy of Southern Africa in the colonial and regional division of labour. The attempted forced creation of rural ethnic identities and citizenship by the apartheid state failed, as economic, political and social attempts at legitimising ethnic identities were challenged by an African nationalism which promised not only freedom in the nation, but also, as part of this process, to address the economic penury associated with ethnic identity and rural life. Free movement to cities was now said to provide jobs so that freedom was explicitly or implicitly identified with urbanisation, a view which dovetailed nicely with the 'market freedom' advocated by neo-liberal thought as markets are predominantly urban phenomena.

The understanding of 'nation' which was politically asserted by the nationalist movement was thus a fundamentally urbanised one. It was also a conception for which the 'migrant labour system' was seen as the basis of apartheid. In other words, apartheid was not so much a form of state but a form of labour control based on rural migrant labour, moreover a labour which was kept in dormitory areas (Bantustans) against its will by the pass system, and hence 'tribalised' in the process. What this eventually led to is a conception for which the restriction of migrant labour from the Southern African sub-region (the restricting of would be migrants to their own countries) could be justified as part of the dismantling of apartheid itself, and as such as a democratic process. As a state discourse, this conception fed into creating the conditions for popular xenophobia as we shall see in chapter three. This process of creating a whole class of non-citizens excluded from claiming rights was common to the post-colonial situation in Africa and was not unique to South Africa (Mamdani, 1991, 1996).[4] What has arguably been unique in the South African case, has been the extent and depth of the problem. These features resulted both from the character of the apartheid state and from the nature of the understanding of it and opposition to it, by the exiled nationalist movement. They resulted from a political relationship.

In sum then, the form of ideological resistance to the apartheid state, which was founded on a conception of citizenship upheld by a nationalist organisation which largely equated migrant labour with oppression, could relatively easily form the basis of a discourse of national chauvinism, or at least was perfectly congruent with it. Thus, an understanding of post-apartheid xenophobia must elicit the history of the relations between apartheid state politics and the politics of resistance. It is with this issue that the present chapter is concerned.

State and Citizenship in Southern Africa

It could be asserted, although perhaps rather boldly, that the recent history of Southern Africa has been a history of the structuring and de-structuring of nationalities both in the 'subjective' sense of the formation and dissolution of national or ethnic identities and in the apparently more 'objective' sense of the destruction and making of nations and nationalities through struggles over state formation. One need only recall how the form of colonial state known as apartheid was built around an attempt to de-nationalise a large proportion of South African citizens, how relations between this state and its subjects were structured around 'ethnic' nationalities as were the relations between mining companies (and others) and their employees, and to observe how in the post-apartheid period a South African identity is still very much in the process of formation. This latter process includes an attempt by the new South African state to demarcate its own citizens from 'foreigners' – often peoples from the region from which the erstwhile national liberation movements refused to consciously demarcate South Africans during the liberation struggle in that country. While the post-apartheid state is attempting to construct a 'culture of rights' in various ways, this process has often been seen by state functionaries of the new state as not being applicable to non-citizens as we shall see in detail in chapter three.

The current process of formation of a South African identity has also included more or less sophisticated attempts by large numbers of individuals in the region to show a 'South African connection' in their family backgrounds in order to acquire access to jobs in South Africa (similarly to the ways in which East Europeans have attempted to prove a German family connection in order to acquire access to the European Union). Indeed, under the current conditions of economic and political crisis which the region is experiencing, 'national identity' is showing signs of extreme fluidity, contrary to the rigidity sometimes ascribed to it by many anthropologists in the past and by those who wish to imply some kind of essential African 'ethnic' nature in the present ('economy of affection', 'politics of the belly' etc.).

There are at least two dimensions to the way in which citizenship in particular has been structured, de-structured and restructured in the Southern African region. The first and most obvious is the historical dimension just referred to. The nature as well as the function of citizenship has drastically altered, not simply between a colonial/apartheid process of 'the making of ethnicity' and a post-colonial one of 'nation building', but also along with the greater or lesser fluidity (or rigidity) of the process of identity-formation itself. The second dimension of the structuring of citizenship, although perhaps less obvious, is nonetheless crucially important. This is a 'vertical' dimension along which the state (colonial or post-colonial) as well as the people over whom it attempts to secure its rule, have both participated and continue to participate in the structuring and transforming of citizenship, according to the forms taken primarily by their political relations to each other (coercive, authoritarian, democratic etc.) in the socio-economic context within which these relations play themselves out.

This context has been changing over the years, but one constant has been the centrality of labour migration in the political economy of the region from the time of the main mineral discoveries in the second half of the nineteenth century. Rural peasant labour from throughout the region has built, in the mines and elsewhere, the economic structure of South Africa into what it is today. Under apartheid itself, the denationalising of the African population was a corollary of the attempt to reverse the urbanisation process occasioned by increased industrialisation, and to permanently institutionalise 'oscillating migration'. While labour migration has linked the rural peripheries of the region to its metropolitan centres (mainly Gauteng and the western Free State), rural peasants have combined ethnic and national identities as well as rural and urban ones in successive periods. Indeed it was these identities, often combined into an overarching anti-imperialist ideology which, at least up to the 1960s, provided the main ideological impetus behind the struggles for liberation of the masses of the people. It was in these struggles, as well as in those of the 1980s, which became dominated by the fully urbanised, that conceptions of nationality and citizenship were forged by the people themselves in opposition to a state, which had attempted to secure its rule through expanding 'indirect rule' to the extent of de-nationalising its subjects. After liberation the state itself took a much more dominant role in this relation. Both from the perspective of the state and from that of the people, it is the migratory phenomenon which has provided the most important context for the development of democratic conceptions of citizenship in the region.

This chapter will be, therefore, mainly concerned with the connections between labour migration on the one hand and citizenship on the other, as the these processes resulted from, and in turn impacted upon, the relations between state and people. As this process has historically been a regional one, it will address the history of forms of state rule in South Africa within the regional context in which they unfolded. In fact it is rarely noted today (unlike say in the 1980s) that, given the economic predominance of the South African economy in the region, the country's economic relations with its neighbours have historically been very much those of a sub-imperialist power in relation to its regional periphery. Indeed the dominant perspective of the regional economy during this period, which I shall address in some detail below, was wont to emphasise this point given its affinities with dependency theory. The collapse of a critical political economy perspective in the post-apartheid period has meant the failure to analyse critically the relations between South Africa and its neighbours. It has also enabled the dominance of an official discourse for which the economic intervention of South African capital in the region, and indeed further afield, is overwhelmingly portrayed in a positive light, as contributing to the 'development' of a poverty-stricken continent.

However, in order to understand political identities and by extension xenophobia, it is not helpful to restrict oneself to an analysis of the political economy of migrant labour, but it is also necessary to understand this migrant labour from a perspective which emphasises politics, particularly the politics of citizenship. Consequently, I will first address the issue of the character of the apartheid state and will then move to a discussion of the importance of migrant labour from the region for the political economy of apartheid. Here I will assess the links between the economics and politics of South African society under apartheid in order to bring out some of the contradictions of citizenship as the state attempted to construct it for Africans. A third section will consist of a critical assessment of the African nationalist conception of apartheid as an economic form of labour control and its effects within intellectual and political discourse; while the final section will briefly outline the inclusive conception of the South African nation emanating from the popular resistance movement of the 1980s within the country which stressed a different conception of citizenship.

The Apartheid State

Mamdani's (1996) argument that the colonial state ruled through a distinction between citizens and subjects is of particular importance to the argument developed here. In Mamdani's formulation the state which developed during the colonial period as an answer to the 'native problem' was a 'bifurcated state'. As this state evolved especially after the 1930s:

> Direct rule was the form of urban civil power. It was about the exclusion of natives from civil freedoms guaranteed to citizens in civil society. Indirect rule, however, signified a rural tribal authority. It was about incorporating natives into a state-

enforced customary order... direct and indirect rule are better understood as variants of despotism: the former centralized, the latter decentralized (Mamdani 1996: 18).

The point well argued by Mamdani is that the mode of rule of the colonial state differed between the urban and the rural. While in the former the state ruled citizens and excluded natives from citizenship, in the latter subjects were ruled through state-transformed 'tradition'.

> The rights of free association and free publicity, and eventually of political representation, were the rights of citizens under direct rule, not of subjects indirectly ruled by a customarily organised tribal authority. Thus, whereas civil society was racialised, Native Authority was tribalised. Between the rights-bearing colons and the subject peasantry was a third group: urban-based natives, mainly middle- and working-class persons, who were exempt from the lash of customary law but not from modern, racially discriminatory civil legislation. Neither subject to custom nor exalted as rights-bearing citizens, they languished in a juridical limbo. In the main, however, the colonial state was a double-sided affair. Its one side, the state that governed a racially defined citizenry, was bounded by the rule of law and an associated regime of rights. Its other side, the state that ruled over subjects, was a regime of extra-economic coercion and administrative driven justice (ibid: 19).

Under indirect rule in particular, independent peasant communities could be preserved and controlled through excluding the market from the land relations which were to be founded on customary communal rights. The market would only regulate the product of labour and labour power itself would only marginally be affected by the market (ibid: 17). It was on this system that apartheid was founded. In late nineteenth century South Africa in particular, but continuing right up to the 1980s, the problem arose of how a minority was to retain state power in the face of a rapid process of industrialisation which would create pressures of urbanisation, 'integration', and the 'swamping' of the ruling urbanised minority by an oppressed overwhelmingly rural majority. The resolution of this problem was seen by the state as the 'reproduction of autonomous peasant communities that would regularly supply male, adult and single migrant labour to the mines' in particular (ibid: 18). It was this mode of rule which began what South African historiography and political economy has referred to as the period of segregation (basically referred to as 'indirect rule' in Africa) from the late 1920s to the late 1940s, and the period of 'apartheid, an extension of the indirect rule system of "segregation"', from 1948 up to the early 1990s (Wolpe 1972). Mamdani shows very well how apartheid in South Africa was simply a variant of an existing system of rule applied with success throughout the continent, and was by no means unique or exceptional to South Africa.

In sum therefore, Mamdani argues that the colonial and apartheid states distinguished between citizens and subjects and ruled each group differently. At independence, the state in Africa was 'deracialised' but not 'democratised'. It was deracialised primarily through what was then called 'Africanisation' and what is today called 'affirmative action' (ibid: 20). It was not democratised because that would have required a democratic transformation of the form of rule in rural areas. When such transformation was attempted it was not democratic but rather 'it was to reorganize decentralized power so as to unify the "nation" through a reform that tended to centralization. The antidote to a decentralized despotism turned out to be a central-ized despotism' (ibid: 25). This was the reform attempted by 'radical' regimes. The 'conservative' regimes merely continued with the dual state inherited from colonialism.

> The bifurcated state that was created with colonialism was deracialised, but it was not democratised. If the two-pronged division that the colonial state enforced on the colonised – between town and country, and between ethnicities – was its dual legacy at independence, each of the two versions of the post-colonial state tended to soften one part of the legacy while exacerbating the other. The limits of the conservative states were obvious: they removed the sting of racism from a colonially fashioned stronghold but kept in place the Native Authorities, which enforced the division be-tween ethnicities. The radical states went a step further, joining deracialisation to detribalisation. But the deracialised and detribalised power they organised put a pre-mium on administrative decision-making. In the name of detribalisation, they tight-ened central control over local authorities. Claiming to herald development and wage revolution, they intensified extra-economic pressure on the peasantry. In the process, they inflamed the division between town and country. In the process, both experi-ences reproduced one part of the dual legacy of the bifurcated state and created their own distinctive version of despotism (Mamdani 1996:26-7).

If post-colonial states continued with a despotic form of rule of the people and excluded to one degree or another overwhelmingly rural inhabitants from civil soci-ety and the rule of law – ie. if they reproduced in one form or another the colonial division between citizens and subjects – then presumably the latter category applies even more obviously to non-citizens. These are those classified by the state as 'for-eigners', '(legal or illegal) immigrants', 'international migrants' and 'refugees' which are such an obvious feature of the political economic landscape of Africa in general and of Southern Africa in particular. In one of his earlier writings, Mamdani had remarked that:

> It is with the second partition of Africa – 'independence' – that the significance of cross-border migrant labour becomes enormous. Entire communities now migrate to labour as 'non-citizens' in foreign territories: the Bourkinabe in Ivory Coast, the Ghanaians in Nigeria, the Rwandese in Uganda, and a whole string of border na-tionalities inside South Africa... This vast and growing group of producers on the continent is caught between the devil and the proverbial blue sea. For received no-tions of 'rule of law' have little relevance to their position since the 'rule of law' is said to govern mainly relations between citizens. On the other hand, reigning con-ceptions of citizenship in Africa are carried over from modes of thinking shaped by pre-capitalist social realities: thus, the right of citizenship is often seen as principally a birth right, an extension of the principle of clan right by birth. But where there is a radical rupture between the place of birth and the place of work, should rights

derive wholly from the fact of birth and not the contribution of labour? Should it be possible for states to hold to ransom large sections of their resident working population under a 'non-citizen' status, and then to expel them when expedient, as with the Ghanaians in Nigeria, and the Rwandese in Uganda? (Mamdani 1991:244).

The issue of citizenship being primarily a political issue – one affecting both the state and the people, particularly the latter's inclusion or exclusion from the nation and more broadly from rights inherent through community membership – it cannot be comprehended by starting from economic questions. The point of departure must be the historically changing forms of rule in Africa as Mamdani's analysis makes clear.[5] If we understand apartheid as a variant of the colonial state in Africa, we can begin to make sense of the identities which it attempted to create through interpellating its citizens and its subjects. Mamdani (2001) distinguishes primarily between the creation of racial and ethnic identities by the colonial state; here I wish to stress the attempt at 'denationalising' or alienating (in the literal sense) the African subjects of the South African state through the creation of nominally independent countries within the confines of South Africa on the foundation stone of the administrative districts of ethnically governed societies.[6] Whereas the British colonial state in particular had created districts in order to territorialise the 'tribes' they had systematically re-structured or created during the colonial period, the apartheid state, successfully for a period, created four legally independent countries founded on ethnic territorial divisions manufactured by its 'Native Affairs Department' so-called.

In sum then, the fundamental political difference between apartheid as a mode of state rule from its historical antecedents in segregation or indirect rule, was not so much its increasingly repressive legislation or its increased exploitation of migrant labour – in fact large proportions of this labour had in fact become permanently urbanised in huge townships around Johannesburg in particular – but its attempt to manufacture foreign ethnically-based political identities along the lines of the BLS countries, particularly of Swaziland where a highly repressive ethnic citizenship ruled.[7] This is evident in the way the state addressed – or interpellated – black South Africans in particular, and is especially so in the legislation it developed for that purpose.

Peberdy and Crush (1998) have traced the chronology of legal enactments regarding immigration. Such legislation started with the 1913 Immigration Act contemporaneous with the Land Act of the same year which restricted movement within the country. Black South Africans were defined as non-citizens subject to the same legislation which governed entry to the country by non-South Africans. But it was with the introduction of the 1937 Aliens Act which was meant to exclude Jewish immigration that the term 'alien' became synonymous with 'unwanted immigrant' (ibid: 26). This legislation had strong anti-Semitic undertones and governed immigration policy until the mid 1950s. Peberdy and Crush show that immigration legislation was used a racist means to manufacture black aliens. It developed a complex system of categorisation and control between and within racial groups. They show that during the 1950s and 1960s Germans and British were actively encouraged to immigrate in order to boost the white skill base of the country, while Portuguese, Italians and Greeks were actively discouraged during this period.

While some white foreigners were classified as aliens, black foreigners were not classified as such during much of the apartheid period. The reasons for this had mainly to do with the dependence of the South African economy on migrant labour from surrounding states and because of the centrality of race, they argue, rather than nationality as such as the basis of discrimination. Black foreigners were wanted as sources of labour rather than as immigrants so apparently the term 'migrant' was introduced into legislation to denote a temporary resident (ibid). By the 1970s, and the construction of the 'independent' TBVC states, the categories of foreign black aliens were expanded to include residents of these 'Bantustans'.

Consequently a large number of South Africans were denied South African citizenship so that they now were forced in a sense to 'emigrate' to the TBVC states in order to migrate back to urban South Africa as foreigners. By the time the Aliens and Immigration Laws Amendment Act of 1984 was enacted, the state was systematically denationalising its citizens in large numbers and attempting to create ethnic citizenship and national ethnic identities of foreigners from among its people. In 1985 the population of the TBVC states was given as in Table 1. The table gives an indication of the numbers involved. Although the figures underestimated the number of Africans they do give some indication of the numbers involved. It can be assumed then that around six million South Africans were turned into foreigners in this manner, but this number was far lower than the fifteen million black South Africans, a large number of whom were urban residents. There were clearly plans to alienate another twelve million when the non-independent 'homelands' were to be eventually provided with independence.

This process of de-nationalisation had two fundamental consequences. First it effectively made no distinction between say a citizen of Lesotho and a citizen of the Transkei, a citizen of Mozambique, a citizen of Swaziland and a citizen of Venda, and thus it interpellated most black rural inhabitants (in particular) of the region and of the country in the same way and oppressed them in the same way. Second, and largely as a result of this oppressive interpellation, the ideology of resistance by the black majority tended to provide a mirror image of it. Bonds of solidarity were developed between all Africans in the region and beyond, so that the struggle against apartheid was very much conceived by those resisting oppression as a fight of all Africans and their allies against the apartheid state. The concept of 'nation' thus developed tended therefore to be inclusive rather than exclusive of Africans from the region in particular. This Pan-Africanism thus largely resulted from resistance to the mode of domination rather than from a consciously propagated ideology. There is little evidence that any such ideology was consciously propagated by the ANC as it was equated with the PAC (Pan-African Congress) whose organisational presence inside the country was minimal.

Table 1: Population of South Africa by 'Race' and Population of 'Bantustans', 1985

Official South Africa Excluding Bantustans	Number	Percentage
African	15 242 828	65
Asian	793 978	3.4
Coloured	2 825 094	12.1
White	4 576 690	19.5
Total Official RSA	23 438 590	100
Total Official RSA Includes		
non-independent 'homelands'	12 832 400	54.7
Bantustans		
Bophutatswana	1 627 475	
Ciskei	925 095	
Transkei	2 947 058	
Venda	454 797	
Total Bantustans	5 954 425	
Total South Africa	29 393 015	

Source: South African Race Relations Survey 1985: 1.

At the same time however, the system of distinguishing migrant labour and 'alienating' it also contributed to further drawing distinctions between permanently settled labour in the cities (those with so-called 'section 10 rights' of urban residence which was indicated in people's passes) and temporarily visiting migrant labour housed in hostels.[8] Accounts of township life under apartheid are replete with economic, cultural and political distinctions between urbanised township dwellers and male migrant workers who were never fully integrated into urban communities (Ramphele 1993; Mamdani 1996: chapter 7). Both these features had deep effects on the character of popular resistance to apartheid in the 1980s as we shall see in a following section. I have argued so far that the apartheid state must be understood politically and that if we do so, the issue of citizenship becomes central to the manner it regulated its relations with its citizens and subjects. I have also argued that this state attempted to create an ethnic citizenship among its African subjects, much as existed in other countries of the region. I now need to turn to a discussion of migrant labour as such, going back to its origins, in order to link the political economy of the region to the mode of state rule which I have so far only introduced. It should be also stressed that this political economy and state interpellation were fiercely resisted not just in South Africa, but given the tightly knit character of the region, such resistance was geographically widespread.

Apartheid, Migrant Labour, Citizenship and Resistance

In this section I will go back in history to begin from the introduction of the system of indirect rule/'segregation' from the late twenties onwards and in doing so I will lay emphasis on popular struggles against the state in its different forms in the formation of migrant labour and ethnic citizenship. The struggle over national citizenship is treated in the next section.

The Origins of Migrant Labour and Ethnic Citizenship

The historical origins of the South African 'working class' have been sought in the proletarianisation of peasant labour (see for instance Bundy 1988, Morris 1979). However, the creation of migrant labour from the 1890s to the 1930s by direct state legislation which undermined peasant accumulation in the region did not amount to a process of proletarianisation similar to that of Europe at the dawn of capitalist development. Rather, more and more it came to be based on the reproduction of peasant production on the one hand while undermining the possibilities of peasant accumulation on the other. This period saw the creation of the 'oscillating' migrant labour which has persisted to this day. This tying of worker-peasants to the land was accompanied by the strengthening of an authoritarian 'tradition' founded on an oppressive chieftaincy and a despotic patriarchal and gerontocratic system of 'custom' (Vail 1989a; Neocosmos 1995). The peasantry had to suffer this oppressive system for survival if they wished to have access to land only available through such 'customary' relations:

> Independent access to land was dependent on access to chiefly patronage. Only through the institution of chieftainship could access to resources be legitimated. Although clothed in the garb of 'tradition', there was in fact very little historical continuity in the new foci of legitimacy and patronage that were emerging under the auspices of the industrial state in the new segregationist era (Keegan 1988: 149).

It should be stressed that the function of the 'traditional' powers of land allocation by the chiefs were completely different in the pre-colonial context where land was seen as 'the place of the ancestors', so that land represented the continuity between the past and the present, as well as a place to live in relative abundance. Now the functions of these 'traditional' powers were directly aimed at securing the powers of the chieftaincy (the state) over a worker-peasantry which depended on this land for its subsistence. It was this control over land which provided the basis for all the other powers of the chief. Evidently it was very difficult for the oppressed people to resist successfully the combined forces of the colonial state and the local state of the emerging new ethnic nationalities, yet they did resist as the rural success of the Industrial and Commercial Union (ICU), in both South Africa and Zimbabwe, in particular shows.[9]

Increased coercion on the peasantry however was regularly met with increased resistance especially by poorer peasants and youth. This resistance found expression in the act of migration itself as the powers of the chieftaincy were weakened with urban residence; it also took more open forms of resistance with the rural spread of the ICU in the 1920s for example. Some episodes from these struggles surrounding the formation of nationalities are worth recounting.

Up until the late 1920s and the spread of the ICU among workers and peasants, the dominant response of the state towards the 'native problem' in South Africa (with the exception of Natal) had been influenced by the need to destroy chiefly power and legal systems of the pre-capitalist societies which had resisted colonial expansion. This tendency had been typified by the Cape Colony's 'assimilationist' policies.[10] The colonial state having by then consolidated its power after destroying resistance based on the remnants of pre-capitalist formations was faced with a potentially more damaging threat, a nationwide (as opposed to an ethnically and regionally limited) rebellion. The result was the Native Administration Act of 1927, 'the first link in a chain of measures leading to the refurbishing of African tradition-alism, with the emphasis on ethnic and cultural separatism' at the same time 'it began to reverse the assimilationist trend of gradually accepting urban Africans into western industrialised society' (Lacey 1981: 85).

The 1927 Act was draconian by any standards and basically generalised the Natal Native Code of 1891 to the whole of the Union. Like the Natal Code it designated the Governor-General of the Union as the 'Supreme Chief' over all 'natives':

> he exercised all political power over Africans in Natal; he appointed and removed chiefs; he could divide and amalgamate tribes; he might remove tribes or portions of tribes and individual Africans; he might call out armed men and levies and he had the power to call upon Africans to supply labour for public works; he might punish by fine or imprisonment, or both for disobedience of his order or for disregard for his authority (Welsh 1968: 82, cited in Lacey 1981: 97).

The powers of the 'supreme chief' were thus despotic in the extreme and he could delegate them to the civil servants of the Native Affairs Department (NAD) who 'could do practically what they liked in the name of the Supreme Chief without being answerable either to parliament or the law' (ibid: 99). Lacey comments that 'the juggernaut was launched as if it were merely carrying on in the spirit of early African tradition'. Mamdani notes that:

> with the passage of the 1927 Native Administration Act, two elements of the triple consensus that would define 'native policy' under apartheid were already in place: the first was rule by decree, the second 'customary law' (Mamdani 1996: 72).

Under the control of the NAD, chiefs would collect taxes, dispense 'justice' and collect tribute:

A chief's tribute was calculated on how many taxpayers he had in his district. This encouraged chiefs to work for closer settlement which in time forced people off the land and into wage labour. It also ensured that chiefs would collect all the taxes, of course so the government knew without having to check that no revenue would be lost... chiefs were prepared to coerce men into jobs to earn money for their taxes if need be, which suited white employers. Not least, since their own income depended on it, the chiefs made people return home to pay their taxes (Lacey 1981: 108).

Mamdani (op cit.:101) argues that the main alterations enacted during the apartheid era through the 1951 Bantu Authorities Act and the Bantu Laws Amendment Act of 1952 were concerned to remove the NAD from rural areas and to replace it with a decentralised form of 'native authority administration', bringing to the reserves an autonomous form of 'indirect rule'.

It should also be stressed that the colonial/apartheid state's concern in 'tribalising' rural South Africa was not simply to establish social control independently of broader economic concerns. Rather this social control was also necessary to enable coercion of rural Africans for the provision of labour power to white capital (as was stressed repeatedly in the political economy literature of the 1970s and 80s) and most importantly, to 'develop' the reserves in line with state ideology of the time. As was the case in colonial Africa, the main features of extra-economic coercion (such as forced labour, forced cultivation, forced sales, forced removals and so on) were supplemented with forced development. The state was not beyond providing land for the purposes of such development after 1913, and not simply for 'consolidation'. Thus the Native Economic Commission of 1932 (p. 32-3) stated:

> In pursuing the policy of developing the Native Reserves, it is essential to proceed from institutions which are known to the Abantu, and to evolve from these something which will suit the needs of the present (UGSA 1932: 30)... In areas where the tribal institutions are a vital force - and this applies to the greater part of the Reserves outside the Cape Province - the policy should be to strengthen these and to make them centres of progress from within ... In all tribal areas the system of government through the Chief and council should be recognised... in certain areas, e.g. in Northern Natal, some hereditary Chiefs have no land, and this prevents them from keeping their tribes together, and exerting a salutary influence on them...this matter should receive early attention in connection with the provision of more land.

This 'development' was one which involved forced dipping of cattle, forced culling, grazing fees, enforced villagisation and so on and so forth. Thus the 'tribalisation' of rural South Africa was very much linked to its 'development'. At the same time, under such repressive conditions, the 'ethnic community' provided a defence against the predations of an extremely authoritarian form of statism. The chieftaincy provided access to land for a substantial sector of the population; while not usually sufficient (especially after the 1930s) to enable independent peasant production on a significant scale, the provision of land to worker-peasants did provide some security against total destitution. The desire to retain this communal form of security, although shorn of its oppressive aspects contained in the powers of the chieftaincy, is a regular leitmotif in the peasant movements of the region, and is particularly apparent in the actions and demands of the poor peasant movements, such as the Mountain Movement in Pondoland in the 1960s for example.

The centrality of struggle in the development of ethnicity in Natal for example, is revealed from an assessment of the role of African incipient bourgeoisie in Natal in the 1920s. The case of this African elite in Natal in the inter-war period and its role in the strengthening of 'tradition' has been studied at length. This is an interesting case because during the nineteenth century there had been an exceptional degree of accumulation among an African peasantry in Natal, which had led to the development of a class of capitalist farmers from its midst. These:

> larger landowners were no longer simply peasants employing family labour. Many, like Martin Luthuli, were cane-growers, employing either labour-tenants or wage-labour. Thus, Luthuli, for example, hired what he was pleased to describe as '30 or 40 boys... at the same rate of wage paid by Europeans' as togt, or daily paid, casual labour, a process that increased as more of these landowners went over to sugar production in the twenties and thirties (Marks 1986: 51).

This accumulation had quite predictably been ideologically accomplished and justified through a eulogising of private property in land and a corresponding desire to acquire the franchise on the same terms as whites (ibid). While the former proclaimed an antagonism to 'tradition' and a corresponding attachment to 'modernity', the latter expressed an attempt to gain access to civil(ised) society and a rejection of segregation in favour of assimilation as typified by the policies of the Cape. While there had been little restriction on owning land through freehold tenure in Natal other than the simple ability to buy, access to civil society through political rights was denied. Therefore as in the case of other accumulating (or potentially accumulating) classes in Africa during the colonial period, the African (petty-) bourgeoisie in Natal took, in the nineteenth century, a clear anti-'tradition' ideological stance.

A number of processes and events combined to alter the position of this bourgeoisie, starting with the 1913 Land Act which restricted the ability of Black landowners to increase their land holdings and hence their ability to accumulate. Denial of access to increased private wealth removed the economic basis of adherence to liberal ideology. The increasingly obvious effects of the Act on accumulation came to coincide with its effects on proletarianisation of large sections of the peasantry, as increased migration of young men and women to towns took place. The fact that the Act affected all Africans, even though it did so in different ways:

> enabled the landowners and intelligentsia to present their class interests as the general interest, to speak on behalf of the whole African community, and with passion, although even at the time their claims did not go uncontested (Marks op.cit.:64).

Under the circumstances of being squeezed from above by the colonial state, it is not surprising that an alliance was gradually formed between the 'modernising' and 'traditional' African 'elites' which were successfully able to provide leadership to the

African masses against colonialism. This was particularly the case as the alternative claimant to such leadership - the ICU - was defeated. This alliance of the African ruling bloc was cemented in the 1920s, as the increased agitation of the ICU which threatened white and black capitalists from below also coincided with the colonial trend of 'indirect rule' (known in the South African literature as 'segregation') as a form of social and political control.

And it was among rural wage-tenants that ICU propaganda gained the most response. As the ideas propagated by the small band of socialists and communists on the Rand and in Durban, and by the ICU's rural organisers fused with popular consciousness, an almost millenarian expectation suffused the countryside. Popular resistance in the form of work stoppages and individual acts of defiance was transformed into a wave of strikes in which a 2,000 percent increase in wages (8sh. a day) was demanded by labour tenants, brandishing their red tickets and saying they would rather be shot than return to work (Marks op cit.: 95).

Under these circumstances it is not so surprising to see that the African ruling bloc was prepared to ally with the colonial state against its own people. Thus we hear John Dube complain, in identical language to that of the Native Economic Commission (to which he was also a witness), that the victory of 'socialistic' doctrines:

> would mean the breaking down of parental control and restraint, tribal responsibility and our whole traditions, the whole structure upon which our Bantu nation rests ... We have got to maintain ... the sense of paternal and tribal responsibility by Bantu traditions with all its obligations of courage, honour, truth, loyalty and obedience for all we are worth ...

> He then adds a rider to his statement, in case his white correspondent may think that he has given up representing a 'modernising' African bourgeoisie in favour of 'backwardness': Don't think for one moment that am not progressive. I am anxious as any man could be for the development of my people, but on the right lines (cited Marks 1989:222).

Development along the 'right lines' was therefore obviously not class-neutral. It is very interesting to observe that under circumstances where for the first time, the poorest and most oppressed classes and groups of the African people were united irrespective of nationality and rural-urban differences in a popular-national movement - the ICU - the bourgeoisie in South Africa combined across racial barriers to defend its interests by opposing this movement.[11] Under the prevailing circumstances, the solution of this united bourgeoisie was to bolster 'communalism' in the face of 'communism' through the strengthening of an oppressive 'tradition'.[12]

In sum, while the colonial state was instrumental in the making of an oppressive tradition, this process was a site of struggle which was conducted now in hidden, now in open forms. While the state ruled its subjects through an 'ethnic despotism' to use Mamdani's term, the historical evidence shows that these subjects were not always adhering rigidly to the ethnicities ascribed to them by colonial racism. Thus, the well known racial stereotypes which were applied to various 'tribes' during the colonial period, although enabling a differential system of 'divide and rule' and

stratification between 'tribes' in the workplace, also allowed for the changing of
one's 'tribal affiliation' in order to acquire employment (Ranger 1985b:10-13; Vail
1989b; Quinlan 1986:33; Vail and White 1980). While adapting one's ethnicity to fit
the 'needs of the market' must have been easier to undertake when selling one's
labour than in rural areas where one's origins would have been known, the process
itself shows that adhering to a certain 'ethnicity' was often a flexible process. As we
shall see below this 'flexibility' was also recognisable in the 1990s, especially among
the middle classes for whom acquiring a South African connection had become a
way of acquiring well paid jobs.

The Attempted Making of 'Ethnic-National' Citizenship

Along with the development of nationalities/ethnicities went the development of
national identity founded on ethnicity. Most obvious here was the development of
the three BLS ethnic states from the 'High Commission Territories', which the British originally expected would be incorporated into the Union of South Africa. First,
the chiefs of these nationalities resisted incorporation as did the worker-peasantry
of Lesotho organised by the Lekhotla la Bafo or Commoners League, but the coming to power of the National Party in South Africa in 1948 finally put a stop this
idea altogether. The formation of citizenship based on ethnicity was most obvious
in Swaziland. Here an unreconstructed chieftaincy came to power at independence
under the leadership of King Sobhuza. The kind of 'traditional and customary'
culture produced during indirect rule became transformed wholesale into the law of
the land, so that Swazi citizenship became founded on paying allegiance (khonta) to
a chief. The process of acquiring a passport became fundamentally identical to that
of acquiring land. The result was that if descent from a Swazi clan was not obvious,
as with the case of coloured people, then acquiring citizenship was denied. The
notion of a 'non-citizen' or foreigner would then seem, at least on the surface of
things, to be determined by pre-capitalist conceptions of rights. Similar notions could
also be found in Botswana for example where the constitution excludes San-speak-
ing peoples from being one of the nation's constitutive 'tribes' on the grounds that
San speakers did not obviously have a chieftaincy (i.e. a state). Clearly it did not help
to maintain relatively democratic ethnic social relations in newly independent Africa.

Ethnic nationalism was of course what the apartheid state attempted to produce
with its grand plan to turn rural areas denoted as 'traditional homelands' into 'independent' or 'self-governing states'. Dubbed 'Bantustans' by nationalist critics, these
entities failed lamentably to gather any mass support whatsoever and were based on
the exclusive control of the chieftaincy and its clients. In some cases, (for example
Lebowa) even the chieftaincy was divided, with some chiefly families supporting the
ANC (having opposed Bantu Authorities in the 1960s) and being excluded from
leadership of the Bantustan. Having been granted independence by the apartheid
state (the only state to recognise them) the 'TBVC states' (Transkei, Boputhotswana,
Venda and Ciskei) organised border controls for visitors and issued their own passports. In this way large sections of the oppressed South African population were

'denationalised'. They were supposed to migrate to 'White areas' temporarily for work only. Their 'foreign' status was never accepted by themselves, by the majority of South Africans or by the national liberation organisations. Interestingly though, the notion of 'us all being one people' was also regularly applied to Basotho by the same organisations and had entered popular consciousness in the 1980s (much more so than with say Swazis or Batswana).

Table 2 gives an idea of employment figures for certain Bantustans and shows the small size of internal employment relative to employment outside the 'home-land', i.e. in 'White South Africa' in 1982. While this state of affairs was generally analysed as the creation of 'labour reserves', it was regularly forgotten that many of the migrants were not completely proletarianised. Rather they were peasants from various strata ('poor', 'middle', and 'rich') who had access to land and cattle to various extents, although this was more apparent in the case of migrants from the region than in South Africa proper (Neocosmos 1987, First 1983). At this stage therefore it is probably useful to provide a general picture of the extent and form of migration patterns to South Africa from the countries of the region in the 1970s and 1980s.

Table 2: Employment Figures for Certain 'Homelands', 1982

	Internal	Migrant	Commuter
Ciskei	21 807	47 000	37 000
Kwazulu	58 895	300 000	400 000
Gazankulu	15 685	300 000	7 800
Venda	6 872	35 000	2 500

Source: Maré (1983: 81).

Table 3: African Miners Employed at End of Year by Affiliates of the Chamber of Mines by Country of Origin, 1970-1983 (in thousands)

	1970	1973	1977	1980	1983
Botswana	16.3	16.8	19.7	19.3	17.6
Lesotho	71.1	87.2	103.2	109	102.8
Malawi	98.2	128	14.2	14.3	15.9
Mozambique	113	99.4	41.4	45.8	44.8
Swaziland	5.4	4.5	8.1	9.4	11.8
Zimbabwe	--	--	21.4	5	--
Total (inc. Namibia)	304.2	335.9	208	204.3	193.8
South Africa	96.9	86.2	214.2	279.1	289.5
Total	401.1	422.1	422.2	483.4	483.3

Source: de Vletter (1985: 675).

Table 3 shows the number of African miners employed by the companies affiliatedto the Chamber of Mines (the largest companies) at the end of each year bycountry of origin. Apart from the gradual decline of recruitment from abroadand the corresponding increase in the recruitment of miners from South Africa,the other notable point is the importance of recruitment from Lesotho. Minelabour statistics for that country covering the years 1970 to 1990 are featured inTable 4. In addition to numbers employed, these indicate the earnings of theminers as well as deferred pay to the Lesotho Bank as well as total remittances tofamilies. By the 1980s, Lesotho had become the dominant foreign exporter oflabour to South Africa. The increasing tendency for the mining companies tosubstitute South African citizens for foreign labour, which accelerated after the1987 miners' strike, is also apparent. Changing patterns of migration since 1990are dealt with in the following chapter.

Table 4: Mine Migrant Labour Statistics, Lesotho 1970-1990

Year	Average Number Employed ('000)	Total Earnings (millions of Maloti = millions of Rand)	Deferred plus Remittance (millions of Maloti)
1970	87.4	11.9	4.4
1975	112.5	60.4	20
1980	120.7	185.4	42.1
1985	116.5	572.3	235.4
1987	100.3	719.3	321.7
1990	77.5	1029.4	482.1

Source: Lesotho Government (1990:4), cited in Neocosmos (1993b: 138).

The main aspect of much of Southern Africa's dependence on South Africa has historically been through migratory labour which lets off the pressure of unemployment in most of these countries, notably Lesotho and Mozambique.[13]

The Case of Lesotho: Labour reserve economy and peasant production

The recruitment of labour to South Africa has been governed by bilateral treaties between the South African government and the BLS countries. Similar treaties also exist for Malawi and Mozambique (*South African Labour Market Commission Report* 1996, s. 534). This has helped to keep migrants as citizens of a 'sending' country by making them perpetual contract workers:

> The perpetual temporary status of contract migrants reflects government's concern to limit the number of foreign workers to whom permanent status is granted as well as concern for the impact that a drastic change in the pattern of labour supply would

have on the sending countries and on South African employees (*Labour Market Commission Report*, ibid).

Lesotho has constituted a special case in the migrant labour system for a number of reasons: (i) being completely landlocked by South Africa, (ii) having one of the lowest proportions of arable land available to a country; and (iii) having the largest degree of land erosion and highest population density on arable land (more than double the regional average).

Apart from these features, there are also 'institutional factors' which typify Lesotho, including the state neglect of infrastructural development in the rural sector. Although the rise of wages in the South African mines from the mid-1970s has often been mentioned as the prime cause for the neglect of agriculture and for the accelerated emigration on the part of rural people, this does not fully explain the phenomenon if one considers that in the nineteenth century when the Basotho also migrated in numbers, agriculture thrived and mine wages generally escalated all at the same time (Murray 1981; van der Wiel 1977; Winai-Ström 1984; Kimble 1982). It seems rather that the explanation ought to be sought in politico-economic factors including structural relationships with South Africa which render it impossible for the Lesotho state (even if it had wished to do so) to map out is own independent pricing structure to provoke a producer response in the worker-peasantry (Neocosmos 1993b).

Selinyane (1995, 1996c) has argued that new avenues for surplus extraction renewed the state neglect of agriculture in the post-independence period. The undemocratic, neo-colonial character of the state has fuelled this by ignoring the arguments of economic nationalism. The accumulation from above which followed was undertaken on the basis of an alliance between the ruling classes and chiefs and the arbitrary justice that this implied, with the fusion of the powers of chiefs who were the dispensers of statist development as well as administrators in the rural areas. This also restricted accumulation and differentiation from among the peasantry by restricting private property in land. This mode of state rule, coupled with the lack of industrial growth as a result of rentier industrial policy, went a long way to reinforcing the need for migrancy among worker-peasants, the poorest in Lesotho as indeed elsewhere in the region were always those who did not or could not find work on the mines for whatever reason. Kimble (1982) has shown that in the days following the mineral discoveries of the late 1860s, labour migration from Lesotho was encouraged by the state. The chiefs needed guns for defence against colonial encroachment and subjugation, and later the capitation fees which became notorious in Swaziland and Botswana were also paid to chiefs in Lesotho. With time, migration allowed for the state in Lesotho to exercise control over the worker-peasantry, surplus extraction being mediated by co-operation of the apartheid state and mining capital.

This practice of the coercion exercised by the state on people to migrate lasted up to the the 1960s and beyond (Winai-Ström 1986). The miners however did not take this without resistance, as the reduction of deductible deferred pay from sixty percent to thirty percent in 1991 shows (Central Bank of Lesotho 1993). As Mamdani (1991) points out, with the 'second partition' of Africa at independence, migrants became conspicuous as foreign citizens, a factor most visible in periods of tension between the 'sending' and 'receiving' countries, especially during the apartheid era in Southern Africa. One could say from the evidence from Lesotho that apartheid regional sub-imperialism reinforced the view from below of the oppressed peoples of the region as forming 'one oppressed people' with the assent of the black nationalists in the region. The economic importance of migrant labour in Lesotho led to a situation in which, similar only to Southern Mozambique in the region, migrants' remittances made, on average, a greater contribution to rural household subsistence than did agriculture.[14] State revenue in Lesotho still relied heavily on compulsory deferred pay imposed on miners until in the 1990s when revenues from royalties from water exports to South Africa increased. In this context, political struggles in the country have always been affected by the interests of its strong neighbour; and conversely struggles in South Africa have shaped to a larger extent the relations between people and state in Lesotho. Hence the changing conceptions of citizenship in South Africa have had repercussions in Lesotho also.

Migrant worker identities in Lesotho have not simply amounted to a reflection of their economic location in the South African economy. On the contrary, an analysis reveals that a myriad of political views, perceptions and values have been forged among migrants over the years and that these values, although fiercely nationalistic, do not necessarily accord with the hegemonic political values in Lesotho. Part of the explanation for this is that these are hammered out in the context of a different milieu of migrant life in the rural areas (Neocosmos and Selinyane 1996). Of particular significance here was the popular movement known as Lekhotla la Bafo (LLB) or Commoners League which was centrally instrumental, during the colonial period, in developing a national identity founded on the popular-democratic aspects of Sesotho tradition in opposition to the chieftaincy which was seen as betraying this tradition (Neocosmos 1995). From the period of apartheid onwards, and particularly after independence in 1966, Sesotho popular nationalism contained a strong strand of anti-South Africanism given the latter country's economic and increasingly political interference in Lesotho.

The dual class status of the migrant-peasants of Lesotho led to the adoption of forms of identity which may have seemed contradictory in other settings. As a peasant he (and migrants were overwhelmingly male), identified with the culture and economy of small commodity producer in the socio-economic and political context of Lesotho. As a worker the migrant tended to align himself to a workplace political tradition with a history of supporting workers' struggles in a racialised labour market although ethnic identity was systematically reproduced at the workplace by employers who controlled workers through a so-called 'induna system' of 'traditional' headmen. In a depressing apartheid industrial environment which had no social and old age security for the peasant-migrants, the continued access to land, cattle and ethnic identity was vital, and so was the link with the political and cultural authority which regulated and dispensed these crucial resources. Despite over three decades of changing rural administration, the chiefs remain central to village politics because they have managed to retain control over land. On the other hand, the institution of migrant labour initially created by the colonial states in the nineteenth century has been harnessed by its victims who were thereby able to resist total proletarianisation.

Particularly from the 1980s, as a result of their involvement in the anti-apart-heid struggle along with South Africans, miners from Lesotho started taking out ANC membership and becoming elected to positions of responsibility both within this organisation and their union in South Africa, the National (sic) Union of Mine-workers (NUM). As the NUM became a powerful union, miners also became an important support base for the ANC. It was thus natural that the ANC alliance succeeded in persuading the Transitional Executive Council (the transitional execu-tive authority) to allow Basotho migrants to vote in the first South African elections of April 1994. By November 1995 the NUM had secured the right for migrants to vote in the local elections. At the same time the union initiated a motion to secure permanent residence rights for migrants who had worked in South Africa for at least ten years. This was not surprising given that the miners had already passed a resolution calling upon political leaders to work towards the eventual integration of Lesotho into post-apartheid South Africa (op cit). For the miners this apparently did not have citizenship implications, given that they thought they could still live in an area that is Lesotho today, with full access to their land, livestock and families. In this connection the identification of migrants with the rural and not the urban in their ideology, and choice of allegiance to political authority (citizenship) is completely rational. Indeed it could be argued that this identification with the land and the security it offers Basotho peasant-migrants, proffers the single most constant rela-tion between them and the Lesotho state. This point will be pursued in the next chapter when I discuss the offer of South African citizenship to Basotho miners in some detail.

The case of Lesotho shows very clearly that migrant labour, though initiated in the interests of the colonial state and big capital, was central to the reproduction of the rural economy. Indeed in other countries of the region there is even more evidence than that from Lesotho of the enabling of rural accumulation through access to migrant labour earnings. This was particularly so given the difficulties of raising funds for investment in petty accumulation such as shops, transport as well as some agricultural activity. It was only the failure of the political economy of migrant labour to analyse the rural areas of the Southern African periphery which led to the fundamental misconception of migrants as homogeneously migrating for survival. This viewpoint, at the core of South African nationalism, was eventually to lead to an exclusive conception of the nation. This resulted in detrimental effects on miners from Lesotho and elsewhere both economically and in terms of their subjec-tion to new forms of xenophobic exclusion in the post-apartheid period, as we shall see in the next chapter. However, before we do so we need to deconstruct the political-economic perspective hegemonic in the 1970s and 1980s in greater detail.

National Liberation and the Urban-Economic Understanding of Apartheid

It is important to subject to critical scrutiny the dominant intellectual paradigm which structured our view of the political economy of the Southern African region during the 1970s and 1980s. Although this perspective correctly insisted on the importance of migrant labour within the regional economy, it did so by one-sidedly concentrating on the importance of economic forces understood in a simple, non-contradictory manner. Its economism correspondingly failed to comprehend either the contradictions inherent in the migratory process, or for that matter the importance of an understanding of politics and the state in the region. I have examined this perspective in detail elsewhere (Neocosmos 1987, 1993a, 1993b, 1999) so that only the more salient points need be repeated here.

Basically, the dominant political economic discourse in Southern Africa over this period was one which stressed the industrialisation of South Africa and the corresponding formation of a working class through a process of the linear proletarianisation of the peasantry from the rural peripheries of the region, from the late nineteenth century to the present (a similar process on a smaller scale was deemed to have occurred in Zimbabwe also). Simply put, this approach visualised the character of the region from both an urban-biassed and an economic perspective. Its urban bias maintained explicitly or implicitly that rural-urban migration was a sign not only of temporary but of soon to be permanent proletarian status by a majority of the regions peasants. The pre-capitalist peasantry was understood to be proletarianising in a linear fashion, but the process was being held up by apartheid through the pass system. This had the effect of reproducing the pre-capitalist modes of production in rural areas in order to cheapen the value of labour power in the interests of South African capital (see for example Bundy 1988; Wolpe 1972).

The economic side of the perspective stressed inter alia that only in the urban industrial areas of South Africa were production relations to be found. Rural areas were simply seen as 'dormitory areas' for a 'reserve army of labour', bereft of production relations, classes or any social contradictions (other than 'tribal' ones). The politics of these regions and countries tended therefore to be understood as reflections of events in the South African metropolitan centres.[15] At the same time, 'apartheid' was explained economically as a form of labour control, the apogee of so many forms of labour control historically present in South Africa (from slavery to indentured labour to labour tenancy). It was a mechanism for providing super-exploited cheap labour for white capital in the interests of an expansive industrialisation process under pressure from popular struggles (Wolpe 1972; Legassick and Wolpe 1976). The main component of this control mechanism was the 'migrant labour system' in which the gradual impoverishment of the rural hinterland provided the conditions for a compliant 'reserve army of labour'.[16]

On the other hand, Ruth First also made the important point that in some areas of Mozambique peasant production had been virtually destroyed as a result of extensive land alienation, but that in other areas where mining capital had extensive influence, the peasantry was systematically reproduced alongside wage labour (First 1983: 130). This was an important remark for it seems that in many instances mining capital reproduced petty commodity production to an extent where other forms of intensive capitalist development could not. Thus it is reasonably apparent that, far from just having a proletarianising effect, the development of mining capital in particular had much more contradictory effects, one of which was to produce and reproduce such small scale productive activities. In fact, analyses of rural production relations showed evidence of considerable peasant differentiation in the rural economy of the region including in South Africa, and not a homogeneous impoverishment; by and large this evidence was ignored in debates at the time (First 1983; Neocosmos 1987a, 1987b, 1993a, 1993b; Levin and Neocosmos 1989; Levin and Weiner 1994 *inter alia*).

A number of consequences followed from the perspective of the 'linear proletarianisation' of the peasantry. Given the absence of contradictions at the rural periphery, the population of those countries and regions was seen as socially homogeneous while a simple reason was provided for migration, namely the impoverishment of the peasantry and labour reserve nature of the rural economies – i.e. simply capital-induced 'underdevelopment' along the lines of Gunder Frank's analyses of Latin America (Bundy 1988). In addition, no ways were found to explain the state and politics in these areas other than in simple technical or conspiratorial terms (Neocosmos 1987, 1993a, 1993b). The state ended up being seen as an external imposition from South Africa. Local people were given no role to play in their own histories. At the same time in South Africa itself apartheid was simply accounted for in economic terms, as a system of labour control based primarily on migrant labour, as instituted simply because it was in the interests of South African capital to do so or so intertwined with capitalism itself that the demise of the one could only mean the collapse of the other (Saul and Gelb 1986). Thus, because the region was seen as composed overwhelmingly of proletarians or 'proletarians to be', socialism was visualised as inevitable and 'just around the corner'. For example:

> In our country – more than in any other part of the oppressed world – it is inconceivable for liberation to have meaning without a return of the wealth of the land to the people as a whole. It is therefore a fundamental feature of our strategy that victory must embrace more than formal political democracy. To allow the existing economic forces to retain their interests intact is to feed the root of racial supremacy and does not represent even the shadow of liberation (ANC 1969: 32-3, see also Slovo 1976: 139ff; Arrighi and Saul 1973).

Under these circumstances, a host of crucial processes for the region were ignored and/or left unexplained. At the level of political economy, these included the differentiation of the oppressed South African population (whether rural or urban) along class, gender and ethnic lines, the differentiation of rural dwellers (including worker-peasants) and possibilities of accumulation among the people and the reproduction of petty commodity production (rural or urban) and the fact that the proceeds of labour migration might be a source of accumulation for peasants.

At the level of the understanding of politics, the specificity of both popular politics and state forms in the countries of the periphery, as well as the forms of state rule during the apartheid and post-apartheid periods, could not be adequately grasped.[17] After the collapse of apartheid, discussions of the state in South Africa (much as in the immediate post-independence period in Zimbabwe) were systematically reduced to assessments of policy and management questions (Neocosmos 1998, 2005). Finally, it became extremely difficult to recognise the fact that the people of the region could show extreme inventiveness in their struggles against colonialism and apartheid, in the making of their own histories, so that even the struggles of the 1980s in South Africa have been said to have been the simple result of decisions taken at the leadership level of the ANC in exile (Mbeki 1996).

This discourse then had positive and negative features. On the positive side, it emphasised the imperial character of the South African economy through its reliance on a dependency-type perspective which stressed the accumulation of the South African centre at the expense of the rural regional periphery. The positive side of this economistic nationalist perspective was also that, as it emphasised the proletarianisation of rural labour in general, no distinction was ever drawn between the ethnic or national identities of that labour. Migrant labour was migrant labour, irrespective of where it came from. Thus it was clearly understood and regularly asserted that labour from throughout the region had contributed to the building of the South African economy.

On the other hand, the process of regional migration was viewed exclusively in negative terms, as the 'migrant labour system' was seen as the *sine qua non* of apartheid. It enabled the super-exploitation of labour, forced migrants to live in inhuman conditions in single sex hostels and led to prostitution and to the break up of the family. It therefore combined economically exploitative as well as social pathological features which were seen as purely negative (Wilson 1972; Wilson and Ramphele 1989; Ramphele 1993). This overwhelmingly negative view of the migrant labour system followed because apartheid, as I have noted, was understood primarily as a form of labour control and not as a form of state, and also because migrant labour was seen as escaping to the cities in order to survive from uniformly impoverished and oppressive rural areas. With a few exceptions such as the work of First on Mozambique, rural areas were rarely studied and rural migrants were rarely questioned. As we shall see in the next chapter, it followed from this perspective that the demise of apartheid must entail the demise of the migrant labour system irrespective of whether it could have been in the interest of sections the Southern African peasantry or not. In addition, the effect of this discourse which was the central ideological pillar of the nationalist perspective in the region was to place a major obstacle in the way of the understanding of politics in general and democratic politics in particular. Only very gradually is this obstacle starting to be overcome, although with the collapse of political economy discourse, there has been a tendency to throw out the baby with the bathwater.

This perspective was also combined in nationalist discourse with a view which tended to see ethnicity in a blanket way as reactionary, backward-looking, atavistic, and generally as a conspiracy by white employers (for example on the mines) and by the 'apartheid regime' more broadly, to divide and control the oppressed in general and the working-class in particular.[18] It was seen as somehow 'visited from the out-side' on an unsuspecting population, as 'invented' to use Ranger's expression, and not produced from within rural political relations of domination (Neocosmos 1995). In broad terms therefore, the basic theory provided little in terms of a perspective to understand questions of ethnicity, nationality and citizenship at all. This was to be developed in practice only by the mass movement of the 1980s insofar as the struggle for a 'new nation' in South Africa was concerned as we shall see below. In addition, as I have noted elsewhere, no way was devised at the level of theory to politically unify the various national or ethnic components of a working class, as the latter was assumed to be already given as a unity (constant references to the South African (black) working-class testify to this; for example, Neocosmos 1999). The only arena in which it was seen as important to overcome ethnic and nationality divisions was at the workplace itself, through trade union organisation to confront employers. Outside of the workplace, the issue of ethnicity or nationality differ-ences was simply seen as resolved by ANC membership/support which was itself supposedly sufficiently unifying.

Popular Struggles and National Citizenship in Countryside and Town

What was characteristic of nationalist ideology at the independence of the BLS countries in the 1960s was a form of ethnic citizenship based on concepts of tradition and community defined to a greater or lesser extent by the chieftaincy. This meant inclusion in, or exclusion from, the community in terms of relations which were authoritarian, patriarchal, gerontocratic and oppressive of minorities. On the other hand, the struggles which led to the independence of the Portuguese colonies in the mid-1970s and to that of Zimbabwe in 1980, as well as the struggle for the liberation of South Africa in the 1980s, developed different conceptions of citizen-ship. I shall comment briefly on the case of Zimbabwe and then on that of South Africa in greater detail. While in the former the national struggle was mainly rural and in the latter overwhelmingly urban, both gave rise to popular democratic con-ceptions of citizenship – i.e. of people's relations to the state - which were both inclusive and active rather than exclusive and passive in content.

Rural Struggles in Zimbabwe and the Issue of Citizenship

The literature on the struggle for liberation in Zimbabwe has given rise to a lively debate on the nature of peasant consciousness. The writings of Ranger (1985a) and Lan (1985) in particular, argued for a unitary conception of peasant consciousness which harboured deep resentments towards the Rhodesian colonial regime, thus providing fertile ground for nationalist guerrilla activities. The collaboration of chiefs in Shona-speaking areas in particular with the colonial regime, and the consequent expression by the spirit mediums of the 'spirit of national struggle', consequently meant that the former lost legitimacy among peasants and that the latter took over many of their functions. At the same time, spirit mediums were not only instrumental in 'delivering' peasant support to guerrillas, but also redefined conceptions of community to include the latter (who always originated from other areas than their field of operations). This is explained by Lan as follows:

> The factor that persuaded the majority of the mediums to convert their symbolic resistance into practice was the undertaking given by the guerrillas that if their efforts should succeed they would reverse all the legislation that limited the development and freedom of the peasantry. Of all the promised reforms the most important for forging unity between guerrillas and mediums was the undertaking to free the land from the grasp of the whites, to return it to the peasants who had barely enough to keep their families alive... the guerrillas were 'strangers'. In other words, they were not descendants of the royal ancestors who 'owned' the land, either as members of the royal lineage itself or of any of the commoner lineages which held rights in land but whose members could not succeed to the chieftaincy. Therefore... the guerrillas held no political authority at all... But despite their lack of political authority, the guerrillas claimed the land... all the land in the whole territory of Zimbabwe... [through their alliance with mediums] by observing the ancestral prohibitions the guerrillas were transformed from 'strangers' into 'royals', from members of lineages resident in other parts of Zimbabwe, into descendants of the local *mhondoro* [royal ancestor] with rights to land. They had become 'at home' in the [local community] (Lan 1985: 148, 164).

In other words, even 'traditional' culture and custom which always traced community membership through descent and through descent alone, could be transformed to include erstwhile strangers into the community. This was done by those who spoke for tradition and the nation/community through giving symbolic rights to land to the guerrillas. It seems therefore that even under apparently pre-capitalist or pre-modern cultural conceptions, rights of citizenship can be conferred on foreigners, and the concept of community can be thereby democratised.

Contrary to Ranger and Lan who treat peasant consciousness as homogeneous, more recent work by Kriger (1991, 1992) and Maxwell (1993), emphasises the importance of divisions among the peasantry in understanding popular reaction to ZANU guerillas during the liberation war. This work operates at different levels showing not only that the oppressed people are capable of making their own histories under extreme conditions, but that they were doing so through attempts to transform their own social relations as well as the powers of the local state. This work largely debunks the nationalist myth of a homogeneous peasantry willingly assisting their guerrilla liberators from ZANU. The people were not just 'helping' the guerrillas, but were attempting to address their own grievances which did not always fit within the narrow nationalist conceptions of the latter.

Without denying that peasants had common grievances against the central colonial state, Kriger shows that struggles within peasant community played a crucial mobilising role in the independence war. She looks at generational, class and gender struggles, as well as conflicts between dominant and dominated lineages/'outsiders'.

At the level of generational relations, she shows how unmarried youth over fifteen years (overwhelmingly male) were organised separately and thus were gradually constituted (and constituted themselves) into a distinct grouping of 'youth'. They challenged the control which elders had over their daily lives and this was one of the reasons motivating them to participate in the war. In addition having no cattle or land, the youth were among the poorer strata of the peasantry (Kriger 1991: 126-133). These poor peasants also acted independently, defied guerrilla instructions to raid only white farmers for cattle and attacked rich peasants even though such measures may have been individualistic, unorganised and undisciplined. As with the generational conflicts, these attacks on the wealthier occurred largely independently of formal organisation, but they did suggest a struggle towards some form of equalisation of wealth and power within the community (ibid: 133-136).

Kriger makes similar points with regard to why other oppressed groups within peasant society participated in the war, namely women and dominated lineages/strangers. The former were attempting to improve their domestic lives, and for a brief period wives were able to democratise household relations somewhat. The latter attempted to democratise village politics through taking over the chiefs' powers to judge court cases and allocate land (ibid: 137-145). In particular these struggles involved attempts by dominated ethnicities or lineages to play a more direct role in village politics. In actual fact, all these struggles can also be read as attempts by the weakest members of the community, for inclusion into local state 'community structures' principally through an equalisation of community relations.

> The revolutionary initiative to reconstitute local politics in a more democratic way came from rural people themselves. The guerrillas opposed 'traditional' rulers (i.e. primarily chiefs and not spirit mediums – M.N.) because of their involvement with government, but never challenged the institution of hereditary offices. When they killed incumbent rulers or encouraged committee members to take power from them or share power with them, the intent was to punish individual 'traditional' rulers for collaborating with the government and give some status and power to the new committees. The guerrillas' agenda never included eliminating the lineage-based, hereditary pre-colonial political system and broadening the basis for political competition for local power (Kriger 1991: 145).

ZANU therefore was only interested in transforming rural social relations insofar as these concerned the whites and their state. Like other nationalist organisations in Africa, they were not concerned with a democratisation of social relations within peasant society. But in order to be successful in their venture they needed the support, enthusiasm, hard work (and even the dominance for a period) of the most oppressed or exploited sectors of the rural population, because the economically better off and politically more powerful were unreliable. They were unreliable supports of the nationalist movement because they had achieved their relative wealth and power within a colonial context. They were therefore (more or less) compromised in the eyes of the nationalist movement and more importantly in those of the people. ZANU practice was therefore typical of nationalist movements. A recent text notes that:

> Because those shifts in local power relations which brought women and youth to the fore, were never institutionalised, their new found status was short lived. The latter years of the 1980s have seen a revival of rural patriarchy with increased subsidies for chiefs and the reconstitution of traditional courts. Guerrillas did secure local legitimacy, but their lack of a concrete programme meant that they lost the opportunity to bring about lasting changes in rural areas (Maxwell 1993: 386).

Authors such as Kriger and Maxwell (1993) understand that the various groupings of rural society, although in favour of independence and liberation and the 'return of the land to the tiller', support such demands for ultimately different reasons and not just because of an overall peasant or national or even 'ethnic' consciousness. In actual fact peasant action was directed both against the colonial state (nationalism) and the local state (the chiefs), while operating clearly within the limits of an 'ethnic' Shona culture. On the other hand, it seems that in the period immediately following independence, chiefs in both Zimbabwe and Mozambique were soon able to successfully re-establish themselves by leading a coalition of rural forces against what were the obvious statist predations of the 'modernising' and bureaucratic development strategy of the post-colonial state (Alexander 1993; Abrahamsson and Nilsson 1995: 86ff). Alexander puts the point succinctly:

> Though traditional leaders may have been partly or largely motivated by their own ambitions, their appeal to tradition gained support from a constituency which perceived state-defined 'modernization' as a threat either to its autonomy, economic interests or social standing and which had no alternative institution through which to express its objections (Alexander 1993: 153).

In brief, peasants in the Shona-speaking areas of Zimbabwe attempted to systematically democratise rural social relations during the independence war. In particular, the collapse in authority of chiefs through their association with the colonial state meant that it was the peasants themselves who withdrew state powers from them and gave these to others including both spirit mediums and guerrillas. The former would be entrusted with land allocation for example, while the latter would engage in arbitrating and adjudicating disputes (Lan 1985, especially chapter 8). The whole process was at the same time a 'struggle over tradition', an attempt at reassertion of Shona cultural ('ethnic') values which the chiefs were seen to have betrayed. This can be seen in particular with regard to the link between the present and the ancestors which the chiefs had broken and which the spirit mediums now came to express (Lan op. cit.: passim). The process can also be seen as a struggle for inclusion in the community as the poor, youth, women and outsiders were asserting their status as community members, as part of a process of re-arranging community relations. The re-establishment of chiefs into positions of power and their re-emergence as the dominant figures in rural areas in the post-independence period has meant a reassertion of authoritarian, patriarchal and gerontocratic tradition along with a narrowing of the dominant concept of community.

Citizenship and Popular Struggles in Urban South Africa

While the rural struggles of the peasantry in Zimbabwe revolved around a discourse of 'tradition', those of the urban township dwellers in the South Africa of the 1980s utilised a discourse on 'rights'. This distinction stressed by Mamdani (1996) seems essentially correct, although I would suggest that the South African popular movement was not simply demanding entry into an existing civil society; within the complex discourse within which demands were formulated (Lodge et al., 1991), there was a trend - although never consistently a dominant one – which geared its demands and practice towards a transformation of society and of the state itself. Central to this trend which gave rise to the demand for 'people's power' was a specific conception of active citizenship which exhibited two main components: first an actively participatory conception of citizenship in which politics became the day-to-day business of ordinary people, in which civil society organisations were politicised, and thereby inaugurated a popular realm of political society outside the state. The second aspect of this active citizenship was a specific inclusiveness in which national citizenship was to have a non-racial and not simply a multi-racial character. Both these components were to be found to a greater or lesser degree within the discourse and practices of township and trade union organisations. They never existed in isolation however and had to struggle to assert themselves against authoritarian and generally undemocratic practices within the same organisations. The fact that they failed to consistently dominate within these organisations does not decrease their importance from the perspective of understanding the struggles over citizenship in South Africa and the region (Neocosmos 1998).[19]

The popular mass upsurge started in earnest in September 1984 and took the form of bus and rent boycotts, housing movements, squatter revolts, labour strikes, school protests and community stay-aways. This change in the focus of protest was not the result of any strategy or of a change in policy by the UDF (United Democratic Front) leadership – the umbrella organisation in whose name the protestors were organising, and which had originally been set up 'from above' to combat the apartheid state reforms of the 'tricameral' parliament and the 'Koornhof Bills'. The radicalisation and democratisation of the struggle seems ultimately to have been forced on the leadership from below (Swilling 1988: 101). Indeed, by mid-1985 it was becoming clear that the UDF leadership was unable to exert effective control over developments despite its popularity. In Lodge's words:

> The momentum for action came from the bottom levels of the organisation and from its youngest members. It was children who built the roadblocks, children who

led the crowds to the administrative buildings, children who delegated spokespersons, and children who in 1984 told the older folk that things would be different, that people would not run away as they had in 1960 (Lodge et al. 1991: 76).

According to Swilling, local organisations:

exploited the contradiction between the state's attempts to improve urban living conditions and the fiscal bankruptcy and political illegitimacy of local government. They managed to ride a wave of anger and protest that transformed political relations in the communities so rapidly that the UDF's local, regional and national leaders found themselves unable to build organisational structures to keep pace with these levels of mobilisation and politicisation (ibid: 101-2).

He also stresses that mass actions mobilised unprecedented numbers of people. These succeeded in mobilising:

all sectors of the township population including both youth and older residents; they involved coordinated action between trade unions and political organisations; they were called in support of demands that challenged the coercive urban and education policies of the apartheid state; and they gave rise to ungovernable areas as state authority collapsed in many townships in the wake of the resignation of mayors and councillors who had been 'elected' onto the new Black Local Authorities (ibid: 102).

The declaration of the first state of emergency in 1985 which lasted until 1986 was the state's response as it attempted to control this mass upsurge and reassert control over 'ungovernable areas'. Interestingly both popular rebellion and political organisation grew during this period which saw the setting up of 'street committees' in particular. These took over the functions of local government especially in ungovernable areas. One local activist in the Port Elizabeth area stated:

We said [to our people]: In the streets where you live you must decide what issues affect your lives and bring up issues you want your organisation to take up. We are not in a position to remove debris, remove buckets, clean the streets and so on. But the organisation must deal with these matters through street committees (cited in Lodge et al. op cit.: 82).

The view of the ANC in exile as expressed by their spokesman Tom Sebina, was that street committees 'grow out of the need of the people to defend themselves against State repression...and in response to ANC calls to make the country ungovernable and apartheid unworkable [so as to forge them into] contingents that will be part of the process towards a total people's war'. Contrary to this view which saw street committees as tactical adjuncts to the development of a militaristic process and as simply 'oppositional' to the apartheid state, local activists spelt out a different assessment:

The people in Lusaka can say what they like... we know that the purpose is to enable people to take their lives in hand. Local government has collapsed. The state's ver-

sion of local government was corrupt and inefficient in any case, but local government is necessary for people to channel their grievances. The street committees fill the
vacuum. They give people an avenue to express views and come up with solutions
(cited in Mathiane 1986: 13).

These popular state structures were proliferating in urban townships. Marx (1992:
167) notes that by 1987, forty-three percent of the inhabitants of Soweto for example were reporting the existence of street and area committees in their neighbour-
hoods. In many townships, rudimentary services began to be provided by civics and
youth congresses, while also crime began being regulated through 'people's courts'.
These developed in some areas originally to regulate dispute between neighbours (as
in Atteridgeville in Pretoria) and also as attempts to control the proliferation of
brutal Kangaroo courts (for example in Uitenhage and Port Elizabeth). In Alexandra
outside Johannesburg, five members of the Alexandra Action Committee were nomi-
nated in February 1986 to sit in judgment over cases of assault and theft, while
street committees were empowered to settle quarrels. In Mamelodi, one of Pretoria's townships, a number of 'informal' systems of justice operated in the 1970s and
1980s and there were long term struggles over the setting up of popularly accountable courts, which were also highly influenced by traditional African custom (for
instance the importance of elders etc.).[20] Lodge concludes that:

> Of all the manifestations of people's power... the efforts of local groups to admin-
> ister civil and criminal justice were the most challenging to the state's moral authority.
> More than any other feature of the insurrectionary movement, people's justice testi-
> fied to the movement's ideological complexity and to the extent to which it was
> shaped from below by popular culture (op cit.: 135).

In addition to popular control of townships and popular justice, there was a comple-
mentary development of institutions geared towards the provision of 'people's education'. These included in particular attempts to bring local schools under community control through the establishment of Parent Teacher Student Associations
(PTSAs) and even attempts to develop a new curriculum in response to 'Bantu
Education' – the central plank of the apartheid state in this sphere. The struggle for
people's education was seen as intimately linked to establishing 'People's Power'. In
the words of Zwelakhe Sisulu:

> The struggle for People's Education is no longer a struggle of the students alone. It
> has become a struggle of the whole community with the involvement of all sections
> of the community. This is not something which has happened in the school sphere
> alone; it reflects a new level of development in the struggle as a whole... The struggle
> for people's education can only finally be won when we have won the struggle for
> people's power...We are no longer demanding the same education as Whites, since
> this is education for domination. People's education means education at the service
> of the people as a whole, education that liberates, education that puts the people in
> command of their lives. We are not prepared to accept any 'alternative' to Bantu
> Education which is imposed on the people from above. This includes American or

other imperialist alternatives designed to safeguard their selfish interests in the country... To be acceptable, every initiative must come from the people themselves, must be accountable to the people and must advance the broad mass of students, not just a select few (Sisulu 1986: 106, 110).

Or again:

I want to emphasise here that these advances were only possible because of the development of democratic organs, or committees, of people's power. Our people set up bodies which were controlled by, and accountable to, the masses of the people in each area. In such areas, the distinction between the people and their organisations disappeared. All the people young and old participated in committees from street level upwards (ibid: 104).

What stands out in particular from the ideology and practice of the mass popular movement of the mid-1980s is an attempt to develop genuinely popular forms of democracy founded on active citizenship in both ideology and practice. In particular the general characterisation of the mass struggle as national and democratic combined both territorial as well as popular democratic aspects of the process. In fact the two were regularly combined in attempts by leading activists to theorise the process of struggle. Thus Murphy Morobe, the 'Acting Publicity Secretary' of the UDF in 1987 famously stated:

We in the United Democratic Front are engaged in a national democratic struggle. We say we are engaged in a national struggle for two reasons. Firstly, we are involved in political struggle on a *national*, as opposed to a regional or local level. The national struggle involves all sectors of our people – workers (whether in the factories, unemployed, migrants or rural poor), youth, students, women and democratic-minded professionals. We also refer to our struggle as national in the sense of seeking to create a new nation out of the historical divisions of apartheid. We also explain the *democratic* aspect of our struggle in two ways... Firstly, we say that a democratic South Africa is one of the aims or goals of our struggle. This can be summed up in the principal slogan of the Freedom Charter: 'The People Shall Govern'. In the second place, democracy is the means by which we conduct our struggle... The creation of democratic *means* is for us as important as having democratic *goals* as our objective... When we say that the people shall govern, we mean at all levels and in all spheres, and we demand that there be a real, effective control on a daily basis... The key to a democratic system lies in being able to say that the people in our country can not only vote for a representative of their choice, but also feel that they have some direct control over where and how they live, eat sleep, work, how they get to work, how they and their children are educated, what the content of that education is; and that these things are not *done for them by the government of the day*, but [by] the people themselves... The rudimentary organs of people's power that have begun to emerge in South Africa (street committees, defence committees, shop-steward structures, student representative councils, parent/teacher/student associations) represent in many ways the beginnings of the kind of democracy that we are striving for... Without the fullest organisational democracy, we will never be able to achieve conscious,

active and unified participation of the majority of the people, and in particular the
working class, in our struggle (Morobe 1987:81-83, emphasis added).

I have cited this passage at length because it clearly sums up the systematisation of
popular experiences and demands which some leaders were able to eloquently make.
Clearly this statement has more the character of an ideal to be struggled for rather
than a simple description of reality, nevertheless it indicates the centrality of popular democracy within the ideology and practice of the movement. It is important to
note first that the main slogan of the Freedom Charter ('The People Shall Govern')
is given a specific interpretation by the UDF, namely to mean a popular form of
democracy and not simply an electoral multi-party system, or for that matter a one-
party system (as its vagueness could also have implied). In fact the former is explicitly rejected as the exclusive form of representation, and as too limited a form of
democracy. Thus an evidently vague and indeed 'populist' slogan could in the circumstances of the time be given an unambiguous popular-democratic content. It
would be a fundamental error to confuse the content of such democracy with its
own slogans and its self-presentation, as many who at the time dismissed the UDF as
a 'populist' organisation, in fact did. In practice, the social movement was giving rise
to a form of mass democracy and a form of state unique in South Africa (and
probably also in Africa as a whole); these forms of democracy and state have
arguably gone largely unrecognised by most intellectuals, by the party of state nationalism, the ANC, and even by many of the movement's own leaders.

Two features of this democracy worth noting were a detailed system of control-
ling leaders to be accountable to the rank and file membership, and a different way
of demarcating 'the people' from 'the oppressors'. Attempts at instituting internal
democracy within organisations were strongly followed, although they obviously had
various degrees of success. The important point however was that such a struggle
for democracy existed within organisations.

The various dimensions of this democracy were, according to Morobe (1987):

1) Elected Leadership. Leadership of our organisations must be elected (at all
   levels), and elections must be held at periodic intervals... Elected leadership
   must also be recallable before the end of their term of office if there is
   indiscipline or misconduct.

2) Collective Leadership. We try and practice collective leadership at all levels.
   There must be continuous, ongoing consultation...

3) Mandates and Accountability. Our leaders and delegates are not free-floating
   individuals. They always have to operate within the delegated mandates of their
   positions and delegated duties...

4) Reporting. Reporting back to organisations, areas, units, etc. is an important
   dimension of democracy...We feel very strongly that information is a form of
   power, and that if it is not shared, it undermines the democratic process. We
   therefore take care to ensure that language translations occur if necessary...

5)   Criticism and Self-criticism. We do not believe that any of our members are
     beyond criticism; neither are organisations and strategies beyond reproach...
     (Morobe op cit.: 84-85).

However, by February 1989 it had become clear that some individuals were beyond
criticism, as when an attempt was made by the UDF (and COSATU) to publicly
censure Winnie Mandela it was blocked by the ANC in Lusaka. In fact, the danger
posed to popular democracy by the lack of control of the popular movement over
a number of 'charismatic' leaders who felt they had the authority to speak and act
without being mandated, was one of which many were aware. Thus, *Isizwe*, the main
journal of the UDF, made a rather prophetic statement in 1985:

> One thing that we must be careful about... is that our organisations do not become
> too closely associated with individuals, that we do not allow the development of
> personality cults. We need to understand why we regard people as leaders and to
> articulate these reasons. Where people do not measure up to these standards they
> must be brought to heel – no matter how 'charismatic' they may be. No person is a
> leader in a democratic struggle such as ours simply because he or she makes good
> speeches... *No individual may make proposals on the people's behalf – unless mandated by
> them*... We need to say these things because there are some people and interests who
> are trying to project individuals as substitutes for political movement (United Demo-
> cratic Front 1985: 17, emphasis added).

The practices of 'mandates and report-backs' which had been adopted largely as a
result of trade union influence were taken particularly seriously in the mid-eighties,
although there is evidence that they started to decline at the end of the decade.[21] By
1991, the position had changed substantially so that *Mayibuye*, the journal of the
ANC, now pompously proclaimed:

> accountability is the basis of democratic organisation. Accountability means that
> leadership must discuss decisions with the membership. Decisions must be ex-
> plained so that members understand why they are made (*Mayibuye*, December 1991,
> p.36).

We are a far cry here from 'People's Power'. The manner in which the popular
movement demarcated its members ('the people' or 'the nation') from the oppressive state, is also worthy of note. This largely surrounded the notion of 'non-racialism' as a way of characterising the ideology of the movement as well as the nature
of the state which was being fought for. Originally inherited from Black Consciousness discourse which used the term to refer to all oppressed racial groups in South
Africa under the characterisation 'Black', 'non-racialism' was adapted by the UDF
to include whites who supported the struggle. This struggle was visualised as uniting
into a national opposition the disparate groups which the apartheid state divided,
hence the main slogan of the UDF: 'UDF Unites, Apartheid Divides!' One important aspect of non-racialism was the fact that rather than distinguishing 'the people'
or 'the oppressors' on racial grounds, it did so by demarcating on political grounds:

popular-democrats from anti-democrats. The former were those who supported change 'from below', the latter those who proposed some form of 'tinkering from above' and who had by this period, lost the confidence of the majority. Democrats were all those who opposed 'minority rule' and supported 'majority rule' through popular democracy. In the words of a UDF discussion document from 1986:

> The essential *dividing line* that we should promote is between supporters of *minority rule and majority rule*. The common ground between the Botha (sic), the PFP (Popular Federal Party, the main White, big business-backed liberal opposition at the time – MN) leadership and big business is that they all seek solutions within the framework of adapting minority rule. Although they differ fundamentally on who to involve in negotiation and how much adaptation is necessary, these elements all agree that the system must be changed from the top down, with the solutions being decided over the heads of the people. All those who accept the right of the people to determine the process of change are allies of the people and part of the NDS (National Democratic Struggle – MN) (UDF Cape Town Area Committee 1986: 10, emphasis in original).

This meant that the conducting of the popular struggle should also be 'non-racial'. Terror Lekota, a senior UDF figure put it this way:

> In political struggle... the means must always be the same as the ends... How can one expect a racialistic movement to imbue our society with a non-racial character on the dawn of our freedom day? A political movement cannot bequeath to society a characteristic it does not itself possess. To expect it to do so is like asking a heathen to convert a person to Christianity. The principles of that religion are unknown to the heathen let alone the practice (cited by Marx op cit.: 124).

Such a position was possible precisely because the social movement was not an elite movement and because white 'progressives' (to use the jargon of the time) provided invaluable work both in the trade unions as well as the UDF, thus becoming known and appreciated by the people of the townships. It served to divide a minority of white democrats from white racists (while forcing the uncommitted to commit themselves), in the same way as affiliation to popular organisations divided blacks between collaborators with the state (so-called 'sell-outs') and the majority of the oppressed.[22] This attempt to create the unity of a 'new nation' can be contrasted with the attempts to do so 'from above' by the post-apartheid state via 'reconciliation', 'nation building', the Reconstruction and Development Programme, 'affirmative action' or Black Economic Empowerment. Thus, the much maligned 'populist' character of nationalist discourse in the 1980s allowed for the development of genuine forms of popular democracy; unfortunately, such popular initiatives were to be systematically precluded by the 'statism' of nationalist discourse in the 1990s, as the state gradually arrogated to itself the monopoly of the nationalist project – 'liberation'.

Similar points can be made with reference to the history of the trade union movement during the same period. As is well known, the history of the modern trade union movement in South Africa largely originates in 1973 when 100,000 workers went on strike in the Durban area. These largely spontaneous mass strikes revitalised trade union activity which had been dormant during the 'decade of peace' after the banning of the ANC/SACP (and the PAC) along with that of SACTU (South African Congress of Trade Unions) which was largely the organ of the 'Congress Alliance'. The unions which developed as a result of the Durban strikes saw it as crucially important to maintain their independence from nationalist organisations in order to avoid the same fate as SACTU. Rather they concentrated on developing strong shop-floor structures and a system of worker representation based around shop-stewards. Apart from being intrinsically democratic, it was argued that such a system would enable a small union organisation to better withstand state repression (Webster 1988, Lambert and Webster 1988).

This fiercely independent stance became the dominant position in FOSATU (Federation of South African Trade Unions) which was launched in 1979, and actually came to be adhered to rigidly like an article of faith (until the formation of COSATU in November 1985) theorised by the intellectual high priests of the 'White Left' who had been instrumental in servicing the development of the new unions. Basically the view was that 'working class politics' should grow out of shop-floor struggles. Unions should not identify with any nationalist political organisation as union members belonged to different organisations, and also because it would mean accepting the dominance of a petty-bourgeoisie who supposedly dominated the township-based organisations, which in any case were said not to be as democratic as trade unions. With the increasing development of popular struggles in the townships (in which trade unionists lived after all) the question which was to occupy the centre of the intellectual stage on the Left in South Africa came to the fore, namely the question of the relationship if any between trade union struggles and township struggles or workers' organisations and national politics. This single question has given rise to a large volume of debate covering not only the above issues, but also ranging more broadly to include the question of class alliances, the 'road to socialism', the nature of the Freedom Charter, the question of 'unity in the struggle', 'liberation versus transformation' and so on.

More briefly it is known as the debate between 'workerists' and 'populists' and was also conducted far beyond the confines of popular organisations, where it became transformed well beyond its original spheres of concern regarding the relationship between civil society and politics into an often acrimonious academic debate where arguments merely served to further entrench already rigidly adhered to positions. Shortage of space precludes an assessment of this debate here although it is proposed to study it in detail as part of future work. Rather a very brief account of the changes to the trade union movement which paralleled this debate is of greater importance to our immediate concerns. Briefly, the pressure for unions to become more involved in township nationalist politics came overwhelmingly from workers themselves as they experienced not only oppression in the workplace but the same urban problems and coercion as all other residents at their homes. The main organisations which voiced these pressures were the Local Shop-Steward Councils (known simply as 'locals') which brought together shop stewards from a given urban area and which originated in the East Rand (Germiston, Wadeville, Katlehong). According to Webster (1988: 183): 'founded as a way of involving shop-stewards in the organisation of unorganised factories, these councils spread rapidly during the 1981-2 strike waves... At the centre of this social movement in the East Rand hostels was the migrant worker'.

Although the locals were originally founded as a way of spreading union organisation to other factories and to fight against scabbing, organised as they were in urban townships, they were bound to become involved in township issues. They started to become involved in questions of housing, unemployment benefits, adequate pensions and maternity rights inter alia (ibid; Swilling 1984: 118). In the words of Jeremy Baskin's study of a Shop-Steward Council in 1982:

> The shop-stewards' council is characterised by its militancy, mutual support... and strong grassroots organisation... All this is made possible by strong local organisation. Workers in the area share many problems. They use the same buses and trains, they live in the same areas and they know other workers in neighbouring factories. The common conditions which workers face at local level becomes a major spur to militancy, once organisation gets started... The fact that workers began presenting common demands generally strengthened their position in the area... Workers are encouraged to see beyond their own union to the struggles of workers as a whole (Baskin 1982: 47-8).

In addition, the locals became bases for democratic control over unions as more power lay in the hands of shop-stewards and these structures were not bureaucratic. One shop-steward explained:

> We talk of unity... what kind of unity and how far we should go as a local. What sort of help, what sort of things we should do, and the disciplinary procedures. Because if we are to be united we have to have disciplinary procedures and some clear objectives... As workers, then we are involved in political issues, so we have to be clear on how to react to such things... Problems like rent have come up... we have to do some things outside the factory (cited in Baskin 1987: 52).

As a result of these developments, the 'FOSATU line' came more and more into conflict with its own shop-stewards, especially after the formation of the UDF and the intensification of community struggles, and the greater and greater pressure from below for joint community-trade union action. What had been a very correct tactic in the early 1980s had become by the middle of the decade a sterile dogma, as the objective situation had fundamentally changed. One shop-steward from the Metal and Allied Workers Union (MAWU) argued:

> The situation of the worker in South Africa is that they are oppressed and exploited. The struggle goes beyond the factory gates. Workers must address themselves to the problems of rents, shacks, electricity tariffs, schools, recreation, etc. In FOSATU and MAWU workers have been openly discouraged from taking up these issues and

political organisations have been openly criticised. We recognise that the trade unions are not political organisations. But for them (MAWU) to say no politics in trade unions is nothing else but to keep their politics of reformism inside the trade unions (cited in Swilling 1984: 119).

It was this pressure from below which ultimately led to the formalisation of what Webster has called 'social movement unionism', finally expressed in the formation of a new giant union federation, the Congress of South African Trade Unions (COSATU) in 1985. Unlike its predecessor, COSATU encouraged the politicisation of trade union activity and collaboration between unions and the UDF, even adopting the Freedom Charter as a guiding principle. COSATU therefore became involved in building 'worker control' (the equivalent of democratic 'People's Power' in the factories and unions) and insisted on contributing to the 'working-class leadership' of the 'national democratic struggle' (although what precisely what was meant by such leadership was not always clarified). Thus Jay Naidoo, the general secretary of COSATU:

> Non-political unionism is not only undesirable but impossible in South Africa. Therefore we believe that though COSATU is not a political party COSATU has a responsibility to voice the political interests and aspirations of organised workers and also more broadly the working class. To do this we have to look at how WE BUILD WORKERS [POWER] and how do we locate workers as the leading force in our struggle for national liberations (sic)... The key element in the building of the labour movement was, and still remains, the democratic principles of worker control... In real terms it means that the members of the trade union must have absolute control over all decision-making in the organisation... COSATU has high regard for those communities and organisations that are building strong grassroots organisation in the form of area and street committees. We encourage this and see it as COSATU's policy for members and local structures of COSATU to play an active role in building such structures (Jay Naidoo 1986: 3, 4, 8).

In this way, COSATU was politicised and its national campaigns made a conscious attempt to address issues which were pertinent to the interests of the poor and unorganised in general, and not simply to those of the organised workers (the most famous being the 'Living Wage Campaign'). A survey on the state of the unions published in 1985 noted that in a sample of twenty three of the largest industrial unions, there were 12,462 shop stewards, with 1,443 shop-steward councils in place (Collins 1994: 35). Not surprisingly then, COSATU placed much emphasis on the role of 'locals' which were seen as the foundation of the organisation: 'In particular the role of the shop steward councils was crucial. They assisted in organisational work and developed ordinary worker leadership. The local confronted the political issues of the day and developed resistance in practice' (ibid: 36).

Both township and trade union struggles in the South Africa of the 1980s developed a popular conception of citizenship which I have suggested above had two components: first a notion of active citizenship founded on the direct participation in politics of ordinary people, and second a concept of national unity based on non-racialism. This popular movement re-made a political truth most clearly formulated by Fanon (1990: 165), namely that 'the living expression of the nation is the moving consciousness of the whole people, it is the coherent, enlightened action of men and women'; the symbols of the nation cease to be the 'empty shells' of 'the flag and the palace where sits the government', they become embodied in active citizenship.

Fundamentally then, the popular movement gave practical content to the initial statement of the Freedom Charter, the flag of the Congress movement that 'South Africa belongs to *all* who live in it' (emphasis added). The Freedom Charter consisted of a number of popular prescriptions on the state collected in one document. It included prescriptions in addition to the one above such as 'The People Shall Govern', 'All National Groups Shall Have Equal rights', 'The People Shall Share in the Country's Wealth' and 'The Land Shall be Shared Among those who Work it' inter alia (Suttner and Cronin, 1986). The important point here is that the popular movement of the 1980s provided an active conception of citizenship while it gave, in its practice, a universal content to these prescriptions which were absolutely clear to all within the popular nationalist politics of the time.

What was missing from this conception however was a notion of citizenship founded on place of work rather than descent. Such a conception was not developed systematically in South Africa in particular and this showed, as Mamdani (1996: chapter 7) has pointed out, in the exclusion of migrant workers in particular and the countryside in general from the concept of community which the urban movement adhered to. This point is important and should be expanded. As both the township and union movements faced the wrath of the state towards the late 1980s, they gradually lost their characteristics associated with popular control and came gradually to respond more and more to directives from above. The loss of powers of 'local' shop-steward committees for example was accompanied by a dominant trend towards corporatism in the 1990s, while civics dropped their political role in favour of the ANC at the latter's unbanning. The women's and youth organisations were incorporated into the ANC (Neocosmos 1998). Concurrently, the dominant political discourse became more and more defined by a leadership not always closely linked to the rank and file and informed by popular experience. At the same time, neither the popular urban movement nor the ANC in exile had developed a link between the rural and urban sectors of the country in their political programmes.

The result of all these factors was the uncritical adherence to an ideological perspective for which migrants were seen simply as workers, and migrant labour was seen solely as a 'system' devised by apartheid to acquire cheap labour for white capitalists. While there was much truth in this nationalist perspective, it was dominated by the economistic paradigm discussed above. Its one-sided emphasis on proletarianisation and capitalism meant that it could not understand the fact that migrant labourers were only half workers and that as peasants they may draw some crucially important benefits from the migrant labour system.

This can be understood clearly if we realise that not all migrants to employment in South African (mines etc.) did so in order to achieve subsistence or for simple survival needs. As we have seen, a significant proportion migrate in order to acquire funds for their reproduction as middle peasants (First 1985), and also for purposes of accumulation whether in agricultural, merchant, transport or other economic activities (Neocosmos 1987, 1993a, 1993b, Johnston 1996). It follows from this that not all migrants wished to be settled in urban areas nor did they wish to see the 'migrant labour system' abolished – as they saw their stay in South Africa as purely temporary – male hostels destroyed and family housing being put up in their place. In fact Mamdani shows clearly that this latter policy of emphasising family housing, which the ANC and COSATU pursued vigorously in the early 1990s, was instrumental in driving migrants from Kwazulu-Natal into the arms of a political organisation based on mobilising ethnic nationalism – Inkatha (Mamdani 1996, chapter 7).

As we shall see in the next chapter, the National Union of Mineworkers (NUM) (as well as the Presidential Commission on the Labour Market), pursued a similar form of reasoning in the mid-nineties in raising the issue of an offer of permanent residence followed by full rights of South African citizenship to Basotho miners with many years labour in South Africa. While seemingly 'progressive' and democratic, such an offer did not take the wishes of migrants themselves into account, and failed to look at the issue as one of providing rights for all workers, native and foreign, and not only to citizens. Basotho miners would have to lose access to their Lesotho citizenship as well as to their resources in Lesotho in order to acquire South African citizenship (Neocosmos 1999). The reason the NUM pursued this line was because free movement to cities was assumed to provide jobs as the economic poverty of rural and ethnic life was seen as endemic and urbanisation restricted by the apartheid state. Access to cities, it was assumed, would mean access to jobs, and freedom was explicitly or implicitly identified with urbanisation. The understanding of 'nation' (and hence citizenship) which was politically asserted by the nationalist movement was thus a fundamentally urban one.

Of the two components of citizenship developed by the popular movement, the former in particular, i.e. that of active participation in political activity, had become so much of a truism by the early 1990s that academic writing in South Africa seemed at times to take such a notion of citizenship for granted (for example Orkin 1995). Unfortunately however this was largely wishful thinking as this conception soon became inapplicable as state institutions substituted themselves for popular activity. As already noted, from the mid nineties, the state directed a process of 'nation building' and hence citizenship formation from above, basically via legislative activity and other practices. I shall return to review this process in the final chapter. For the present it is important to stress that the experiences of the liberation/independence struggles in both Zimbabwe and South Africa, despite their differences, illustrate the view taken in here that citizenship is not merely an effect of state interpellation, but is also established as an effect of active politics from among popular or subaltern forces. In actual fact, its final form appears as an outcome of precisely a political relation between state and people. What is also important to note is that in both the case of rural Zimbabwe and in that of urban South Africa, popular conceptions of citizenship stressed not only national unity vis-à-vis state divisions, but also and more fundamentally an inclusive conception of citizenship not based on indigeneity. Indeed it is particularly to note that guerrillas in rural Zimbabwe were treated as fully fledged community members as, contrary to assumptions that citizenship by descent or indigeneity is a pre-capitalist or pre-modern conception, rural communities had clearly devised ways through tradition to include strangers.

Mamdani (1998a) is thus mistaken to assert that the members of one ethnic group can never become members of another, that the settler into another ethnic domain cannot acquire another ethnicity as this is defined by an 'ancestral area'. He stresses: 'you were obliged to follow the custom of your ethnic group. Your rights and obligations were defined by your custom, and that custom was enforced as a "customary law", by a Native Authority whose seat was the local state. The local state spoke the language of culture not rights' (ibid: 1). Thus ethnic citizenship for Mamdani cannot be acquired it can only be inherited. However there are numerous examples of 'strangers' being accepted as fully fledged citizens of ethnic communities in Africa. An example among many is precisely Zimbabwe during the liberation struggle.[23] Lan (1985) shows clearly how guerrillas who were strangers to their areas of operation during the liberation war in Zimbabwe, became accepted as full community members through the intermediation of spirit mediums. Moreover, such ethnic citizenship could, in many cases under tradition, be bestowed on foreigners through a declaration (sometimes accompanied by payment) of allegiance to a chief. As I have argued elsewhere, there is always space for democratic politics within both a constantly changing 'tradition' as well as within a domain of civic struggles (Neocosmos 2003).

Conclusions

I have shown in this chapter that citizenship is in fact the outcome of state interpellation on the one hand and of popular politics on the other, often in contradiction with such interpellation. It is apparent that the apartheid state systematically manipulated citizenship in order to literally de-nationalise black South Africans, thus turning them into foreigners. Thus there was no fundamental distinction drawn by this state, especially as Bantustans came to be granted independence, between black South Africans and Africans from other parts of the region. All were largely oppressed in the same manner and restricted in various ways at different times from both acquiring South African citizenship and urban residence as much as possible, given the demands of an expanding industrial sector. The idea was to expand the reliance on migrant labour from rural peripheries, but of course this came into contradiction with the same demands for skilled labour, as has been noted at length in the literature (Lipton 1985).

On the other hand, the hegemonic nationalist perspective which governed the intellectual as well as the nationalist discourse adhered to by the exiled movement (Neocosmos 1999) was founded primarily on a political economy which equated the migrant labour system with apartheid, and which saw the former exclusively as negative and in need of abolition at all costs. We shall see that this made it possible after 1994 to think of the exclusion of migrants as a progressive politics precisely because this meant dismantling the migrant labour system. The positive side to migrant labour from the point of view of rural life - namely that it enabled development, survival and even accumulation for some in peasant agriculture in the periphery – was systematically ignored. Ironically the regional worker-peasantry became economically threatened and politically excluded by liberation in South Africa.

Popular conceptions of citizenship were generally developed in direct opposition to state oppression and exclusion and often ended up being mirror images of state forms of oppression in particular. As a result, popular nationalism tended to be inclusive as it saw no distinction between citizenship and anti-apartheid politics by anyone in the region and beyond. In particular, popular nationalism equated citizenship with an active citizenship founded on direct democratic control and popularly controllable leadership. In this manner, popular nationalism saw national identity as not in any way founded on a conception of indigeneity but on universal popular-democratic political activity. This was the case in the rural struggle in Zimbabwe in the 1970s as well as during the urban popular upsurge of the 1980s in South Africa where it was the most marked. There was therefore very little room for xenophobia within this discourse and politics. In the post-apartheid period, the state in South Africa has, on the contrary, defined citizenship in terms of descent so that right of access to the South African labour market has been increasingly defined in terms of indigeneity (for example, Davies and Head 1995; Labour Market Commission Report s. 534). 'Foreigners' then came to be conceived as the non-indigenous, while the importance of migrant labour has declined in post-apartheid South Africa, both economically and politically, it is historically in relation to migrant labour that citizenship as indigeneity has been 'imagined'.

Finally, the South African popular struggle of the 1980s was not without its contradictions either. Popular identities were overwhelmingly urban-biassed and there did not develop a strong bond between urban and rural popular interests. In fact the struggle of UDF activists versus Inkatha cadres in Natal and on the Rand in the early 1990s contained within it a major rural-urban contradiction (Mamdani 1996). It was an indication of the overlap between political, ethnic and urban-rural contradictions often involving generational and cultural contradictions as well. While this violence was eventually contained, one of the manners this was done was to bring the Inkatha leadership, particularly its overlord Buthelezi, into government after 1994, in fact as minister of home affairs, the ministry charged precisely with issues of immigration and relations with 'foreigners'. While this appointment did help to reduce the slaughter between UDF/ANC and Inkatha supporters, it also helped to develop a state discourse of xenophobia which this minister in particular expressed virulently.

CHAPTER THREE

The Construction of a Post-apartheid Nationalist Discourse of Exclusion: Citizenship, State, National Identity and Xenophobia

> African unity, that vague formula, yet one to which the men and women of Africa were passionately attached, and whose operative value served to bring immense pressure to bear on colonialism, African unity takes off the mask, and crumbles into regionalism inside the hollow shell of nationality itself (Fanon 1990: 128).

The migrant labour system became transformed in the post-apartheid period not so much as a result of a democratic development but rather as a process of nation formation led by the state which then organised a distinction between citizens and foreigners. This distinction differed from both the apartheid state's distinctions as well as from the popular nationalist one founded on political agency and forged in the crucible of popular struggle in the 1980s. Citizenship now became reduced to indigeneity and formalised by legislation. It now became overwhelmingly formed by state prescriptions rather than popular ones. Nevertheless, this required the defeat of popular-democratic ideology and politics and its replacement by state politics which rapidly achieved hegemonic status. Along with the de-mobilisation of popular organisations in the 1990s went the de-politicisation of society, and a 'civil society' now develops as an NGO-dominated realm whose function becomes one of supplementing or taking over state activities (particularly in social welfare provision). As a result the hegemony of a state domain of politics is rapidly secured over a popular-subaltern domain (Neocosmos 1998, 2005). The process of citizenship-building by the state was facilitated by the economic and urban perspective which I have already discussed, and which now became a state discourse associated with the more social-democratic RDP-aligned Left within state structures. I shall show below that this view equated the end of migration with a process of 'democratisation' and thus ended up in the paradoxical position of justifying exclusion on democratic grounds.

In South Africa, the process of nation formation was one which went against the trend of globalisation which is usually said to encourage regional/ethnic identities along with a corresponding decline of central state power. In South Africa, the process of state-nation formation was explicitly and intransigently opposed to the democratic recognition of ethnic divisions which had been the basis of oppression under apartheid. The right of self-determination for minorities was interpreted in itself as conducive to the maintenance of privilege for the previously dominant ethnicity (Afrikaners), and the fear of threats of Zulu secession were real in the 1990s. This right was only grudgingly put in the constitution and not in the Bill of Rights. This state-nation formation perforce had to exclude those not seen as belonging to the nation as defined by the state, in other words 'foreigners'. This process provided one of the conditions within the configuration of power relations for post-apartheid xenophobia. State legislation and practice, the former criminalising migration, the latter left untransformed from the apartheid period, have operated within a discourse and practice which not only have reduced citizenship to indigeneity and denied a history to migration, but also enabled state arbitrariness towards 'foreigners' through the excessive power provided to state personnel and the reproduction of racism in a modified form.

At the same time, class, gender and racial distinctions made possible the actual practice, if not the formal idea, of 'degrees of citizenship', whereby some come to possess greater claims to being part of the nation than others, and others are often close to being foreigners or largely 'rightless' because politically weak and marginalised. These latter groups can therefore always turn to even more vulnerable groups of 'non-citizens' such as children and foreigners in order to assert some power. The fact that it is only working people from Africa and not Whites from the West who are the objects of xenophobic practice testifies not only to the inherited racism of the state apparatuses and weakness of the latter, but also to the inability of workers organisations such as unions to state politically the commonality of all working people in South Africa irrespective of communitarian origins. The inability of a universalising ideology such as Pan-Africanism to take hold of the population, despite the government's propagating a (neo-liberal) notion of 'African Renaissance', has resulted partly because the term 'African' has been conflated with 'Black' in state discourse, so that national and racial categories have been collapsed into one another. It has thus so far become impossible to develop a sense of nationhood founded on non-racialism, a perspective which is simply reproduced by continuous attempts by Whites to hang on to their privileges, not least through the discourse of neo-liberalism.

Constructing the Nation and Moulding Citizenship from Above: Nationalism, Indigeneity and Exclusionary Legislation

Nationalist politics, insofar as they concern popular organisations in post-1990 South Africa, have two fundamental characteristics which are, first, the de-politicisation of popular organisations and the corresponding loss of democratic control by rank and file members within them, so that they no longer reflect popular concerns and culture as of nationalist politics is now the monopoly of the party of nationalism, the ANC, and second, their re-politicisation as they gradually became part of a state-corporatist project. The former process was finally completed by 1992 as civic organisations and trade unions withdrew from the political arena in favour of the ANC. The latter was finally consolidated by 1995 as either unrepresentative (the National Women's Coalition) or politically emasculated organisations (SANCO and COSATU) for example, tied themselves to a formal 'alliance' with the ANC and to bargaining structures such as NEDLAC (National Economic and Development Labour Council, the successor to the National Economic Forum) along with the state and employers organisations (Neocosmos 1998, 1999, Marais 1998). This gradual move towards corporatism was accompanied by a top down conception of development (with admittedly a populist gloss) which had found its clearest expression in the RDP (Reconstruction and Development Programme) (Neocosmos 1998). By the second half of the nineties, in a complete volte-face, President Mandela announced that 'privatisation' was a 'fundamental policy' of the ANC, reneging on what the Left had believed were fundamental social-democratic tenets (Bond 2000, Baskin, ed., 1996, Marais 1998). As a result, the RDP was replaced by GEAR – a neo-liberal programme similar to the Structural Adjustments Programmes introduced in Africa, in that the market rather than the state became the motor of growth. Since then this kind of neo-liberal programme has been extended to the rest of Africa in the form of NEPAD.

State corporatism, state-induced development in 'partnership' with private capital, along with state-driven 'affirmative action' and Black Economic Empowerment programmes, form the main pillars of the post-apartheid state process of 'nation building'.[24] As in the rest of Africa after independence, the overall process has been one where the popular forces which exploded in the 1980s have been systematically defeated, and replaced by a top down process of nation building albeit within a neo-liberal multiparty system, while a systematic attempt is being made to enrich a black middle class. The main economic debate in South Africa was thus conducted exclusively between orthodox statist (social democratic) developmentalism on the one hand, and neo-classical liberalism on the other as the third popular democratic alternative. The former was by far the weaker partner in the debate, although the inability to overcome poverty in any meaningful way has meant that considerations on social and infrastructural investment are currently being reconsidered in the wake of the 2004 elections. So far this has not meant a return to a full blown social democratic discourse.

In fact, the undermining of meaningful popular involvement in decision making is nicely illustrated by the story of the change from RDP to GEAR. Following the experience of other African countries, 'development' in South Africa was understood by the ANC in particular in a top-down way, along with what can be best described as a 'participatory component'. It is this contradictory combination of statist (public or private sector) 'leadership' and populist 'participation', finding expression in corporatism, which provided the parameters of the debate on the RDP. This debate concerned the relative role of the state and that of the market in the process. As the people were never considered as independently active components of the process, the choice ended up being between two forms of statist development: state-led or market-led (usually with some participation by NGOs which are unelected and hence popularly unaccountable bodies anyway).

While the arguments of neo-classical economics, especially as institutionalised in the International Financial Institutions, stressed the 'freedom' of the market in the process of development, those of the opposing position, that of 'social democratic statist developmentalism', stressed the centrality of state intervention in redressing historical grievances and in the general the equalisation of access to resources and incomes as a prelude to, or concomitant of, economic growth. The two main documents in which this latter position was elaborated were the MERG (Macro-Economic Research Group) document of 1993 and the RDP 'base document' of 1994. In the RDP document in particular, which is largely written along the lines of 'Five Year Development Plan' documents of the post-independence period in Africa (i.e. full of abstract state-directed 'good intentions' but short on concrete programmes, the main effect of which was largely propagandistic) the combination of statism and populism characteristic of the ANC was evident. For example, the document noted that:

> Our history has been a bitter one dominated by colonialism, racism, apartheid, sexism and repressive labour policies. The result is that poverty and degradation exist side by side with modern cities and a developed mining, industrial and commercial infrastructure. Our income distribution is racially distorted and ranks as one of the most unequal in the world - lavish wealth and abject poverty characterise our society (ANC 1994:2).

It continued to warn that: 'without thoroughgoing democratisation, the whole effort to reconstruct and develop will lose momentum', and that the state itself must foster 'representative, participatory and direct democracy' (ibid: 120). This 'fostering' we were told, should be undertaken 'in partnership with civil society on the basis of informed and empowered citizens (e.g. the various sectoral forums like the National Economic Forum)' (ibid: 121). So in brief, the idea was for the state to develop the democracy necessary for 'popular' development through state-controlled corporatist institutions. Needless to say such 'popular participation' never materialised, while the accent from then on was on 'delivery' (usually of infrastructure) to a passive populace.[25]

Later the arguments of neo-classical economics acquired so much dominance within the state that advocates of the 'developmentalist statist' (orthodox statist) position began to complain that popular concerns had been all but left out of the equation. Thus, Adelzadeh and Padayachee (1994) outlined the distance between the original RDP 'base document' and the state legislative RDP White Paper, pointing out the lack of continuity between the two, the latter being uniformly governed by the 'logic of the market' so that:

> while some of the individual principles, policies and commitments are sound, re-construction, development, growth and redistribution (along the lines set out in the Base Document Vision) has been significantly changed. The current White Paper is incoherent and fragmented. The possibility of retrieving the earlier vision is eroded daily in the cut and thrust of 'reconciliation' and of compromise-making politics within the GNU. This is evident too in the irresolute style characterising negotiations with international financial agencies and representatives of organised domestic (mainly white) capital, and by the dramatic decline in the significance which top policy-makers appear to be according to the trade unions, civics and the tripartite developmental forums, as partners in economic-policy making (op.cit.: 15).

While bemoaning the gradual defeat of the Left-statist project associated with the original RDP 'vision', the authors failed to analyse the reasons for such a defeat and merely restricted themselves to measuring the distance between the two 'visions' of growth. Evidently, the rapidity of the replacement of the initial 'state-developmentalist vision' of the ANC and its supporters on the Left by a kind of 'structural adjustment' package clearly expressed in the (1996) 'National Strategy for Growth and Development' (GEAR) document which finally supplanted the RDP requires some explanation. Such an explanation would need to provide an examination of the fundamental similarities and continuities between the two sides of the 'state versus market debate' which Adelzadeh and Padayachee ignore. While limitations of space preclude a detailed assessment here, a few central points which were overlooked in the debate can profitably be stressed.

Perhaps the most important of these is that in the debate between state and market, between 'state developmentalism' and 'market-led growth', the most important factor, namely 'the people', was left out. For neither position in whatever variant were the working people – who were deemed by both positions to be the main beneficiaries of growth and development - given an independent role to play either in development or indeed in the wider political process which makes it possible. For 'economic liberalism' the market is the people so that the expression 'people-driven' for example is simply used as a synonym for 'market-driven'. For 'statist developmentalism', the state or party itself is usually substituted for the people as not only does it know what is best for them, it also acts on their behalf. This position which until the 1990s had been dominant in the state in Africa is clearly captured in the identification of the nation with the state as in the notion of the 'nation-state'; in such a perspective, it is the state and not the people which constitutes 'the nation' (Olukoshi and Laakso 1996).

In the case of South Africa as I have noted, the statism of 'radical' development thinking had been apparent in the setting up of a complex corporatist structure whereby erstwhile people's organisations had either been systematically collapsed into the party and unrepresentative state organisations set up in their place, or incorporated into state structures at both national and local level. It is noteworthy that Adelzadeh and Padayachee actually bemoan in the above quotation the fact that the state is showing a tendency to ignore its own corporatist structures, and suggest this as a sign of defeat for the Left. Interestingly for both 'development visions', it is accumulation among ordinary working people (what some authors have termed accumulation 'from below', see Neocosmos 1993a; Mamdani 1987), which was ostensibly the principal concern of 'development'. Yet the people only featured insofar as we were told that 'communities' should 'identify their needs' to government through their representatives in local state structures ('development forums', local councils, 'traditional' authorities, civics, or unelected NGOs), and the government and/or the private sector will then 'deliver' roads, electricity, water or whatever other infrastructure was deemed necessary.

Therefore the issue from the 1990s onwards was not one of investment in popular initiative, nor for that matter was it about creating the conditions for the people themselves to mobilise openly and freely around development issues. Whether therefore it was the government or the market which was supposed to 'deliver', the common approach prevalent to this day is ultimately 'top-down'; it is an approach which demobilises and disempowers the people as it ultimately treats them as passive recipients of state or white largesse (Neocosmos 2005). It was this overall environment of 'statism' which was constructed in the 1990s which provides the context for the gradual hegemony of human rights discourse within which xenophobic discourses were allowed to develop.

Nationalism, Democracy and Exclusion: The Construction of State Xenophobic Discourse

It was within this context of the gradual dominance of neo-liberalism in the 1990s that the issue of migrant labour was being reviewed within the state with various individuals, state institutions and trade unions entering into the discussion. The fundamental assumption was that migrant labour was a bad thing which could not be allowed to persist in the 'new' South Africa as it was contaminated by apartheid. The democratic transition meant in effect the 'nationalisation' of migrant labour so that rather than recruiting regionally, mining capital would be expected to recruit 'at the factory gates'. This policy had two basic components: first the replacement of foreign labour by South African labour, and second the replacement of migrant labour by urbanised labour. The latter was to take place through the provision of 'family housing' for miners. What this meant of course, was that the replacement of 'foreign' by South African labour on the mines (and by extension elsewhere) as well as the urbanisation of migrants, were both understood as fundamentally 'democratic' processes. We must begin the discussion with an assessment of the economics of migrancy.

I have already noted in chapter two, how the nationalist conceptualisation of apartheid stressed the 'evil' of migrancy on which it was said to be founded and how this view saw democratic progress as necessitating permanent urbanisation of labour and the provision of family housing. This particularly affected the single-sex hostels in urban townships where most migrant workers lived. Mamdani (1996: chapter 7) has spent time discussing the position of migrant labour in the townships on the Reef in Johannesburg in the 1990s in order to make sense of the violence which erupted, particularly during August and September 1990 between ANC supporters on the one hand and Inkatha supporters on the other. He notes:

> Following the Reef War of August–September 1990, public attention focussed on hostels. Behind sharply drawn lines, two political groups defended two sharply opposed proposals. For the ANC and allied forces, the answer to hostel violence lay in converting hostels into family units. For the IFP and its supporters, hostels had to remain as single sex facilities and be upgraded as such. Conversion and upgrading were the code words for these opposing standpoints. Neither solution was predicated on the idea that hostel residents would want the right to choose between alternatives, let alone the possibility that they might have the right to participate in defining alternatives. Whereas the ANC claimed to represent some sort of general will, the IFP advanced an identity claim, the claim to represent the specific needs of Zulu migrants (ibid: 277).

Mamdani shows that the majority of Zulu migrants wished to retain a foothold in the rural areas and hence wanted to keep their family there in order to do so, mainly because 'agricultural degradation was less advanced in [Kwazulu-Natal] than in any other reserve' (ibid: 274). He argues convincingly that 'without the series of ANC demands regarding hostels – first that they be vacated for exiles, then that they be converted into exclusive family units, and finally that the violent ones be fenced – it is difficult to believe that the IFP could have secured more than a toehold in most Reef hostels' (ibid: 275).

The point here is not to dwell on the Reef violence in 1990 other than to point out as Mamdani shows that it directly reflected an rural-urban contradiction whereby the temporary presence of the rural 'other' in the cities seemed not to be tolerated. As the new liberal democratic state was being constructed, this alternative of total exclusion or inclusion on fully urbanised terms was to become ingrained in left-nationalist thinking in particular. The approach of the ANC in dealing with migrant labour in townships was thus held by the 'liberation movement' as a whole including unions and civics. We shall see below how the National Union of Mineworkers (NUM) in particular was heavily influenced by this position in its arguing for the provision of an 'amnesty' to migrant mineworkers from Lesotho, during which time they were to decide whether to become permanently urbanised residents in South Africa or remain in Lesotho and largely forego their migratory status and become 'foreigners'. As I have noted in chapter two, this position was a direct consequence of the nationalist critique of apartheid, quite simply democratisation and hence some notion of 'progress', however ill-defined, was uncritically equated with urbanisation. This notion is directly related to a typically South African discourse of exceptionalism which is systematically critiqued in Mamdani's work (especially his book in 1996). This discourse is not simply founded on the belief that South Africa is an exception in Africa because of its industrial development, but includes a tendency to see the rest of the continent as rural, backward, immersed in poverty and politically unstable and corrupt. From this notion follows the conception of

Africans as wanting to acquire the benefits of 'our' democracy, economy and so on. South African nationalism by and large failed to address the problems of the rural poor.

This argument was prevalent in various forms in the early nineties, including on the political Left of the nationalist spectrum. It was reflected in the thinking on migrant labour in mining, for example in the work of Wilmot James and Jonathan Crush whose joint and individual writings operated within the same paradigm, stressing that in the mining industry, movement away from migrancy was 'progressive' and that family housing was necessary (Crush and James 1991, Crush and James 1995). Even Guy Mhone, at the time the Labour Department's Chief Director of Market Policy, declared that 'the suggestion is that the migrant labour system needs to be phased out because of its negative economic and social consequences' (Business Day, 24 December, 1996). This position is also evident among ANC activists and particularly in the work of Davies and Head (1995), where trends in the migrant labour system are analysed in some detail along with reference to 'undocumented migrants'. Their arguments are therefore are worth reviewing in some detail as they are largely typical of the nationalist perspective vis-à-vis migrant labour at the time, and these provide a useful review of the 'problem of migrant labour' as seen by the post-apartheid state in the mid-1990s.

Taking a policy perspective, Davies and Head are concerned to tackle the twin issues of the South African 'democratic government' showing commitment to 'reconstructing regional relations on new lines' on the one hand, and the threat apparently posed by escalating clandestine migration to such restructuring along 'equitable and mutually beneficial' lines, on the other. The perspective taken is one of regional international relations among states/countries (not peoples) by long-time ANC supporters. No indication is given that the orientation of states and migrants themselves on these issues may differ; rather the perspective is one which seeks to outline background trends and the concerns of the states of the region which are 'bound to recur as an item in bilateral or multilateral negotiations' (op cit.: 439). By this time in terms of numbers, legal migration to the mines was no longer the main form of migration to South Africa and was being overtaken by the numbers involved in clandestine migration. Although Davies and Head are careful to stress that there are no reliable figures on clandestine migration, they note that the only reliable figures are those for numbers of deportations which only assess the 'tip of the iceberg' insofar as 'illegal immigrants' are concerned. These indicate that 'half as many people were deported from South Africa in 1992 as there were citizens of neighbouring countries working legally in the mining industry' (ibid: 440).

Insofar as legally recruited mine labour is concerned, Davies and Head note that the decline – especially since 1987 – in recruitment of 'foreign' mineworkers continued to accelerate. Thus:

> the average number of SADC citizens employed on gold and coal mines owned by members of the South African Chamber of Mines was 71,224 less in 1993 than it was in 1986 – a figure equivalent to almost a third of the total number of SADC

citizens employed in 1986... The number of men employed from Lesotho on the gold mines reached an all-time high of 105,506 in 1987. In 1993 the figure stood at 79,530. The reduction of Basotho labour on Chamber-affiliated coal mines is even more dramatic. Whereas in 1981 on average 12,314 men were employed in 1993 only one quarter of that number, 3,186 were employed (ibid: 442).

They remark that the main reasons for this trend were the cheaper cost of local labour, the decline in employment due to mechanisation in the mines, and presumably the not insubstantial nationalist pressures and xenophobia emanating from the post-apartheid state itself (which they ignore). On the other hand they argue this trend is slightly tempered by the industry's unwillingness to be dependent on one source of supply in case of strikes (ibid: 441). Insofar as undocumented migrants to South Africa are concerned, the authors summarised the existing information as follows:

> More than one citizen of a SADC member country was deported in 1993 as an 'illegal immigrant' for every two employed legally in the mining industry. The number of legal migrants employed in the mining industry in 1993 was equivalent to just over 5% of the three million 'illegal immigrants' estimated to be living in South Africa. In the case of Mozambicans, the number of deportations was equivalent to more than one and a half times the number of workers legally employed in the mining industry, who made up less than 2% of the total number of the 2.2 million Mozambicans thought to be in South Africa (ibid: 445).

For the authors, 'the migrant labour system' was simply seen to be an effect of apartheid and therefore viewed negatively as a way in which super-exploited labour was provided to South African mining capital. Hence, it had to be scrapped. At the same time, they argued that the decline in employment of foreign labour in South Africa was a long-term trend which had been occurring 'irrespective of the [post-apartheid – MN] government's wishes' and that this restructuring of the labour force had resulted 'from the breakdown of apartheid and [the] beginnings of a transition to democracy' (ibid: 448). As from the perspective of the authors, apartheid was a form of labour control, and a mechanism for the provision of cheap labour for South African capital, the gradually more expensive nature of migrant labour for this same capital was seen as an indication of democratisation.[26] As a result of this process of 'democratisation' of economic forces, they predicted that:

> a permanent labour force – hired at the gates of the mine irrespective of where it actually comes from – seems likely to emerge in South Africa's mines as a result of a combination of economic and political factors related to the dismantlement of apartheid and independent of the new government's thinking on the question. These processes were already underway by the mid-1980s. There is every reason to believe that they will now be accelerated (ibid: 449).

The authors then noted that according to estimates by the Chamber of Mines itself, its half a million employees support family members totalling 3.1 million people, so that each retrenchment of a legally employed miner 'potentially affects the livelihood of anything up to sixteen people' (ibid: 450). Thus, given the lack of employment opportunities in the 'rural peripheries', the likely outcome will be increased pressure for families to migrate clandestinely to South Africa. 'In other words, there could be a multiplier relationship between loss of mine employment and clandestine migration'. The conclusion the authors arrive at is that 'mine management should be pressured to take on its historic responsibility towards the supplier states and invest significantly in large job creation schemes' (ibid: 450).

In commenting on the perspective of Davies and Head, it is worth making a number of points: first, the extent to which state-nationalist discourse in immediate post-apartheid South Africa dovetailed nicely with economic liberalism: an abstractly 'free' labour market is seen by Davies and Head as democratic, while the recruitment of migrant labour was not; labour recruitment from 'home' (South Africa) was equated with a democratic practice, while recruitment of foreign labour through 'the migrant labour system' was visualised as undemocratic. The latter view in particular unconsciously fed the prejudices of South African xenophobia.[27] Contemporary statements from ANC spokespersons made it plain that human rights were largely inapplicable to foreigners in general and to migrants in particular:

> 'There are very few countries in the world which would extend human rights to non-citizens', [said Lockey]... Lockey also accepts the law – considered unconstitutional by many lawyers – which permits suspected illegal aliens to be detained without trial for 30 days. 'What else can we do?' He asks' (ANC MP Desmond Lockey, Chairman, Parliamentary Portfolio Committee on Home Affairs, cited in *Mail and Guardian* vol. 12, no 23, 7-13 June, 1996).

Second, it is also worthwhile considering the fact that Davies and Head throughout their piece absolved the South African state from any responsibility regarding the democratisation of migrancy or regarding the people who helped it defeat apartheid in the first place. Rather, the effect of their perspective was to divert all responsibility towards mining capital and to call for it to invest in job-creation schemes irrespective of their profitability. At the same time, the authors failed to consider the reasons for migration from rural areas other than their apparent economic stagnation. These objectively included both the need to reproduce household production at home as well as to make possible accumulation (although not necessarily in arable agriculture). Davies and Head's urban-biased and economistic assumptions made them unable to visualise migration from the perspective of the rural people. Finally, in any case the change in recruitment patterns from a reliance on migrant labour to a concentration on urbanised local labour was not unique to mining. Changes in mining were part of the same trend which had affected other sectors such as the manufacturing industry in the early 1980s, and to which the unions had failed to respond adequately (Mamdani 1996: 243-55). In that earlier case migrants were marginalised from the unions which became dominated by the fully urbanised, the same trend was being replicated in the mining industry after the 1990s.

For Davies and Head, although the 'internalisation' of migrant labour was an inevitable process as it was an aspect of the 'democratisation' of economic relations which predates the new South Africa, the speed of this process should be slowed down in order to cushion its effects on the peripheral economies of the region, and reduce the pressures for clandestine migration. They stressed that retrenchments would have multiplier effects on illegal migrancy to South Africa and argued that improving 'point-of-origin conditions' would reduce migrancy. However it must be stressed that it was the reinvestment of migrant labour earnings which had provided in the past one of the main conditions for rural economic reproduction as well as the possibilities for accumulation 'from below'; this had been the case especially as there has been no post-colonial state investment in petty agriculture throughout the region. There was no reason to suppose that its effects had changed so that in the post-apartheid period migrant remittances were not simply necessities for survival but also investments for popularly-based development. There was and still is little evidence to suggest that business investments in such areas – even if they were profitable – would provide any substitute for petty commodity production. The Lesotho Highlands water project is an evident testament to that. Davies and Head's concerns were primarily those of politicians removed from the social realities of life of working people which were not elucidated through analysing those conditions themselves. As a result the hegemonic discourse of nationalism was one which equated democracy with the exclusion of foreigners from citizenship rights and which re-duced the latter to indigeneity.

Bending the Rules of Indigeneity: The Post-apartheid State and Migrants from Lesotho

The debates on citizenship in South Africa however were overwhelmingly taking place within the confines of state institutions. In June 1996 it was reported that in the South African Parliament 'politicians from all parties lashed out at illegal immi-grants... calling them a threat to the Reconstruction and Development Programme, a drain on South Africa's resources, and branding them potential criminals, drug smugglers and murderers' (*Mail and Guardian*, 7-13 June 1996).

While the crassness of politicians can always be blamed for raising chauvinistic hysteria, the fact that these outbursts were not confined to politicians from any one party, along with the evidence of petty chauvinism on the streets of major South African cities, and the xenophobic utterances of newspapers, were an indication of growing xenophobia in the country in the early 1990s. It is with little shame that completely unreliable figures concerning 'illegal migration' were bandied around in parliament, various sources mentioning figures between 2.5 and 8.5 million people (ibid). More sober minds however noted that it was not known 'whether it is the immigrants themselves who are a drain on resources or whether it is the implemen-tation of bad policy which is costing the taxpayer' (ibid).

The government attempted to reduce the 'problem' by giving citizenship rights to undocumented migrants from the SADC countries who could prove that they had lived in South Africa for longer than five years, had jobs or were married to a South African and had no criminal record. This one-off 'indemnity' was closed in

September 1996. This offer, although not affecting large numbers, had a certain importance because it showed the context in which the offer of permanent residence to Basotho miners was subsequently made. In fact the first time this idea was made public was just before the local elections of October 1995, when all Basotho mineworkers who had entered the country before 13 June 1986 and who had been issued with temporary voting cards to vote during the April 1994 elections were allowed to apply for permanent residence in South Africa. In other words the normal stipulations of the Aliens Control Act were waived in their case (Department of Home Affairs Circular No. 9 of 1995). A further notice from the Department of Home Affairs provided for exemption from the conditions under which permanent residence in South Africa may be acquired by those SADC citizens who could show evidence of continuous residence in South Africa from 1 July 1991 (and evidence of marriage to a South African citizen or who are engaged in productive economic activity in the country or who have dependent children resident in the country). The closing date for those applications was extended to 30 November 1996. These offers of permanent residence clearly affected miners primarily and it was under pressure from the NUM that the South African government acceded to them. It was also under pressure from the NUM (whose president James Motlatsi was himself a Mosotho), as well as by the understanding that Basotho miners were overwhelmingly ANC supporters, that they were given citizenship rights during the 1994 elections. This showed clearly that it is indeed possible for the state itself to conceive of citizenship rights in terms other than indigeneity. In this case of the Basotho voters, citizenship was founded on place of work: 'you worked in South Africa, you are entitled to full citizenship rights'.

The influence of the NUM also comes across in the report of the Presidential Commission to Investigate Labour Market Policy (or Labour Market Commission in short) published in June 1996. In the chapter dealing with labour migration, it is noted that the NUM, in its submission, wished to end the discriminatory practice which denied miners from foreign countries the right to South African citizenship. 'In particular, it is proposed that migrant workers should have the right to permanent residence status and to acquire citizenship after five years of work in South Africa' (s. 544). Permanent residence rights would have allowed miners to qualify for various housing schemes and other social benefits. The NUM was therefore clearly arguing for a concept of citizenship based on place of labour rather than indigeneity. The NUM also demanded the abolition of the compulsory deferred pay scheme to the Lesotho state which undermined the basic right of workers to receive their full pay (s. 548). In both these instances the Commission concurred with the NUM's submissions. At the same time, the Commission recommended preferential access to the South African labour market by Southern African Customs Union countries and Mozambique (s. 560), while arguing for the phasing out of the migrant labour system, contrary to the wishes of the Chamber of Mines in its submission (s. 583, 584).

Finally it is also relevant to note the position taken by the Commission on the SADC Draft Protocol on the Free Movement of Persons in the SADC Region of June 1995. The objective of this agreement was the progressive abolition of border controls on citizens of member states. Reminiscent of some of the resolutions adopted in 1958 in Accra and influenced by Pan-Africanism, the Draft Protocol calls on member states *inter alia* to confer, promote, and protect in relation to every citizen of a member state:

- the right to enter freely and without a visa the territory of another Member State for a short visit;
- the right to reside in the territory of another Member State;
- the right to establish oneself and work in the territory of another Member State. (section 566).

While identifying 'itself with the ultimate objectives underlying the Draft Protocol', the Commission distanced itself from its recommendations 'in the current circumstances of highly uneven development in the SADC region' (s. 568). What this meant of course was that despite its asserted willingness to support the integration of the regional labour market, the Commission simply backed the South African chauvinist fear of being 'swamped by foreign immigrants' rather than seriously addressing the issue of how such integration was to be achieved. At the same time, the Commission saw the abolition of the 'migrant labour system' as an injunction to 'liberalise' the regional labour market which it said should only operate along with increasing the free flow of capital and trade in the region (s. 562). Like Davies and Head therefore, it ultimately ended up agreeing with the neo-liberal economics being propagated at the time by the International Financial Institutions, that the democratisation of the relations of migrancy in practice meant 'freeing the market'. Neo-liberal discourse seems not to have been seriously challenged.

Both the Commission Report as well as the arguments of Davies and Head (1995) outlined above suggest that even for the most progressively minded South African intellectuals and politicians concerned with democratisation, the wishes of those most affected by the migration process and a change in citizenship were not being addressed. Rather, while paying lip-service to the democratisation of regional relations including the migratory labour system, their perspective was one of 'democratisation from above' and they preferred to hide behind a short-term narrow conception of 'national interest' insofar as regional relations were concerned. This amounted to a conception of nationalism defined by the state and its apparatuses. With the sole exception of the abolition of the compulsory deferred pay scheme, the recommendations of the Labour Market Commission on the issue of regional migration simply confirmed ANC and NUM prejudices, and offered little openings to democracy other than a temporary and very specific relaxation of notions of indigeneity. Oddly (and sadly) enough, it was the interests of the Chamber of Mines who wished to have access to migrant labour from the region to keep its price and militancy down, which seemed more in tune with those of the peasant-migrants, as at least these argued for the retention of migrancy.

In fact, the historical case of Lesotho shows a long struggle between popular and state conceptions of citizenship and nationality which are not so apparent in Swaziland or Botswana. The reason for this struggle was mainly the development of popular organisations of civil society in colonial Lesotho such as the Lekhotla la Bafo. Such popular conceptions of citizenship and national identity died at independence with the passing of LLB and its replacement by the Basutholand Congress Party (BCP) and the exclusively party conception of politics to which it adhered. The question for the BCP as with other post-independence parties in Africa was one of 'nation building,' of 'nation-state formation' from above, and this was equated with the particular party attaining state power, as only it was said to represent the nation. Whether the formal political system ended up being a no-party, a one-party, or a multi-party system was largely irrelevant to this question.

From the perspective of the peasant migrants in Lesotho, the 'migrant labour system' should have been allowed to continue (and arguably be expanded as a way of improving their conditions of life). In the words of Coplan and Thoahlane (1995: 149): 'a very large majority of migrants and ex-migrants...prefer to carry on or resume migrating'. For such migrants, it is the corrupt practices of Lesotho state officials and the lack of democracy which have been responsible for the absence of development, not their own absence from the country through migration or even economic dependency or environmental degradation. Witness a few statements from Basotho Miners interviewed by Sechaba Consultants in Welkom, South Africa in the mid-1990s:

> Lesotho has economic problems which will be worsened if migrants take up South African citizenship but still, there is free land which could balance the situation if well utilised.

> Lesotho is unable to provide for her peoples because of poor governance, and this would ensure that many miners would seek permanent residence... Lesotho will face disastrous economic problems as she will lose all her earnings from migrant labour.

> Migrant workers like everybody else are disgruntled by the fact that their expectations to improve economically have been shattered. Our voices to the government to use the deferred pay money to improve and make education accessible to all, and pensions for the aged and disabled, have not been heard. Government officials use our hard earned money to enrich themselves...

> Many miners who applied for [South African – MN] IDs did so because they feared that they would lose their jobs unless they voted for the ANC. The move to provide permanent residence some say was taken without consulting them (Sechaba Consultants 1996).

The states of the peripheral rural countries of the region (most evidently in Lesotho), have since independence systematically neglected investment in rural areas, using the miners forced savings for dubious enterprises (speculative, real estate or commercial transactions) justified as 'national development'. However, for my purposes the significant factors must be those which influence the perception of migration or citizenship from the standpoint of the migrants. It seems that the migrant-peasants from Lesotho continued to desire association with the industrial world of South Africa to the extent that such association enhanced the benefits already established by their access to land and means of production, and by the ability to acquire those needs whose satisfaction could only be acquired through the market. It did not make sense for the migrant-peasant's partial and tenuous independence from the market to be totally eliminated by a change in his status from that of semi-proletarian (part-proletarian and part-peasant) to fully-fledged proletarian living in urban South Africa. This would have meant total loss of his economic 'reserve base' – the loss of survival capacities under crisis conditions for some, and of possibilities of accumulation for others. The differentiated 'peasant side' of migrant life was likely to be the more important determinant of their willingness to move permanently to South Africa.

In addition of course it was abundantly clear that the Lesotho state's opposition to migrants taking up South African residence and citizenship was founded on its fear of losing access to deferred pay and the effects of remittances on the economy.[28] The Basotho miners on the other hand were opposed to the compulsory deferred pay scheme and had expressed their opposition on a number of occasions. The following comments are taken from interviews with miners in 1996:

> The deferred pay savings scheme is benefiting the banks and government officials who take loans because interests received by the mine workers is not only insignificant but an insult to those who contribute: mine workers have for years complained about this... it would have been better if the interest was improved to benefit old people and pensions. It would have still been far better if miners had been asked to pay twenty rand monthly to make education free for all...

> The money form the fund cannot be withdrawn more than once a month. The most disgusting thing about the deferred money is that the interest that accrues is meagre to think of doing anything with it: it would have been far better to have one's money and bank it himself (sic) (Sechaba Consultants 1996).

In a survey by John Gay at the time, sixty-three percent of a sample of 500 miners preferred the deferred pay scheme to be optional (Gay 1997: 30). From a democratic perspective therefore, the significant factors must be those which influence the perception of migration or national identity from the standpoint of the migrants. It seems that the migrant-peasants will continue to desire association with the industrial world of South Africa to the extent that such association enhances the benefits already established by their access to land and means of production, and the ability to acquire those needs whose satisfaction can only be acquired through the market.

We should not therefore be surprised to discover that survey data of migrant opinions in the 1990s showed that only a minority of respondents were keen to move permanently to South Africa, and to the ANC's and NUM's dismay, only a minority took up the offer even after the deadline had been extended. Between seventy to eighty percent of miners interviewed said they refused the offer (Neocosmos 1999: 288). A survey undertaken by the Central Bank of Lesotho (CBL 1995) found that only thirty percent of Basotho migrant-peasants wished to become South African citizens, even though they may have been members of the NUM, which saw the move as beneficial to its members. Another similar more recent survey (1996) of 493 miners interviewed in the TEBA (the acronym of the apartheid period mine labour recruitment agency 'The Employment Bureau of Africa') offices undertaken by Sechaba Consultants found that the proportion of miners wishing to move permanently to South Africa was just under nineteen. Some of the more important reasons mentioned for wishing to remain in Lesotho concerned the fact that no land was available for settlement in South Africa and that migrants possessed assets in Lesotho which they did not wish to lose (Gay 1997). Clearly peasant-migrants did not wish to become permanent residents and South African citizens if this meant that they were to be proletarianised as a result. Coplan and Toahlane (1995: 148) also note that the extent of the willingness of migrants, ex-migrants and their wives whom they interviewed, to leave Lesotho permanently for South Africa, varied in inverse proportion to 'their social and material investment in their homesteads'.

These data confirmed both the validity of the analysis regarding the differentiation of the worker-peasantry in the region and particularly in Lesotho (Neocosmos 1987, 1993a and 1993b, Levin and Neocosmos 1989), as well as the view that migrants should be consulted before any transformation to the migrant labour system was undertaken. Clearly peasant-migrants did not wish to become permanent residents and South African citizens if this meant they would be proletarianised as a result. This was confirmed by the low numbers who actually applied for permanent residence and which were noted above. The South African Green Paper on International Migration recognised this and noted that the figures of those applying for and those receiving permanent residence were 'much lower than anticipated and indicate that the scale of unauthorised migration might be smaller than originally estimated' (James 1997: 16). All these results flew in the face of the NUM's view (both in South Africa and in Lesotho) which was founded on a conception of miners as proletarians. A couple of remarks from miners illustrate the point:

I have laboured under very difficult conditions to make South Africa what it is and so, have earned some reward. South Africans earn pensions at old age and blue card earnings for six months while looking for jobs. This blue card money is the money deducted from the salary while one works. Unlike in Lesotho where our deferred pay is not benefiting us as contributors, here at least there is something to wipe off one's tears... [Respondent has no intention to bring his family even if he is granted permanent residence] Life in South Africa is garbage... working here is like going to the cattle post where you take your livestock in summer and bring them back in winter. [He does not want to be a citizen of South Africa. He will only use the ID or permanent residence as passport to getting his worked for benefits]...

Another [does not want to stay permanently in South Africa because there is no free land...] while another [wants to bring his family because he does not own fields or anything of value in Lesotho] (Sechaba Consultants op. cit).

Clearly therefore migrants tried to get the best of both worlds – the rural security and status of Lesotho and the access to cash in urban South Africa. However the majority made it absolutely clear that they were only interested in having access to South African benefits – jobs or IDs – temporarily. This response can be understood as being completely rational and had two major reasons: first because miners had access to material resources (mainly land and cattle) in Lesotho, which they would never have been able to access in South Africa (unless Lesotho became integrated into the latter); second because the proletarianisation entailed by becoming permanently South African also entailed a complete decline in conditions of life, including in moral standards which were seen as incomparably lower than rural life from the perspective of rural dwellers. It is this latter conception – recurring systematically in interviews – in particular which was often expressed as an adherence to Sesotho cultural values (as expressed in songs, music etc.) and is interpreted by Coplan (1994) as a romantic attachment to national identity.

Defending 'Fortress South Africa': A Brief Review of Legislation

Clearly the process of 'nation-building' (whether explicit or implicit), is not simply about the creation of 'national unity' around a common political project, it is also about demarcating that unity from others – from 'foreigners'. The opposition citizen-foreigner denotes both the creation of a new community as well as the exclusion of some from community. As this community is based not only on a common 'identity' but also on also on legal prescriptions (rights and duties) and socio-economic benefits (access to social services, bank loans, etc.), it is certainly not 'imagined' but materially experienced. It is not only an ideological but also a fundamentally socio-material object embedded in social relations and is experienced as such, most obviously by 'strangers'/'foreigners' who are excluded from community rights and access to resources.

How is this process of inclusion/exclusion arrived at? To what extent is it/has it been democratic? Clearly these are crucial questions, as the ability to sustain this community (the nation) including the ability to justify exclusion, is largely determined by the democratic nature of the process (both in its objective and subjective dimensions). The crisis of the state in Africa today is largely attributable to the fact that this process was constructed undemocratically during the post-colonial period in such a manner that the nation was reduced to the state (the 'nation-state') (Olukoshi and Laakso 1996). Moreover it has really to be questioned whether a concept of 'citizen' developed in 1789 in a context when nationhood and birthplace coincided, is still applicable in the 1990s when this correspondence no longer exists and has ceased to exist for some time, most notably in Africa. Perhaps it is time to replace such a concept by one of 'people from all walks of life' or 'persons from every-where'.[29] Unfortunately South Africa has not yet reached this point. Arriving late into the realm of (bourgeois) democracy, the dominant view in that country is still one which sees concepts such as 'the market' and 'citizenship' as democratic. The contradictions to which this gives rise can be seen in the Draft Green Paper on International Migration submitted in May 1997 to the Minister of Home Affairs (James 1997).

The Green Paper and the Constitution

The build up to the publication of this Green Paper rightly gave the impression that it was expected that this report would suggest the liberalisation of the existing law. Of course, given the extremely repressive character of existing legislation, only liberalisation had any meaning, so that the publication of the Green Paper was hailed as signalling a 'Break with [the] Racist Past' (Williams 1997) in that it recog-nised that migrants and immigrants can be an asset to South Africa. Yet at the same time the report was very disappointing from a democratic perspective and its break from the past was only partial. In fact the report was largely hamstrung by the assumptions internal to its discourse as well as by the external constraints of the constitutionally enshrined Bill of Rights itself. These constraints can be seen in three different areas.

First, the report assumed without providing any evidence that the reason for the 'negative view of immigration' held by South Africans whereby immigrants are viewed as illegitimate competitors and as a security risk to the country, is simply a left-over from the period of apartheid (James 1997:4). This inference is clearly mistaken and indeed absurd as the struggle against the apartheid state in the 1980s linked oppressed South Africans with other Africans and especially those from the region very closely politically, as I have shown above. Rather, the reasons for South African chauvinism should be sought elsewhere, particularly in the statements and actions, in other words the politics, of its state agents and politicians and in the failure of the state party, the ANC, to provide democratic leadership on the issue within the context of its programme of nation building and reconciliation. The Green Paper in fact confused state policy and practice, especially in the Ministry of Home Affairs, which has indeed been influenced by apartheid on this issue, with popular attitudes. Even the 1996 constitution, as we shall see, makes important distinctions between the rights of citizens and those of persons (including foreign-ers), and as such provides a basis for 'legal' discrimination against foreigners by making the distinction in the first place.

Second, the Green Paper noted that the challenge in South Africa was to replace a racially-motivated policy on immigration (whereby immigration of Europeans was encouraged and African immigration prohibited under apartheid) by a 'non-racial and rational' one – not it should be stressed by a democratic one. In other words it assumed, as with so much South African official reasoning, that 'non-racial' equalled 'democratic', as if immigration policy cannot be non-racial, oppressive and undemocratic at the same time. For example, although the Green Paper was rightly concerned to restrict the hitherto arbitrary actions of Home Affairs officials with respect to migrants deemed to be 'illegal' by the state, it did not consider nor did it encourage any form of self-empowerment by 'foreign' residents (or even people including 'foreigners') as a counterpart to the arbitrariness of state power. Rather, it merely stressed the importance of formal/legal 'checks and balances in the form of appeal and review procedures and access to information', as a way of restricting the 'administrative discretion' given to the executive and bureaucracy in immigration matters. Although these checks are useful, the point regularly made by democracy activists everywhere in relation to this is of course that the poor, from whom most 'illegal' suspects emanate, do not have the power or knowledge to use such legal avenues. Clearly, the self-empowerment of 'foreigners' raises the question of the nature of citizenship rights, and how citizenship is defined and codified in law. This issue is posed directly by the Bill of Rights in the South African Constitution.

The third point therefore concerns the manner in which the Green Paper was hamstrung by the statements of the Bill of Rights on this matter. All foreigners (whether legally employed or not, or whether they pay taxes to the state or not), are denied all political rights, including voting at local, regional and national elections. They are also denied the 'freedom to trade, occupation and profession' which is also exclusively restricted to citizens. In these instances in particular, the most fundamental law of the land, constantly paraded in the media as 'one of the most democratic constitutions in the world', demarcates people resident in South Africa between 'citizens' and 'foreigners' regarding some of the most basic rights in existence, including the right to make a living and to survive through employment and trade. The logic behind this is unsustainable on democratic grounds given the regional history of Southern Africa and the regular patterns of migration and the arbitrariness of the drawing of borders which have characterised such a history. Given this history, a significant proportion of South Africans have either lived, been born or are descendants of those who have lived and/or have been born outside the confines of South African borders, often for several generations. Given this distinction in the constitution, the power to decide who is denied political and commercial rights now rests with that lower level legislation which defines citizenship. As in many other African countries, most notoriously Zambia and Côte d'Ivoire, people can be denied their political rights simply by withdrawing their citizenship through legislation introduced for the purpose.[30] Presumably people could even lose their right to work by similar methods. Clearly, there is no sign of this happening at the moment, but the danger is there for the future.

Denying foreigners trading rights in particular is evidently discriminatory and affects migrants directly as many engage in petty-trading activities. Reitzes (1997b: 17) comments that 'all people should be assured of the necessary rights to engage in economic activity' as such a right is a human right – an attribute of human existence – which is 'territorially transcendent' as 'all human beings are rights bearers, when they cross borders they carry their rights with them'. She argues that research shows that these kinds of rights are the ones which immigrants claim: 'their expectations of the state are primarily to be left alone to make their own way' in civil society. She continues:

> At present, in terms of the Aliens Control Amendment Act of 1995, the South African government fundamentally negates... [such]... rights by subjecting illegal immigrants to continual harassment, bribery and corruption; divesting them of their property and earnings; imprisoning them without trial, and deporting them. Furthermore, in granting the right to freedom of trade, occupation and profession exclusively to citizens, the revised bill of rights deprives migrants of a fundamental... human right (ibid).

But it could also be argued that denying foreigners who work in South Africa citizenship rights (such as rights to organise) is also discriminatory, although I realise this point is contentious. The apartheid state provided full citizenship rights to foreigners after a few months if they were white. Why could the present state not do the same for others? In fact we shall see below that this indeed happened in 1994 during the first general election and in fact an argument can be made that rights should be linked to work rather than to indigeneity. However, whatever the case may be with regard to the constitution, the Green Paper on Immigration was clearly restricted by both conceptual and legal constraints. It was this which ultimately accounted for the contradictions between its democratic intentions and genuine attempts to liberalise migration policy on the one hand, and its fundamentally nationalist-statist preoccupations and concerns on the other. For example, while dismissing the SADC protocol on the free movement of persons, it attempted to suggest 'freer' access to the South African labour market by SADC citizens in ways regulated by its narrow conception of South African 'national interest' (regulation of migrants through quota systems and of immigrants through 'point systems' which again will give discretionary powers to the bureaucracy) (James, 1997: 11). While recognising that all available evidence shows that SADC migrants do not wish or intend to stay permanently in South Africa (i.e. that they are migrants and not immigrants) (ibid: 16), it insisted on restricting migration through quotas and entry and trading permits. As a result it was unable to address the issue of discrimination squarely and democratically and to suggest ways of overcoming it.

I have already noted in chapter two and have argued extensively elsewhere (Neocosmos 1996), that a clear distinction is apparent in the way the process of national unification in South Africa was conducted in the 1980s from the way it has been conducted in the post-apartheid period. While during the former period this process was founded on concerted attempts to involve ordinary people (including many of those now deemed to be 'foreign') in its production so that a popular democratic process would be unleashed and sustained, today this process is exclusively state-directed and controlled. National unity now means primarily unity 'at the top' within the state and its apparatuses and within the new 'non-racial elite' as the 'patriotic bourgeoisie' of black accumulators now join their white counterparts in accumulating in the 'national interest'. While during the 1980s we could speak of a process (however flawed, however partial) of the construction of national democracy, it is difficult nowadays to refer to anything more than state democracy. While the former involved a national debate within all sectors of community regarding the nature of democracy, the latter no longer does so and is exclusively a state discourse. While distinct from the African experience in many ways the South African process of 'nation building' has been fundamentally founded on the same conception that the state is the nation, so that unity at state level is equated with national unity in society. Of course this amounts to a clear substitution of the state for the people which can be said to have been the main characteristic of statism throughout Africa.

The fact that the citizenry has the opportunity every five years to elect the party of its choice is not in itself an indication that the party represents in the intervening period, in all its pronouncements, the popular will. One way in which this will is expressed and which is regularly emphasised these days is through the existence of a 'vibrant' civil society. However the latter is not itself a guarantee of democracy and is compatible with the existence of authoritarianism (Neocosmos 2005), but in any case civil society organisations in South Africa have been incorporated through a complex corporatist structure (for instance NEDLAC) into the state itself. As a result there are few avenues independent of the state open for the expression of popular grievances and discontent. There are no direct controls over the people's representatives, any more, only elections every five years. The latter are controlled from above, by the party leadership, by patronage.

Examples of this from the 1990s were not simply the money spinning activities of ex-trade union leaders which we had been told would 'represent workers' interests' in government, parliament and so on, but the revelations in which leading ANC women were said to be investing in a deportation centre for 'illegal immigrants' called 'Lindela' (*Mail and Guardian*, vol. 13, no. 5, February 1997). It is in this context that the Green Paper on Immigration must be situated and evaluated. While the liberalisation of the existing immigration laws was long overdue, the fact that such a review took place so late after the repeal of all other apartheid legislation was indicative of the fact that any change in this area has not been a priority. As with previous government commissions on related issues, the authors of the Green Paper seem not to have been concerned to go beyond a narrow conception of the 'national interest', and did not provide an opening to democratic popular perspectives. Clandestine migrants and 'foreigners' are the weakest members of any society, having few rights. It seems that the old concept of citizenship in Southern Africa is thoroughly outdated. In order to move forward to a new non-discriminatory vision in a democratic way, 'migrants' and 'foreigners' should be taken seriously and asked their opinions, but that can only happen when politics are reintroduced into society and foreigners are politically organised. Despite all its flaws however, the Green Paper was an attempt to democratise immigration legislation. The fact that it failed and was then rejected by the Government meant a hardening of immigration policy.

More Recent Legislation

Harris (2001: 7) in her comprehensive report on violence, crime and xenophobia in South Africa is categorical in her statement: 'racism is a key feature of South Africa's immigration legislation and practice, both historically and, despite the country's transition to democracy and equality, currently'. This can be seen, for example, in deportation figures cited by Valji (2003: 7) who notes that in the first months of 1996, 26,000 people from Germany, Britain and the United States overstayed their visits, yet in the whole of 1995, only 49 people from these three countries were deported. Harris states that the discriminatory apartheid legislation between black and white immigrants in effect remains in place. Of course this is not formally the case yet, state legislative practice is clearly biased against the poorer immigrants on the basis of class criteria (qualifications, etc.) while state employees themselves are highly xenophobic towards migrants whether documented or not from Africa as we shall see below. While indeed state practice and some legislative assumptions are indeed inherited from the past, I have been at pains to argue here that xenophobia as practised by state institutions cannot simply be understood exclusively in those terms. In the past exclusion was regulated by an apartheid logic as we saw in chapter two, today exclusion is often justified on the grounds of economic necessity. The argument goes something along the lines of: 'poverty is high in South Africa and unemployment has been growing, we must look after our own first; it would be disastrous to "open the flood gates" and allow the poverty of Africa to overwhelm our economy'. In other words, the arguments usually adduced to defend 'fortress South Africa' are economic ones, but since restrictions on economic grounds (for example on the basis of lack of appropriate skills) tends primarily to affect Africans, de facto the system takes a racist form.

There has however been continuity in what Crush refers to as a 'fortress' perspective where South Africa is seen as having to defend itself against 'invading hordes' of immigrants (Crush 1999). The legislation which has basically been governing immigration in South Africa for most of the past decade is the Aliens Control Act of 1991, passed just as the new state was being formed. It focuses on control and expulsion, keeping unwanted foreigners out and deporting them if they have been able to enter the country without documents. The amendments to the Act in 1995, it has been noted, actually increased the repressive powers of officials (Valji 2003: 12). The history of legislation since then has been a confused one of attempting to amend, supplement and transcend the provisions of the Act - which is draconian by any standard. For example section 43 of the act gives any police or immigration officer the power to declare anyone suspected of being an illegal immigrant a 'prohibited person'; section 55 stipulates that the courts have no jurisdiction over 'any act, order or warrant of the minister, an immigration officer or master of a ship performed or issued under this act' (Reitzes 1997b: 2).

After the rejection of the Green Paper, the next piece of attempted legislation was the Draft White Paper on International Migration of 1999 which was criticised for assuming that South Africa had been flooded by illegal immigrants. This assertion was based on the findings of a discredited piece of research by the HSRC which put the number of 'illegal immigrants' at five million, while more sober-minded research noted that this was an exaggeration, yet no other estimates were mentioned (official estimates vary between 2.5 to 12 million people, SAMP 2001a: 3; McDonald et al., 1998: 8). Underpinning the White Paper, SAMP (2001a: 3) argued was a crude neo-Malthusian view according to which 'South Africa has reached its "carrying capacity" and cannot accommodate significant further population increase'. The White Paper used the high unemployment rate in the country as a justification for discouraging immigration and it is in the area of enforcement that it shows its preoccupation in line with the Aliens Control Act while research by SAMP shows that for the most part migration to South Africa is highly regularised and orderly (ibid: 20).

By the time the White Paper became a Bill in 2000 it included sections making concessions to the mining industry allowing it to employ 'a wholly foreign workforce' to which SAMP (2001b: 5) objected that this would simply maintain the migrant labour system. Also interesting, and extremely dangerous as we shall see, were clauses which gave the police powers to stop anyone (citizen or otherwise) to prove their immigration status, and which enacted a 'community enforcement policy'. What this latter point meant was immigration and police officers were empowered to organise community-based organisations to involve the citizenry in the application of the Act and to 'educate the citizenry in migration issues' (s 30f). South Africans were being encouraged to 'root out' and report 'illegal immigrants' to state authorities. Apparently, in presenting the Bill, the Minister of Home Affairs stated that 'if they are good patriots, I would hope that they would know that it is in their interests to report [illegal immigrants]' (Valji 2003: 11). As we shall see below, this attempt to 'involve the community' arguably led directly to at least one (and probably contributed indirectly to other) major incident in Zandspruit outside Johannesburg in late 2000, when over one hundred informal dwellings belonging to 'Zimbabweans' were burnt down by local residents, leading, according to newspaper reports, to an exodus from the area of around a thousand people. Occurring as it did just over a month after the World Conference against Racism was held in Durban, this incident elicited rapid state responses and by the time the Immigration Bill was re-submitted for comment in 2002, these sections had been dropped.

Human Rights commentators on this version noted that the bill created 'a situation in which the almost exclusive function of Home Affairs is that of enforcement' (for example Williams 2002: 3). They rightly pointed to the contradiction between this function and the professed concern by the ministry 'to provide for a human-rights based legal framework to deal with matters related to foreigners within the republic'. It was noted:

It is not feasible to believe that the same department that will take such extraordinary measures to 'prevent, detect and deport illegal foreigners' can and wants to take equally energetic measures to prevent xenophobia and/or promote a human rights based framework. Significantly, while the enforcement strategies are clear and explicit, there are no specific strategies to prevent xenophobia or to protect and promote the rights of foreigners (Ibid: 4).

The coercive side of the legislation was thus not removed and the powers of thepolice to harass and intimidate people on the street were not circumscribed whenthe Bill became an Act of Parliament (No. 13) in 2002. Given these powers, theimmigration control system has been and continues to be highly enabling of corrup-tion, and the system is thereby riddled with it at border posts, in Home Affairsoffices, on the street and in police stations, in the Lindela holding camp, in fact inevery state institution dealing with immigration, as the evidence shows. In 2004,after Buthelezi was unceremoniously removed from Home Affairs as a result ofthe poor performance of the Inkatha Freedom Party in the last general elections,the Act was amended in October. This followed a highly publicised disagreementbetween Buthelezi and the Cabinet in which the former was accused of ignoring thelatter before publishing regulations. Anyhow, the new amendments seem primarilyconcerned with removing some of the impediments to immigration of skilled for-eigners. It is still too soon to decide how this latest piece of legislation for whichregulations are still to be gazetted will affect xenophobia.

The importance of legislation is that it consists of the fundamental way in which the sate addresses sections of the population under its control. It is also indicative of a specific form of politics, state politics, and provides one of the main dimensions of state discourse, which moulds the terrain within which discussion and debate within the 'public sphere' takes place. It is clear that South African legislation has systematically provided the basis for a hegemonic xenophobic discourse within the country. The roots of the problem are to be found within the constitution itself which actually distinguishes between two categories of people: citizens and persons. The distinction means that not all people within the country are interpellated in the same manner. Some are said to have rights which others do not have. Clearly, it is now recognised by many in the upper echelons of government that human rights in South Africa are applicable to all and not just to citizens, yet this perception has not become hegemonic and it is certainly not apparently prevalent within either the Home Affairs Department or the Police Services. This largely means that the hegemony of xenophobic discourse has yet to be overcome. At the same time, it is pertinent to note that if a distinction is systematically made in official discourse between citizens and others because the former is reduced to a notion of indigeneity conferred by the state, it seems difficult to see how xenophobia can be overcome at all. I shall return to this point in the conclusion. For the present we must turn to a brief account of the utterances and practices of state personnel and the press and a brief account of popular experience.

Post-apartheid Nation-building Continued: Citizenship and the State Construction of Xenophobia

Evidently government legislation is not the only indication of how a state discourse of xenophobia has been structured in post-apartheid South Africa. Other political agents are also contributing to fashioning this aspect of state politics. In this section, I shall first outline some of the indications and xenophobia among the country's politicians, then I shall move onto assessing some of the experiences of African migrants at the hands of various state institutions followed by the press. Finally I shall end with a brief account of popular attitudes. In this manner a fuller picture of the power relations in the dominance of xenophobic discourse can be painted.

Government Xenophobic Discourse and Its Effects

Perhaps one of the most staggering remarks was made in 2002 by the ANC ex-Director General of Home Affairs. He was quoted as claiming that:

> approximately 90 percent of foreign persons, who are in the RSA with fraudulent documents, i.e. either citizenship or migrant documents, are involved in other crimes as well... it is quicker to charge these criminals for their false documentation and then to deport them than to pursue the long route in respect of the other crimes committed (Billy Masethla, cited Crush and Peberdy n.d.: 1).

Of course, as Crush and Peberdy point out, there are no data whatsoever to support this contention, or otherwise. Nevertheless, Harris (2001: 76) notes that in 1998 according to police statistics, South African citizens comprised on average ninety-eight percent of all arrests made, foreigners arrested rarely exceeded one percent in any crime category, actual conviction rates are, of course, much lower.

After only a few months in office, Minister of Home Affairs Mangosuthu Buthelezi announced in 1998 that 'if we as South Africans are going to compete for scarce resources with millions of aliens who are pouring into South Africa, then we can bid goodbye to our Reconstruction and Development Programme' (cited in Harris 2001: 74). In fact Buthelezi developed quite some notoriety for his infamous xenophobic statements which included *inter alia* the suggestion that all Nigerian immigrants are criminals and drug traffickers (op cit.). He also stated in 1998 at a speech in Cape Town on 12 February that 'it is not surprising that there is in the country growing resentment to most foreigners... just as South Africa was coming to grips on how to meet its people's needs and to develop, it faced a deluge of migrants'.[31] By 1998, Buthelezi was reacting to the Human Rights Watch Report on Xenophobia in South Africa (HRW 1998) which had referred to South Africa's 'increasingly xenophobic public culture' which tolerates 'unsubstantiated and inflammatory statements' by politicians which blame migrants for crime, rising unemployment and the spread of diseases, by accusing Human Rights Watch of wanting 'five-star treatment of illegal aliens while more than 50 percent of South Africans live below the poverty line'.[32] In August 1999, Buthelezi was asked by an ex-MK ANC

MP in Parliament (Ike Maphoge) why refugees from neighbouring countries 'were being treated so leniently'. He replied that he sympathised with Maphoge but every time he had raised similar issues with government he had been accused by the ANC of xenophobia.[33]

Of course, Buthelezi's quasi-fascist opinions are well known but what is more important is that his officials from his Home Affairs Department were thus encouraged to air their xenophobia in public, which was regularly paraded as the official position of the department if not that of the government itself. For example a Home Affairs official called Mr George Orr in a television talk show on 'illegal immigrants' (South African Broadcasting Corporation Television Channel 1, Two-Way, 13 October 1996) stated without apparently even blushing: 'We will grant a grace period for those who have been in the country for five years or more to apply for permanent residence; after which they ('illegal immigrants') will be hounded, using police to trace them, prosecute employers, deny them health, education services and make life unbearable for them'.

Human Rights Watch (1998: 4) has concluded that 'in general, South Africa's public culture has become increasingly xenophobic, and politicians often make unsubstantiated and inflammatory statements that the 'deluge' of migrants is responsible for the current crime wave, rising unemployment and even the spread of diseases. During the campaign for the 1999 elections all opposition parties politicised the issue of immigration (Harris 2001: 74), with one New National Party member stating: '[I]t was no good to take R10 million from the budget of the Department of Home Affairs for the Reconstruction and Development Programme when illegal aliens were removing far more than that from the economy by taking jobs away from South Africans' (cited in Valji op cit.: 10).

More disturbing are the statements made by many ANC politicians,[34] several of which have already been cited, despite the fact that the organisation had by August 2001 expressed its opposition to xenophobia in a public declaration.[35] Published extremely late in the day, this woolly statement did not do justice to the anti-xenophobic sentiments of many serious ANC cadres. On the one hand it stated that 'the instance of xenophobia in South Africa is largely linked to immigration' which was unavoidable given the attraction of 'South Africa's democratic breakthrough in 1994' (p.1) and the forces of globalisation (p. 2); on the other hand it stressed the ANC's commitment to 'a human-rights based system for migration control through legislation' (p.3). In sum then, xenophobia was the result of immigration and was thus inevitable and should be regulated through the law. This seems to be another case of blaming the victims of 'structural causes' beyond control; presumably it is not thought possible to have immigration without xenophobia, and the only political way of tackling this is seen predictably to be through the exercise of state legislation. Given what we have seen regarding the character of this legislation, it is difficult to avoid the conclusion that the organisation is unable to think beyond the confines of exclusion and control, while remaining within the domain of state liberal politics. Popular organisation and militant democratic struggles are clearly no longer within its ambit of thought.

This ANC statement was particularly unhelpful given the fact that it came in the wake of a major xenophobic confrontation at Zandspruit near Johannesburg in late 1990. In fact this disastrous episode was itself the culmination of a whole series of state attacks on undocumented migrants throughout the year beginning in early 2000 when the government announced its 'US-style bid to rid SA of illegal aliens' (cited in Comaroff and Comaroff 2001: 647). Police carried out high profile raids throughout the country in an operation variously named 'Operation Crackdown' and 'Operation Monazite'.[36] In March, 144 suspected 'illegal immigrants' were arrested in Johannesburg, fourteen in Soweto, 212 persons on the West Rand including 92 suspected 'illegal immigrants', 135 alleged 'illegal immigrants' were arrested in the Mpumalanga region, and 87 in Pretoria (ibid: 1-2). In the last instance 14,000 people were searched and over 1000 arrested including many South Africans suspected of being 'illegal immigrants' (Comaroffs, op cit.: 647-8). In a two month period of 'Operation Crackdown', 10,000 suspected 'illegal aliens' were arrested, 7000 of whom were taken to Lindela (Harris 2001: 54). At one point when the Human Rights Commission meekly 'raised its concerns' regarding 'the ill-treatment of "illegal immigrants" in recent police blitzes in Gauteng', a government spokesperson was quoted as saying that the HRC 'was creating the impression of being sympathetic towards illegal immigrants', continuing to state that the government wanted to hold regular meetings with the HRC to ensure that they do not work at 'cross purposes' (*Business Day*, 30 March 2000).[37] So much for a Human Rights culture here. Later in the year South Africans were to be shown a video on prime time television of six police officers setting dogs on suspected 'illegal immigrants'.

In October, a short while after the UN Conference against Racism and Xenophobia had been held in South Africa, Zandspruit, an informal settlement near Johannesburg, erupted in an orgy of looting and destruction, which miraculously had no fatalities. One thousand Zimbabweans were made destitute and residents had torched more than one hundred shacks belonging to Zimbabweans (*Mail and Guardian*, 23 October 2000). Local residents had accused Zimbabweans of being involved in crime and of taking their jobs. According to the City of Johannesburg itself, Zandspuit is an extremely poor area where 1,600 families reside in overcrowded conditions with only basic infrastructure.[38] The news media all moralised on the appalling acts of xenophobia, but few went beyond platitudes. It soon emerged however that the Department of Home Affairs had been aware of the tensions in the settlement for several weeks. One of their spokesmen, Leslie Mashokwe, stated that residents had asked the police to take steps against Zimbabweans whom they had accused of stealing their jobs and killing residents.[39]

A number of committees were formed to deal with trauma, re-housing and complaints. In response to the Zandspruit residents' complaints three weeks previously, Mashokwe was quoted as saying that: 'officials from the departments of home affairs and labour launched a joint operation called Operation Clean Up with the local people and moved into the area to root out the illegal immigrants'. He was reported to have said that between 600 and 700 illegal immigrants were rounded up and deported to neighbouring countries including Zimbabwe and Mozambique. A few days later residents noticed that the 'illegals' had returned and they rushed to the police station to report the matter. On the way back they decided to 'handle it on their own', and called a community meeting in which they gave 'foreigners' ten days to leave or face the music'. The foreigners did not leave so residents burnt them out. Of course a number were then arrested and taken to court, but the important aspect of the story was that state officials from two government departments had been directly involved in xenophobic raids aided by the local population. Only one article made the connection between these events and the statements of the Draft Bill on Immigration which, as I have noted, emphasised 'enforcement at community level' of the 'detection, apprehension and deportation' of undocumented migrants.[40] Mashokwe was later reported to have said that his department condemned the attacks as did the cabinet, the SACP and COSATU, while the ANC did so in *ANC Today* - coming so soon after the World Conference on Racism, this was inevitable.[41]

After condemning the attacks the ANC's principal task seems to have been to absolve the government of any liability in the process, as it stressed that the real causes of xenophobia have to be sought in 'the legacy of apartheid and colonialism, rapid urbanisation and unfavourable economic conditions' (ANC 2001b: 6). Refer-ring to Harris (2001) the ANC noted that her report stressed that 'xenophobia is not peculiar to South Africa', that 'the South African media represents foreigners in a negative and stereotypical manner' and that 'xenophobia, like racism is about the irrational intolerance of people who are different' (ibid). Despite the fact that all these factors have indeed a role to play in the hegemony of xenophobic discourse in South Africa, the conclusion one is inevitably led to is that xenophobia is beyond state control. The ANC commentary unfortunately omitted to mention any of the comments in Harris which were critical of the government, such as the categorical statement that 'racism is a key feature of South Africa's immigration legislation and practice both historically ... and currently' (Harris 2001: 7).

To my knowledge, no South African state institution or representative has so far been taken to court for incitement to commit a crime, and yet it seems abundantly apparent that there may have been some case to answer by the Departments of Home Affairs and Labour in the Zandspruit incident.[42] Of course this seems to be in the realm of fantasy, yet it would be a logical outcome to a consistent 'culture of rights'. The problem however is that xenophobia in South Africa is not about Hu-man Rights, it is an issue of power, of politics; in the absence of an understanding of this fundamental fact, it seems impossible to begin to address the problem, and the utterances of state institutions condemning xenophobia will continue to seem more and more like empty rhetoric, as it is state institutions which have provided the conditions for a hegemonic discourse of xenophobia in the first place. The issue is rather what kind of politics is most conducive to an overcoming of xenophobia? A politics which treats people differently depending on whether they are citizens or not, or a politics which stresses that 'South Africa belongs to all who live' in it as the Freedom Charter stated?

Criminalisation, Policing, Repatriation and the Role of the Media

Research on xenophobia in South Africa, much of which is actually based on interviews with African foreigners, shows a number of regularities which the interviews conducted for this research corroborated.[43] Quite simply, in their contacts with state authorities, African migrants experienced systematic xenophobia, particularly from the police, Home Affairs officials and Lindela employees. This took the form of the arbitrary exercise of power, corruption, extortion, and gratuitous violence and torture, despite the fact that it must be stressed that migrants are rarely convicted of any crimes whatsoever by a court of law. On the other hand, their treatment in the hands of ordinary South African citizens is reported as being much more contradictory, some being sympathetic and supportive, while others have been frankly xenophobic. It is very important to draw this distinction, and we shall see below that the measured attitudes of South African citizens are indeed quite contradictory in relation to foreign migrants, while state practices are reported consistently as being xenophobic. We must therefore draw a line between state and society on this question. I shall discuss society below; for the present we need to end with some illustrations of the typical practices of state agencies.

The usual criterion for arresting suspected 'illegal immigrant' by the police is regularly stated to be a racial stereotype. Usually this is based on the colour of the skin and darker features, and makes people more likely to be arrested as 'foreigners' or asked for identification.[44] Other methods used are language checks and inoculation marks - all clearly left over from apartheid-type practices. The South African Human Rights Commission (1999: 31) comments:

> Anyone, anywhere at anytime can be stopped and required to produce ID documents. Failure to produce an ID document subjects an individual to the exercise of wide discretionary powers conferred on individual police and immigration officers. Failure to produce an ID document, on demand, may and often does result in immediately being taken into custody with a view to removal from the country. The current legislation, combined with its interpretation, has thus effectively created a pass law requirement.

It should be noted that there is no statutory requirement for anyone to carry identification papers on their person in South Africa at present. In any case, it is clear according to respondents that the ID is not the issue:

> The police don't care even if you have an ID with you, if they suspect you they just detain you.
> The way police [apprehend suspected illegal immigrants] is unsatisfactory, because even if you have ID they just tear it up, they don't want to listen to the explanation (ibid: 25).

[The police officer] took it [the ID] and told me that I am 'Kalanga' [illegal from Zimbabwe] (ibid: 26).

The practice of tearing up or otherwise removing official documents by those in power is one which was prevalent under apartheid. The same is true of extortion and bribery which are said today to be 'extremely widespread among apprehending officers' (ibid: 28).

Undocumented migrants commonly use bribery in order to secure their release from the custody of apprehending officers. Extortion also seems to be routinely practised against documented migrants as well as citizens: 'Failure to comply with demands for money resulted in detention and transfer to Lindela, regardless of whether the individual in question was in possession of a valid ID document' (ibid: 28-9).

The Human Rights Commission notes that 'there is strong evidence for the existence of market rates for release' (p. 30). These vary from R50 to R100 depending on conditions and those who are able to pay get released irrespective of the existence or state of their documents. In the overwhelming majority of accounts by foreign migrants, extortion seems then to be the main effect of the powers provided to the police, and not rigorous compliance with the prescriptions of the Act, which seem to be regularly ignored. In any case it seems the police have the power to ignore or apply these as they see fit (ibid, Harris op cit.). This power indeed goes for beyond the police: it seems and there is even evidence of police refusing to protect 'foreigners' against criminals:

> The police accused us of nursing criminal intentions... How could they arrest us on the mere suspicion that we were potential criminals? I got my wife and my lawyer to come to... my rescue. They presented my passport with my documents but even still, they refused to set us free... [I was released] five months after I and the others had been in detention... My other friends stayed there for another five months before they were released without any charges or proof that we were criminals... During one of the instances when my lawyer applied for bail, the judge turned down our request. He was an Indian guy and he said that he wanted us to suffer to the extent that once we are set free we will go home never to come back to South Africa (Interview Sunnyside, 20 March 2003).

> ...the police are encouraging crime... when I got to Shoprite, four tsotsis attacked me just as I came out of the shop... they wanted to take my parcels... I gave them R10 and ran back into Shoprite but they stayed outside waiting for me... Luckily I saw some cops inside the shop and when they were going out I followed just behind them... But when we came out... the tsotsis approached me and I held one of the cops and told them that these guys wanted to rob me. Do you know what the cop told me? Once he realised I was not South African, he told me to leave him alone and settle the matter with the tsotsis... Later that evening I called 10111 and reported the matter to the police, but all they told me was that the next time, I should try to get the police officer's name and tell them. That's why I believe that the police are encouraging crime in this country (Interview Sunnyside, 11 April 2003).

In fact these kinds of stories are never-ending. It seems that everyone involved in the lower ranks at least of the criminal justice system is able to fleece foreigners of money. This includes the criminal gangs in jail, the cooks also in jail, the warders and the police, of course, who have regular rackets in Sunnyside harassing people for money in return for turning a blind eye to them working without work permits and so on. Businesses exist to get people all the papers they need from Home Affairs and elsewhere:

> What happens is that each time a group of policemen succeed to get money out of foreigners, they go back and tell their friends to come and get theirs. So the process never ends (Interview Sunnyside, 7 April 2003).

> I changed from a visitor's visa to an asylum seeker's permit. That was the easiest document to acquire... many people told me that I needed to have good connections with Home Affairs before having any visa other than the refugee papers.... I got my papers in Johannesburg. I paid somebody who paid somebody else before getting the papers... Many people now pay for these documents. I paid one guy R1000 and he in turn paid somebody else R300 to get the documents for me (Interview, Sunnyside, 7 April 2003).

> I also had to pay R500 for my asylum paper even though we're supposed to get the document for free... The thing has been turned into some kind of business. Many people pay to have it, so I'm not the only person. This is quite funny because there is a notice at Home Affairs (in Pretoria – MN) which indicates that anybody caught giving or taking a bribe will be charged with corruption, but that is not enough to scare anybody ... (Interview Sunnyside, 8 April 2003).

> ...in 1999 the state did not require us to provide them with a police clearance in order to seek employment or carry out any activity. But today, they not only require immigrants to provide police clearance in South Africa, but also another clearance from their home countries. I know people in Johannesburg who issue police clearances which bear the stamp and references of the Cameroon government (Interview Sunnyside, 30 March 2003).

By September, 2005 the price for the release of a (legal or illegal) migrant from the Booysens police station in Johannesburg was cited as around R300 when policemen were caught on video extorting funds from friends and relatives for the release of foreigners who had not been convicted of any crime, and some of whom had been unlawfully arrested. The video was shown on prime time television giving rise to protest in the press (*Mail and Guardian Online*, 6 September 2005, *The Star*, 7 September 2005).

Migrants in South Africa are clearly aware of being discriminated against and are usually clear that the same rules are not applied to citizens and non-citizens.

> ...I felt that they were discriminating against me because I was a foreigner. They did not apply the same laws on me as they would have done if they were dealing with a citizen. For example, the police did not even bring a search warrant before coming to search my flat. That's why I lost most of those things. When I tried to complain, one of the policemen even hit me and said I should stay quiet. He insisted that I'll

explain myself at the police station, but when I went to the station, the guys gave me no opportunity to explain myself. Even at the police station they refused me from phoning my lawyer so, that's why I had to look for other means to free myself, such as giving them bribe (Interview Pretoria West, 9 April 2003).

... if the government has decided to write its laws in such a way that foreigners have the same rights as citizens, then I think that they should enjoy the same rights as citizens (Interview Sunnyside, 8 April 2003).

Other state institutions which exercise power in a xenophobic manner are hospitals and the notorious Lindela repatriation centre. Clearly hospitals are run on commercial criteria primarily and migrants rarely have the funds to pay their exorbitant prices. As recently as January 2005 the Johannesburg *Star* (22 January 2005) reported that an 'asylum seeker' from the Democratic Republic of Congo was turned away at the Johannesburg General Hospital as she was about to give birth. After the staff were told that she did not have R15,000 to pay they threw her out and she was forced to give birth in the car park helped by two paramedics. She was then returned to the hospital and forced to stay there for four days after which she was released and provided with a bill for R26,407. Asked to comment, the spokesman for the Department of Health, Mr Popa Maja stated: 'the general policy is that foreigners have to pay for services rendered because we are protecting resources meant for our citizens... (he quickly added) in emergency situations the hospital should not ask for money' (ibid).

Insofar as Lindela is concerned, the stories which emanate from various studies and reports are equally if not even more harrowing. Here are some of the typical statements from the Human Rights Commission's two reports on Lindela (1999 and 2000). It should be kept in mind throughout that immigration detention at Lindela or elsewhere is not supposed to be punitive (SAHRC 2000: 62). Having noted that 'arrested persons were deliberately prevented from providing accurate documents, valid identity documents were destroyed, bribes were taken for avoiding arrest or for release without documentation...', the second report also notes 'that unnecessary violence is used by arresting officers' (SAHRC 2000: 36). In fact the evidence is clear that the Lindela repatriation centre which is a privately owned business which is subcontracted by the Home Affairs Department simply operates within the same repressive culture which we have seen to be structured by the more formal repressive state apparatuses.

When arriving at Lindela they asked for ID and duplicate application or passport. When I produced my duplicate application they said, 'It's forged; it's not mine; anyone can use it'. They said each of us should pop out R100 to take us out. I did not have. Three who had money went out. This was the second arrest [for me] to Lindela, [before] I used money to bribe and got out. I used R250 (SAHRC 1999: 41).

Further it was stressed:

demonstration of identity documents does not automatically guarantee that the person will be released, since the immigration officer must be convinced that the person is telling the truth. Individuals are often asked to produce other forms of proof such as birth certificates, school records, parents ID books etc. Consider next that the burden of proof of entitlement to be in the country lies with the person arrested... Individuals are further asked questions about their perception of South African languages, geography and culture... other persons explain that immigration officers at Lindela had lost their papers or that Home Affairs refused to accept them as valid proof of their identity (SAHRC 2000: 41, 42).

Evidence was also found that:

employees of the private Dyambu Trust (which runs Lindela) extort money from detainees under a wide variety of circumstances. These circumstances include requiring money for fingerprinting, for the use of public telephones, and in order to allow access of family and friends to the Facility... (SAHRC 1999: 44).

Indeed, 'in a number of reported incidents, officials at Lindela abused their positions by extorting money from wrongfully detained individuals... in fact there is no fee required in order to obtain the release of a person legally resident in the Republic' (SAHRC, 1999: 41-2). Staff at Lindela also extorted amounts apparently for the final processing of those who are due to be deported:

at Lindela we were asked to pay an amount of R50 before being deported to Zimbabwe... yesterday we were supposed to go home but they asked for money to take us home. I didn't have any money so I didn't go (SAHRC 1999: 43).

In other words people are kept in what amounts to detention – in conditions worse than prison according to the same reports – and not repatriated on time unless they pay bribes to officials. In fact at this centre, people's rights are systematically denied and they seem to be regularly coerced, including through the use of physical violence for the simple reasons of maintaining control. People are denied a free phone call as required by law, they are not informed of their rights and they are detained regularly for longer than the stipulated maximum of thirty days. For example, on 3 September 1999, it was observed that 102 persons were being held in excess of thirty days (SAHRC 2000: 51), and 'despite repeated assurances from both the DHA and Dyambu that this history would not be repeated, the practice of unlawful detentions had continued' (ibid: 54). It was reported in the newspapers that according to Lawyers for Human Rights, 1,674 people had been unlawfully detained at Lindela between February 2001 and January 2002.[45] Physical assault is common, especially at night:

The security staff here at Lindela randomly abuse us. They assault us. They leave us alone in the Wall and we are not allowed to go to the loo unless given permission. But since they do not enquire as regularly as they should, people often go to the loo without asking. If such a person is caught he is usually assaulted by security officials (SAHRC 1999: 47).

Every night the detainees are woken up between two and five times for security reasons. The guards wake everyone up by shouting and banging on the doors. They also walk into the room and hit those who do not wake up fast enough. The detainees are told to stand in two rows with their heads between their legs. If someone looks up to see what is going on, the guards will according to information received by interviewed detainees, use their belts and batons to beat that person up. It has further been argued that detainees may have to stand in the same position for half an hour while they are count ed. Others explain that they risk being beaten up by the guards if they ask to use the bathroom at night (SAHRC 2000: 65).

Of course detainees rarely report such incidents, which amount to torture, as it would mean an internal hearing and the detainees risk extending their period of detention as a result (ibid: 67). The Zimbabwe *Herald* referred to NGO sources to suggest that three Zimbabweans a month die at Lindela and are buried in paupers' graves (*Herald*, 25 January 2005). In October 2004, the Mozambican consul-general was quoted as saying that 'so far 20 Mozambicans held at Lindela have died for unexplained causes (sic)' (*Business Day*, 12 October 2004). Whatever the accuracy of these statistics, it is clear that people want to get out of this 'hell hole' as rapidly as possible (*Mail and Guardian*, 5-11 November 2004). This it seems is precisely why some detainees rioted in December 2004, although the story as presented by Home Affairs and the media took a different slant. These sources indicated that in late December, the new ANC minister of Home Affairs, Nosiviwe Mapisa-Nqakula, personally postponed the deportation of 2000 'illegal immigrants' on the grounds that they had handed 'themselves over voluntarily so that [they] can get [a] free ride back home' for the festive season. The spokesperson for DHA stated that some 'illegal immigrants' 'deliberately hid their nationalities and identities and pretended to be from war-torn countries so that they could acquire refugee status' (*Mail and Guardian*, 22 December 2004). A guard was reported as saying that:

> inmates had demanded to be deported and when they were told that deportations had been put on hold, seven had gone on the rampage, breaking windows and doors and trying to scale fences while fellow inmates cheered... The instructions came for us to get our batons and donner them. All hell broke loose and immigrants were beaten badly. After 30 minutes we had the situation under control (*Natal Mercury*, 22 December 2004).

After the riot broke out the minister stated that 'some even come with bicycles they want us to transport home with them...[she said to them] There will be no free rides home today – tough luck ...[and] insisted the guards had handled the matter properly' (ibid). A number of human rights organisations threatened the ministry with court action but the minister was able to get a court to agree to extend the migrants stay at Lindela by another thirty days. Interestingly, a month before the same minister was quoted as:

> denying that the government has a policy of xenophobia, but acknowledged that police action was often a problem... she also denied that inmates at Lindela... were ever tortured to death. 'Deaths have occurred, but they died because of illnesses' [she said] ... 'I have given instructions that I want a full report if a death occurs as a result

of torture' [she continued] ... 'I don't want to be defensive ... the police's attitude is a problem' but she added that illegal immigrants must apply for the necessary permits and cannot undermine the law of the country or they will be arrested and deported. (*Mail and Guardian*, 5-11 November 2004).

These comments are important because the attitude of Home Affairs can no longer be blamed on Buthelezi. We now have an ANC minister blaming the victims. Rather than insisting that Lindela staff be brought to book, it is the migrants who are coerced into staying in detention and who are told to 'face the law', even though the law, such as it is, is systematically broken and undermined in an attempt to coerce, intimidate and fleece them of their resources. What is frankly appalling *inter alia* is the minister's statement that if a death were to occur as a result of torture, she should be provided with a report. Presumably torture without death as I have outlined above does not require reporting, and additionally it is the authorities themselves at Lindela who are to draw the conclusion as to whether any death is a result of torture or not, so as to decide whether a report is warranted. This kind of remark is worthy of the most authoritarian regime, and was not picked up by the media. In response to her appalling utterances, a Human Rights commissioner let her off the hook by meekly stating that 'the constitution stood for respect for every person's rights and dignity irrespective of whether they were locals or foreigners. However, the commission understood that every right had its limitations, provided the state used appropriate legal channels to argue otherwise' (*Business Day*, 24 December 2004).

In July 2005 two Zimbabweans died at Lindela, prompting the minister of Home Affairs to suspend three top officials (*Mail and Guardian Online*, 24 August 2005). In the same news report it was stated that until August at least seven people had died at Lindela and twenty-one more detainees had perished at the nearby hospital during 2005.

It is apparent then that an authoritarian culture permeates all repressive apparatuses of the state, and that this authoritarianism is directed particularly towards non-citizens of African origin. The point is not that this is the outcome of policy decision; it is rather that it is an outcome of structural power and state subjectivity today, as well as of state practices left untransformed from our apartheid past. As Mahmood Mamdani (1996) has put it in the context of his discussion of the post-colonial, the post-apartheid state may have been de-racialised but it has not been democratised. This authoritarianism is a major contributor to the hegemony of xenophobic discourse in the public sphere.

Having looked as some of the practices of the South African state's repressive apparatuses, we need now to turn briefly at the comments of one of its ideological apparatuses in the form of the media which also contribute to the hegemony of xenophobic discourse. The mass media in South Africa are clearly a state ideological apparatus despite their many conflicts with government, and in any case government must be clearly distinguished from the state itself. Some of the best work on xenophobia in print media has been undertaken under the auspices of SAMP and is

to be found in the report by Danso and McDonald (2000) which is detailed and
extensive. As a result this section will remain brief and will restrict itself to highlight-
ing the salient points of this study, which was based on an analysis of a representative sample from 1200 migration-related articles from all English-language newspapers and wire services in South Africa from 1994 to 1998. There has been no
indication that there has been any fundamental change in press coverage of the
issues since then.

Danso and McDonald show that two different perspectives characterise press
coverage of foreign migration to South Africa: there is a majority position which
portrays immigration from an anti-foreigner perspective and calls for stringent and
immediate controls and even for 'an outright banning of immigrants' (ibid: 5). At
the same time this section of the press is bereft of analysis, uncritically cites problematic research as fact and uses anti-immigrant terminology. The minority section
of the print media is more thoughtful in its coverage and attitude towards migration
issues. It highlights the positive impact of labour migration on the economy and
national development while its coverage tends to be more analytical. 'However, the
general tenor running through English-language newspaper reportage on foreign
migration issues is more negative, more unanalytical than critical' (loc cit.). Insofar
as the content of the press coverage is concerned regular refrains make the comment that migrants 'steal jobs', that migrants are mostly 'illegal',[46] that they are 'flooding
into the country to find work' while a typical statement was that 'foreigners are
unacceptably encroaching on the informal sector and therefore on the livelihoods
of our huge number of unemployed people' (ibid: 14, *The Star*, 21 July 1997). Other
xenophobic repetitions concern the supposed drain which migrants represent on the
South African fiscus, the links between illegality and migration (occurring in 38
percent of the sample analysed) and the purported links between crime and immigrants such as in the statement in the *Financial Mail* (9 September 1994) that 'the
high rate of crime and violence – mainly gun-running, drug trafficking and armed
robbery – is directly related to the rising number of illegals in SA' (cited in Danso and
McDonald 2000: 16). Harris (2001: 76) puts the facts straight, when she notes that
'out of all the arrests made in 1998, South African citizens comprise an average of
98%'.

Moreover, the image of Africa portrayed in the press and the media more
generally, is one which, very much in tune its Western counterparts, sees the continent as dominated by death, disease, starvation, war, corruption and helpless victims, thus feeding the stereotypical images of the continent as economically backward and as a politically irredeemable failure. It follows that South Africa needs to
'help' the continent out of its morass, through investment and political leadership.
Therefore, a neo-colonial-type discourse vis-à-vis Africa, propagated by the mass
media and regularly underlined by those in power, is prevalent within the public
sphere. Finally it is perhaps important to note that there is no fundamental hierarchy
of xenophobia within society. While Nigerians could have borne the brunt of xenophobia in the recent past, having been associated in the press with drug smuggling,

today it is Zimbabweans who are the main victims of opprobrium. This seems to follow the vagaries of press reporting, in this case on the economic crisis in Zimbabwe.

In sum then it is important to understand that South Africa's public culture and the subjectivities attached to it are constructed in the public sphere. This construction of public discourse involves principally, in the absence of popular alternative politics, state institutions of various kinds which address (or more accurately interpellate) various sectors of the population in differing ways. It is clear here citizens and non-citizens are indeed interpellated in a very specific way by state discourse, and that this discourse has become hegemonic during the post-apartheid period. The evidence I have provided suggests that it is due to such a dominant state discourse in particular that a hegemonic xenophobic culture throughout society is manufactured and structured.[47] Of course, ordinary people participate in (or in some cases may actively oppose, as do some members of parliament for example) this process of discursive construction, but the dominant perspective, backed as it is by the open deployment of power, repressive legislation and the equally open flouting of the law by state institutions such as the police, the DHA and the Lindela Centre, is relentlessly pursued by state discourse and practice. I have argued that this discourse in its current form has been historically produced quite recently, and therefore cannot be understood solely as an 'unavoidable' left-over from the past, but rather that a nationalist discourse of a particular kind also contributed to its production.

Society: Xenophobic Attitudes, Human Rights and the Absence of Politics

In South African society, particularly in urban areas where most research has been undertaken, attitudes towards foreigners are much more contradictory and not as systematically oppressive as in the case of state agencies. Sichone (2001: 10) in his anthropological research on East Africans in Cape Town notes that the 'cultural definition of *makwerekwere* (the derogatory term African foreigners are referred by) is not the main source of xenophobic hatred'; rather immigrants who create wealth or provide jobs are welcome, while those who are seen to 'take away jobs are not'. In other words, xenophobic discourse in society, unlike its equivalent in the state, is more directly concerned with economic survival rather than with exclusion or the exercise over the less powerful as such. Similar results were apparent from a more quantitative study (SAMP 2004: 2) which compared the attitude of South African citizens to those of other SADC countries in 2001-2002. This survey found that 'citizens are prepared to accept and welcome non-citizens if their economic impact is demonstrably positive'. More detail is provided by a SAMP attitude survey of a representative sample of 3,500 South Africans (Mattes et al. 1999).

The survey predictably found that the majority of South Africans are indeed xenophobic and that opposition to immigration and foreign citizens is widespread: twenty-five percent of South Africans want a total ban on immigration and forty-five percent support strict limits on the numbers of immigrants allowed in (op cit.: 1). Other findings include: just under half of the sample support an expulsion policy restricted to people involved in illegal activities (p.10), while fifty-nine percent of the population surveyed were opposed to the legalisation of migrants as a general principle as with an amnesty (p. 14). Large percentages of respondents opposed offering African non-citizens the same access to a house as a South African (54 percent), the right to vote (53 percent) or the right to citizenship (44 percent) (p. 13); 61 percent felt that immigrants put additional strains on the economy, but 24 percent 'said that they had nothing to fear from foreigners living in South Africa' (p. 18), while 85 percent of Africans and 88 percent of whites agreed with the statement that 'one should listen to various points of view before making a judgement about what's going on' (p.22). At the same time the authors comment:

> Also somewhat surprising , given the nature of press reports on attitudes towards immigrants, is the small but important, cadre of South Africans who support a more liberalised immigration regime and accept immigrants and immigration. Although this group is clearly in the minority, the fact that such a minority does exist – and that all racial, economic, gender and ethnic groups are represented in it – suggests that there is at least some support for a more ... service-oriented approach to immigration in the future (ibid: 1).

We can therefore say quite clearly that xenophobic attitudes, although dominant in certain respects, are much more contradictorily distributed in society. Thus although one does hear of foreign migrants being abused and even physically attacked at times, there is also an indication throughout of support for migrants. In addition of course the whole methodology of attitude surveys is problematic, not least because it is a-contextual and gives the impression, because of its individualism, that attitudes are somehow psychologically ingrained and hence unchangeable. In actual fact discourses and practices can be transformed and are constantly being changed through interventions in the political arena; in this sense methodological individualism contributes to the removal of politics from public and intellectual discourse, it is completely congruent with political liberalism.

The issue then is not so much one of commenting on the 'cognitive links between media representation and public attitudes' (Danso and McDonald 2000: 6), in other words, the question is not a psychological one affecting individuals, but rather a political one regarding the shaping of public discourses. The question should instead be one which asks: what kind of politics is necessary to begin to overcome such a hegemonic xenophobic discourse? I want to argue briefly that a liberal conception of politics and a human rights discourse is unable to do so. What follow are some of the core points argued at greater length elsewhere (Neocosmos 2005).

Liberalism and Human Rights Discourse

Central to liberal discourse has been a conception revolving around the idea that politics is reducible to the state or that the state is the sole legitimate domain of politics. For liberalism, 'political society' simply is the state.[48] This idea has permeated so much into African political thinking for example that it has become difficult to conceive of an opposition political practice that is not reduced to capturing state posts or the state itself to the extent that it seems to be universally assumed that 'politics is the state and the state is politics' (Wamba-dia-Wamba 1994: 250). Nkrumah's famous aphorism, 'seek ye first the political kingdom and everything shall be given unto thee', has been the guiding principle of politics on the continent. In South Africa in particular, state fetishism is so pervasive within the hegemonic political discourse that debate is structured by the apparently evident 'common sense' notion that the post-apartheid state can 'deliver' everything from jobs to empowerment, from development to human rights, from peace in Africa to a cure for HIV/AIDS. As a result, not only is the state deified, but social debate is foreclosed ab initio by a state consensus. The consensual discourse of 'common sense' then restricts politics to certain fields and practices, such as to opinions regarding the practice of 'delivery'. The idea then simply becomes one of assessing policy or capacity, in other words the focus is on management rather than on politics. For liberalism therefore, politics becomes largely reduced to managerialism and thus loses its specificity so that it cannot be thought as a distinct practice. At the same time 'debate' is restricted to a plurality of opinions regarding effective management or 'governance', with the result that there is no real effective pluralism incorporating competing conceptions or modes of politics, as alternatives to liberalism are excluded from the 'public sphere' (Lazarus 1996, Badiou 1998a).

For neo-liberalism 'civil society', the realm within which rights are meant to be realised, exists solely under conditions of mutual recognition between it and the state, only under liberal democracy. It is this mutual recognition which defines the parameters of the state consensus and is itself the result of struggle. A state 'national' consensus is structured within a state domain of politics comprising the political relations between the state and its institutions on the one hand, and the 'official' or 'formal' civil society of citizens on the other. Other forms of politics by unrecognised organisations are seen as beyond the consensus and can thus be de-legitimised in state discourse. These organisations and politics therefore exist outside or beyond the limits (at best at the margins) of civil society. Because of such partiality therefore, 'civil society' cannot be conflated with 'organised society' as the term necessarily implies some form of exclusion (Neocosmos 2004). The distinction between liberal democracy and say colonial/apartheid forms of authoritarianism can be said to concern the extent and forms taken by such exclusion *inter alia*.

Simultaneously, this mutual recognition is given substance by 'human rights' which are visualised as formal and universal (i.e. ahistorical and a-contextual), and therefore not subject to debate or contestation because of the fact that they are deemed to be scientifically, technically or naturally derived. These rights, even though fought for and achieved through popular struggles throughout society, are supposed to be 'delivered' and 'guaranteed' by the state. They are taken out of popular control and placed in a juridical realm, where their fundamentally political character is removed from sight so that they become the subject of technical resolution by the judicial system. Human rights, therefore, do not only depend on a spurious Western philosophical humanism of 'Man' for their conception, an ideology through which individuals are 'interpellated as subjects' by the state itself (Althusser 1971).[49] They also represent the de-politicisation and technicisation of popular victories under the control of the state. The people are forced, if they wish to have their rights addressed and defended, to do so primarily within the confines of, or in relation to, the state institutions of the juridical.

Thus, even though human 'rights discourses can both facilitate transformative processes and insulate and legitimise power' (Krenshaw 2000: 63), the politics of human rights is, at best, a state-focussed politics and is predominantly reduced to a technicised politics, which is limited to a demand for inclusion into an existing state domain. Thus a struggle for rights, if successful, can end up producing the outcome of a fundamentally de-politicised politics. In fact it could be asserted abstractly that while in pre-liberal writings and practice the state expressed the will of God, in liberal writings and practice the state expresses the will of Man; freedom simply consists in obeying that will (Althusser op cit.). In sum, technique and science (the bearers of which are experts and state expertise) are in this manner unavoidably abstracted by the state from the socio-political context and conditions which alone give them meaning, and thus acquire a life of their own, independent of that context and those conditions. To be accessed by ordinary people and democratised, they need to be re-politicised and their technical quality shown to be, at best, only partly independent of socio-political content (Foucault, 2000; Canguilhem 1991).

It has been rightly mentioned on many occasions – this was the essence of the Marxist critique of 'bourgeois rights' – that the poor and oppressed were systematically excluded from exercising their rights because of unaffordability, lack of knowledge and access to all the resources which (bourgeois) state power monopolises and which are necessary for the realisation of rights. Equality of rights it was stressed was simply impossible in an unequal society. Therefore the supposed universality of rights was fallacious as the 'human' in human rights (as indeed the idea of 'Man' as a transcendental human subject) was in fact the Western, white, bourgeois male. Although these points were valid, what was not always added by the critics was that they implied that generally speaking the majority would tend to be excluded from formally legitimated politics under liberal democracy.[50]

If Human Rights Discourse contributes to the maintenance of privilege for the privileged and to the exclusion of the oppressed majority from state politics, it also has the effect of absolving the latter from the responsibility of engaging in political activity themselves. This is because it is maintained that some external body such as the judiciary (or the criminal justice system as a whole), the health system, an NGO, political party or whatever – in other words a state institution – will resolve the political issue at stake on their behalf. As, for example, the judiciary will only deal with individualised subjects and not with the historical context of social structures, issues concerning power relations are rarely raised. Moreover, given that the greatest threat to rights comes from the state itself, we have the interesting phenomenon of one state institution (usually the judiciary, its members unelected and unrepresentative) being charged with defending people's rights against other state institutions; the state is thus meant to police itself, this particular right is removed from the people.

The whole system both materially and culturally thus has the effect of excluding the majority from official state politics on the one hand, while making it difficult if not impossible for them to mobilise politically on the other. It amounts to a permanent system of political de-mobilisation and disempowerment – a process of fundamental de-politicisation of the majority (Englund 2004). It leads to and sustains the complete antithesis of an active citizenship which is the necessary basis of democracy and gives a whole new meaning to the expression: 'the rule of law'. Citizenship is simply reduced to the possession of state documents which entitle the majority to engage in politics at most once every five years or so. Non-citizens, despite the setting up of juridical structures such as international courts, are regularly excluded from rights which can only be claimed through one's 'own' state. Thus, despite the liberal view that it is universal human subjects who are the bearers of rights, these can only be accessed by 'citizens' of a state, as it is the latter which bestows that status upon them. Of course, the apparent benefits of citizenship, as feminist scholars in particular have noted, are differentially distributed, as the powerless are much less able to secure them (Yuval-Davis and Werbner 1999; Hassim 1999).

The effects of political dis-empowerment and the consequent political passivity must not be understood as restricted exclusively to civil life, as they permeate deeply into the constitutive social relations of the fabric of society itself, as the authoritarianism of social structure replicates and makes possible the authoritarianism of state power (Foucault 2000). This is particularly obvious in conditions of post-coloniality in Africa, conditioned as these societies are by the authoritarian legacy of colonialism and apartheid. It is quite unsurprising then that personal responsibility based on power and control over education, housing, and work let alone over desire, sexuality, knowledge as well as over self or personhood, is quite simply lacking. Neo-liberalism which provides the socio-political passivity of empty choices without power, and abysmally fails to even consider the conditions and capacity for its own induced or interpellated subjects to make responsible subjective decisions, is itself the ultimate ideological source of child-like powerlessness. The simple fact that state (or other) power is expected to decide on one's behalf, and that this is systematically internalised in the process of identity formation, is arguably what lies at the root of issues of powerlessness as disparate as those of HIV/AIDS, the alienation of youth from society, the absence of people-centred development and poverty. Conversely and happily for the state, the 'common sense' apparent 'obviousness' of the immutable absence of power to make such decisions means that an even weaker 'other' can always be found to provide a simple and obvious answer to one's powerlessness in those cases where the intervention of power in whatever form (state institutions, market, NGOs, family, etc.) fails to live up to expectations which it has itself cultivated. Xenophobic violence, violence against women, children, babies, the elderly and so on (the weakest sectors of society), as has been noted on innumerable occasions, is closely linked to powerlessness.

Paradoxically then, a Human Rights Discourse purportedly concerned with providing the enabling environment for freedom, within the context of liberalism in a post-colonial society, fundamentally and systematically enables its opposite – political and social disempowerment – through the hegemony of a state-centred consciousness. Having systematically de-politicised the population and systematically disabled their engagement in active politics, state agencies and politicians can then regularly emphasise the 'irresponsibility' of allowing too much free expression and organisation, as this would lead to support for demagogic politics, for capital punishment, xenophobia, racism and so on. In other words having produced political passivity, illiteracy and ignorance, these are then used as justifications for placing restrictions on democracy by calling on 'enlightened despotism' from those in power - much as under apartheid and colonialism, state-induced ignorance among the oppressed was used as a justification for the maintenance of colonial power.

In sum, liberalism in post-colonial Africa systematically militates against the formation of a moral community of active citizens, in other words against the construction of a political community properly understood. In the absence of political agency given the hegemony of political passivity, political choices cannot be made by the overwhelming majority, and political morality disappears. These are of course the necessary conditions for political exclusion and violence, for 'artistic' productions such as those by Mbongeni Ngema which exhibit xenophobic attitudes towards South Africans of Asian decent ('Indians') who are seen as 'different' and hence easily subject to being 'othered'. The moralism of Human Rights Discourse is fundamentally part of these conditions.

Interestingly, some recent comments by those subjected to xenophobia show a high degree of awareness of what needs to be done politically anyway. For example, one Zimbabwean who is legally resident in South Africa and who spent a week in Lindela stated:

> Ultimately I blame the South African government (for conditions at Lindela - MN), which claims to fight for the rights of human beings. We are not animals. Even though we Zimbabweans work among South Africans I always feel a prisoner here. When President Thabo Mbeki talks about Zimbabwe and says we should solve conflict in the region I want him to go to Lindela and see how South Africans treat other Africans. What is the New Partnership for Africa's Development if other Africans cannot be treated with dignity and respect? (*Mail and Guardian*, 5-11 November 2004).

Another was more political in his statement, stressing the need for political agency, but also the dilemma that migrants face in organising in a foreign country:

> What we need more than ever in 2005 is a champion in this country, an organisation that will highlight our plight and be an agency to which individuals can turn when their situation gets desperate... But we do not want to live off charity, we want to do something to help ourselves. As outsiders we cannot do this on our own. We need non-governmental organisations to take up our cause and faith-based organisations to work with us (*Natal Witness*, 17 January 2005).

While a Congolese refugee was cited as saying:

> The South African Government should teach the population to work for themselves and avoid a paternalistic attitude. Since Mobutu we have learnt not to expect anything from the government. We know that we are refugees we just want to survive here (cited in Amisi and Ballard, 2005: 14).

When working on the issue of xenophobia, it is difficult to avoid the conclusion that the difference between South Africa and other African countries is not that the politically weak (in this case undocumented migrants) are not systematically oppressed and exploited, on the contrary practices by state agencies are similar to those under any authoritarian regime in Africa or elsewhere. The difference seems rather to consist in the fact that physical and psychological abuses and corruption of state agencies in relation to migrants are regularly documented rather than remaining undocumented. It is in fact often the form of law itself, and fundamentally the practices of state agencies, the latter carried over unaltered from the apartheid state, which need to be addressed and democratised. This cannot be done by a discourse of rights which largely takes such practices as given. It seems therefore that in South Africa a discourse of rights has so far broadly been restricted to the provision of information on oppressive practices by the state (for those in the legal fraternity and NGOs to comment upon), and does not extend towards eliminating such practices, let alone towards producing a culture of democratic morality. The reason for this is not so much to do with the lack of commitment of Human Rights organisations and activists, but rather with the fact that xenophobia is not primarily a question of individual rights but rather a question of politics. The complete failure of liberalism to provide a democratic future for Africa as a whole is here quite apparent; in South Africa, it is a 'culture of rights' - a passive humanism - which is seen as the ultimate defence of democracy, not a politics of emancipation. The limitations of Human Rights Discourse are dramatically shown up in the case of xenophobia, for it brings out with abundant clarity that democracy and the people's gains cannot be defended by legal-technical rights, but only by political agency by the people themselves.

It is this process of 'disabling', of 'de-politicising', which I suggest lies at the heart of the problem of xenophobia in South Africa. This disabling has provided the conditions for state discourse to become hegemonic largely because it goes unchallenged by alternative politics. Public awareness campaigns such as the much publicised 'Roll Back Xenophobia Campaign' set up by the Human Rights Commission in 1998 cannot undermine this hegemonic discourse through advertising and similar methods: as a respondent noted, the posters at Home Affairs in Pretoria claiming to fight corruption and xenophobia are laughable. Parenthetically, it could in fact be suggested that corruption among officials of the Department of Home Affairs has had some positive results, as without it the oppressive legislation would have excluded many more Africans and prohibited them from making a living in South Africa.[51] In any case, the South African Human Rights Commission is itself, after all, a state institution which therefore shares with other state agencies a specific limited conception of politics. Human Rights NGOs have been good at keeping the issue of xenophobia and rights in the news, yet it seems that all this activity is powerless to finally overcome fundamental structurally determined xenophobic discourses and practices. It has to restrict itself to remaining within legal parameters, so that its ability to engage in political activity critical of other state institutions is highly limited.

There is nevertheless evidence of some political organisation among African migrants. This has been identified among Congolese refugees by Amisi and Ballard (2005). They note that refugees from Congo, particularly in Durban and Cape Town, have organised protests and marches in relation to the politics of the DRC, local NGOs working with refugees, xenophobia, and the Department of Home Affairs. They note however that these protests were largely *ad hoc* and not sustained by organisation and that few demands are made on the South African government. More widespread are ethnically and nationality-based networks, the former of which are more important for 'survivalist' purposes, in other words for mutual help. One network was said to have as many as 500 members (op.cit: 9). One of the main functions of these organisations is to provide help with funerals and other expenses, and generally to safeguard culture and identity (op cit.: 11). It could also be surmised that it is often these networks which are able to negotiate access to papers and permits from the Department of Home Affairs. The point however is that these organisations are not concerned with making political demands on the state and generally asserting the rights of their members. Amisi and Ballard (op cit.: 17) put this down to exclusion from citizenship rights, although it should be pointed out that any serious grassroots political organisation (not necessarily a human rights NGO) could ally with such organisations and push forward political prescriptions on the state, as the restrictions of rights to refugees and other migrants is a political issue which affects all, not just the foreigners concerned.

CHAPTER FOUR

Conclusion:
Theory and Political Agency

In fact, if a political prescription is not explicit, opinions and discussions will be inevitably governed by the yoke of an implicit or hidden prescription. But we do know what lies behind every hidden prescription: the state and the politics associated with it (Alain Badiou 1998a: 34, my translation – MN).

The banning of books is now replaced by self imposed censorship [...] We cannot be celebrating forever [in South Africa - MN]. (Sipho Seepe reviewing Es'kia Mphahlele's *Es'kia Continued, Sunday Independent,* 24 April 2005).

Existing explanations of xenophobia in South Africa – in terms of economic crisis, political transition, relative deprivation, or remnants of apartheid – all contain a grain of truth but none are adequate in themselves; neither is a mere addition of these accounts sufficient. Moreover, for Human Rights Discourse, there is no need to think an explanation as a remedy is already clearly and obviously at hand in the juridical accessibility of rights. The idea then is to passively rely on the magnanimity of the state and on the effectiveness of parastatal institutions such as (most) NGOs. It then no longer is possible to think about democracy critically, it is beyond what seems thinkable.

The central issue in any attempt at explanation is clearly to understand xenophobia as a political discourse as Erasmus (2005) rightly suggests, but this is also in itself quite insufficient because all discourses are not of the same order, or formed by the same set of social relations; it therefore needs to be elucidated what kind of discourse xenophobia in fact is. It is particularly of concern that while the struggle against apartheid because of its universal appeal received the support, not only of the majority of the people of the continent of Africa, but even that of many activists in the world (many of whom had no history of political involvement), South African nationalism should take such a chauvinist turn after apartheid. It should be recalled that the mass support emanating from the West, particularly from the youth and the mainstream pop industry in particular, as well as the declaration by the United Nations that apartheid was a crime against humanity as a whole and not simply an affront to the South African majority, were occurrences with which many throughout the world identified, as the removal of apartheid presaged a better world for all.[52] The struggle against apartheid, particularly its popular forms in the1980s, therefore acquired a universal significance and appeal which that of the Palestinian people against Israeli oppression, for example, was never able to attain, even though both struggles took similar forms in that period. Racism was universally abhorrent of course, and the epithet 'terrorist' did not stick to the ANC as much as it did to the PLO. The popular struggles of the 1980s within the country succeeded in projecting an image in the international media of ordinary people peacefully confronting a violent state, and were thus able to gather widespread support, while at the same time, ANC bombing atrocities against civilians were restricted to a minimum. The point however is that, given the historical universality of the struggle against apartheid in South Africa, the current xenophobic character of South African nationalism is somewhat difficult to fathom. The only way to make sense of this process, I suggest, is as a shift in nationalist discourse from a popularemancipatory subjectivity to a state subjectivity, from an inclusive and active conception of citizenship to an exclusive and passive one. This shift in discourse was an effect of a shift in forms of politics, where emancipation was no longer to be thought as a popular process but one to be led by state power, where democracy was no longer to have a popular character, but to be of the state-liberal type (Neocosmos 1998, 2005).

It should be apparent that xenophobia in South Africa today is a public state discourse.[53] 'Public' subjectivities are formed in the 'public sphere' as an outcome of various struggles in discourse and between various discourses. Clearly, the issue of xenophobia concerns nationalism (Vaiji 2003), but it is more concretely about citizenship as a political subjectivity. It is never obvious that nationalism should be naturally exclusive, and that citizenship in the form of indigeneity should be bestowed by the state on a passive populace. This is only so within a liberal conception of politics, and even this tradition did exhibit a distinct notion of active citizenship among some of its classic theorists (for example in the work of Rousseau and in that of J. S. Mill). Rather, the question which should be asked is as follows: Is the former a function of the latter; in other words, is an exclusive conception of nationalism a function of the hegemonic dominance of a passive understanding of citizenship? I feel that the answer must be a resounding yes.

I have tried to show here that xenophobia in post-apartheid South Africa today is a specifically political discourse with a particular history. It developed as an outcome of a specific relation between state and society. I have also argued that it presupposes a conception of citizenship founded on indigeneity and political passivity. This amounts to a particular form of politics; it is this kind of politics and the necessity of thinking alternatives to it which is the subject of this conclusion. Indeed, as I have already noted, Fanon was keenly aware of how a particular kind of nationalist politics lay at the root of xenophobia in the postcolonial Africa of his day; while indeed private accumulation among the new bourgeoisie is a contributing factor in post-apartheid South Africa also, the fundamental conditions which make xenophobia possible today are those provided by liberal state politics, whether nationalist or indeed those articulated within a discourse of 'Human Rights'.

I have shown in this work the notion of citizenship enforced by the apartheid state on the people of South Africa and how this did not distinguish between Black South Africans and foreign Africans, as all were interpellated and oppressed as foreigners. I have also shown how opposition to this oppression served to unite all those, irrespective of nationality, who were prepared to fight 'the system'.[54] The popular identities thus constructed had a pan-African content and did not distinguish among nationalities, while racial distinctions were fought against within notions of 'non-racialism'. Citizenship acquired a fundamentally active component, in the sense that political agency became its main constitutive aspect. At the same time, the difficulties encountered in building links with rural areas had an effect of creating suspicion, if not direct animosity and conflict, between urban and rural activists, manifested most clearly in the ANC-IFP internecine violence of the early nineties. This suspicion of the rural by a dominantly urban ANC constituency, combined with a partial critique of the apartheid state as a form of labour control which dominated both in exile and among intellectuals within the country, eventually became the hegemonic mode of conceiving migrant labour from the region, and perforce relations with the inhabitants of Southern Africa who overwhelmingly emanated from a rural base. Liberation and democratisation were equated with the demise of the migrant labour system, and adherence to the latter as support for the oppression of apartheid. The alternatives provided by this hegemonic nationalist discourse were either enforced urbanisation, access to family housing and the benefits of a supposedly superior South Africa, or exclusion as foreign migrants. The fact that most of those who were in fact given the option actually chose exclusion if they could not continue to engage in 'oscillating migration', is an indication not only of the misconceptions of progressive nationalist discourse. Even more importantly perhaps, it made it impossible for an alternative inclusive conception of nationalism to be put forward and argued for. This easily melded with a South African exceptionalism which saw the rest of Africa as economically and increasingly politically 'backward'.

Over the years since liberation, Africa, for South Africans, has become the place 'over there', the place of the 'other', to be acted upon, 'led' by politicians, 'studied' by academics, 'developed' by investors or 'visited' by tourists in search of the natural and the authentic. The subjective relations between South Africa and the continent have thus become quasi-colonial, intensified not only by South African economic dominance, but also by the role of South Africa as a bridgehead for Western political liberalism on the continent. Under these circumstances, the slogan of an 'African Renaissance' has become simply a vehicle for South African hegemony. As a result, a hegemonic conception has easily developed according to which all in the public domain, from the Left to the Right of the political spectrum, have been in agreement that the benefits of South African citizenship should be restricted to those who could prove some form of indigenous link with the country and that the others should be kept firmly out.

'Fortress South Africa' was henceforth to be defended against 'hordes of illegal immigrants', barbarians waiting to scale the battlements and to flood the country. It is these assumptions, hegemonic within the state, which have underlain the attempts to construct immigration legislation, as well as the problems with the constitution which distinguishes between rights of citizens and rights of persons. Of course, the valiant attempts by human rights organisations to fight this legal discrimination were not helped by the extreme chauvinism of politicians, not least those ensconced at the ministry of home affairs. The extent of xenophobia practised within the apparatuses of the post-apartheid state is extreme and is consistently shown by all research. The extreme power of state officials over the weak, whether actually foreign or not, has been accurately stated to be a mere continuation of apartheid oppression, while immigration legislation enables the continuation of a pass-like system. Xenophobia is thus a structural feature of state discourse and practice, not an accidental occurrence. Common political accounts of xenophobia, such as that of the ruling party, the ANC, see it as an effect of globalisation, of increased immigration itself or a common occurrence in today's world, all of which conveniently would mean that it is quite impossible to control. While such accounts absolve the state and the ruling party of any responsibility for the prevalence and even dominance of xenophobic discourse, the regular reference to the creation of 'a human rights culture' as the ultimate guarantee of the disappearance of xenophobia is one which is dominantly adhered to. This notion requires extensive commentary.

In fact, a hegemonic xenophobic state discourse arose in tandem with the formation of the post-apartheid state, very much as the xenophobia noted by Fanon (1990) arose as a result of the development of the post-colonial state in Africa. In either case, the rise of xenophobia was part of the process of national state formation and citizenship. It has been my concern to show precisely the manner in which this particular state subjectivity of xenophobia became dominant over time in the case of South Africa. It has not been my intention to adhere to a spurious notion of the monolithic character of the state, indeed it must be recognised that the extreme chauvinism of Buthelezi at Home Affairs was fought by the ANC in government. Rather, my concern has been to document the rise of a hegemonic discourse which structures the parameters within which migration to the country is thought. It is in fact the case that even the most sensitive among those in power tend to see migrants from Africa as potentially making demands on state resources, rather than as contributing to the growth of the economy for example. The overwhelming perception is one of foreigners as 'takers' rather than as 'contributors'. As noted, this is contradicted by all the evidence.

As part of this production of a hegemonic xenophobic state discourse, it is arguably the case that the South African Truth and Reconciliation Commission (TRC) had a profound effect on the making of the liberal post-apartheid state (Wilson, 2001). The functions of this process were to enable reconciliation between the races through uncovering the truth regarding 'gross violations of human rights', but the reconciliation process primarily concerned elites, andwas undertaken on the political foundation of

Human Rights Discourse. It did however provide a forum for the voices of the victims of the apartheid state to be heard, but in doing so it contributed to a discourse of 'victim-hood' whereby South Africans who had become political agents in the 1980s were now overwhelmingly interpellated as victims, passively requesting to be helped by a state commission. Fullard and Rousseau (2003) for example, clearly show that the TRC process failed to transform what they call the 'habits' (i.e. state practices) of the past, by simply relating the contempt with which power treated the powerless during the process itself, an evident continuity from the past if there ever was one. But they are less able to show why this was so as a result of the absence in their work of a theory of the state. For example, they note that 'the most lasting... voices from this period remain those of the victims... ordinary citizens who formed the overwhelming bulk of those who came to the TRC and who paid the price of political violence' (ibid: 83). They also rightly note that having their experience officially recognised was a major achievement for the commission, but these experiences were apprehended ultimately as excesses by individual perpetrators (rather than as the necessary outcome of oppressive state structures and subjectivities) so that 'undoubtedly, the TRC failed to adequately situate the gross human rights violations that it addressed in the wider context of apartheid' (ibid).

It is understood then that 'those who came to the TRC were not organised political activists... but were most often very poor township residents swept up in the conflicts' (op cit.: 90). They got little or nothing from the process, either in terms of much compensation but more importantly neither in terms of a small victory over power, because of a number of factors including the absence of effective prosecution of perpetrators. They were simply recognised for a while and then cynically discarded. The impression one gets from Fullard and Rousseau is that it has been 'a Government choice to keep the TRC on the backburner' (ibid: 97). In fact, the legitimacy of the apartheid state was never challenged by the ANC after 1990, and one could be forgiven for underlining the congruence of interests between apartheid and post-apartheid elites in the maintenance of the system of power. As the authors gently understate the point, this failure could have something to do with 'a more general muting of... transformative impulses' (ibid).

The simple point here the is that the TRC process contributed to the creation of a post-apartheid liberal state through the promotion and legitimation of a discourse on rights, and simultaneously interpellated black South African citizens as victims, passively requesting redress from the judicial apparatus of the state. Concurrently, the fact that the TRC did not devote anything like the same amount of time and effort to an examination of the 'gross violations of human rights' by the apartheid state on the countries of the Southern African periphery, through which a sense of solidarity could have been established between the people of the region, contributed to narrowing a conception of citizenship and 'belonging' to indigeneity. The two defining features of the citizenship of the 1980s popular struggle – political agency and inclusiveness – were thus systematically undermined by the TRC. In this manner, the TRC process contributed fundamentally to the hegemony of a liberal Human Rights Discourse within the country.

It is important to reiterate that this was not always the case, and to briefly refer to the example of the Freedom Charter, in order to remind ourselves of what a politics which prescribes rights and entitlements and demands them from the state can look like. If we put aside much of the romanticisation of nationalist politics surrounding the Freedom Charter (for example Suttner and Cronin 1986), and concentrate rather on simply examining the document, it can be seen that it consists of a preamble and ten demands or 'freedoms' from the state. These demands are prescriptive and require that the state enact them and that they shall be fought for by people until they are enacted. The preamble includes the first statement I have already noted that 'South Africa belongs to all who live in it...', while among the others we may recall the following: 'the people shall govern', 'all national groups shall have equal rights', 'the people shall share in the country's wealth', 'the land shall be shared among those who work it' and so on. The document not only expressed popular national aspirations, it did so in a universal manner appealing to freedom, justice and equality so that it resonated well beyond South Africa's borders. Such prescriptions were very comparable to those emanating from within the Algerian revolution, with which they are contemporaneous, and expressed clearly by Fanon. His statement that 'in the new society that is being built, there are only Algerians...therefore, every individual living in Algeria is an Algerian' (Fanon 1989: 152) suggests that during periods of popular national upsurge, citizenship is a unifying conception.

It should be stressed that the document was not written like a legal human rights declaration, and that in fact, although the term 'rights' appears sixteen times, the expression 'Human Rights' occurs only once and in this case to stress equality. In other words the Freedom Charter is not a human rights document which passively enjoins people to petition the state for the rights due to them by virtue of simply being alive; it is a document which calls on people to engage in politics to fight for their rights, something of a completely different order. It is important to understand this difference, as it has been my main argument here that it is the absence of prescriptive politics in post-apartheid South African society – partly as an effect of the dominance of Human Rights Discourse – which has made possible the hegemony of a state discourse of xenophobia. If this argument has any validity, then it follows that to wait for the construction of a 'human rights culture' whatever that may mean, will not overcome xenophobia in South Africa. What will arguably contribute to overcoming xenophobia is a recovery of active politics, of political agency rather than passivity within South African society. It is the prevalence of such active citizenship which can provide the conditions for a democratic universal emancipatory politics.

It should be recalled that there have been at least three different conceptions of state citizenship in addition to citizenship founded on indigeneity in South Africa over recent years. I can think of citizenship based on race under apartheid, whereby white immigrants were given full citizenship rights after a short period of settlement; the notion of citizenship based on place of work advocated by the NUM and others in the early nineties, and the idea of citizenship based on political activism as advocated by the mass movement of the eighties and the ANC at different times in its history (Joe Slovo, Ray Alexander *inter alia* were not born in South Africa). What this suggests is that even official conceptions of citizenship (let alone 'belonging') are a result of political debate and struggle. Given the facts of labour migration and arbitrary colonial boundaries, the conception of citizenship founded on indigeneity is probably a utopia which is only applicable to a minority. Citizenship as indigeneity suggests the reduction of citizenship to patriarchal descent within a territory, and has its origins in colonial state rule. It is not a democratic notion. A democratic political slogan regarding immigration today in South Africa should stress the central fact that all should be treated equally by the state; everyone should count the same in the eyes of power. Insofar as human rights NGOs are able to push for this state of affairs then their activities are welcome, however as already noted, Human Rights Discourse is hamstrung by the constitution which treats different people differently, and this discourse is itself undermined by the fact that people are never treated equally by state institutions in society.

Of course an opposition of nationals versus foreigners makes it possible during certain situations and contexts to claim that certain groups of national political minorities are 'less part of the nation' than others. Women, the poor and ethnic minorities *inter alia* can be regularly subject to such xenophobia (they become the 'other' in the situation). Politically, the dominance of xenophobia against foreigners means that South Africans become vulnerable to the same oppression. Of course this suggests that citizenship (along with the rights it provides) is experienced along a continuum (as feminist literature rightly argues) and is not an either-or affair. Some conform more to being 'human' (Man) than others who are presumably closer to nature (for example women, children, the poor, 'primitives', etc.; they are 'more emotional', less rational, etc.). Thus, it is the state and only the state if left politically uncontested, which defines who is human or not (or the extent of conformity to the human) through legal and other discourses and practices. It should be noted however that this argument takes politics as simply given; even the 'not-fully-human' can acquire agency when politically organised.

Mamdani (1995) outlines a very important argument regarding the fact that it was central to European rights theory to see the nation as the bearer of the collective right to self-determination and the citizen as the bearer of individual rights. He sees this as having been put into practice from the French Revolution onwards. According to him, the full realisation of the first right implied that the nation establish its own state – the nation-state – while the bearer of individual rights came to be the citizen, a member of the political community as defined by that state. Thus he remarks: '... it is ironic that in its attempt to define a ground for "rights" that cannot be violated by the state, liberal thought became circumscribed within a state-defined logic' (op cit.: 46). He continues by arguing *inter alia* that, because 'states in Africa are not nation-states' and because Africa is 'a land of migrant labour' (ibid: 48, 50) the unmodified application of European legal norms to African conditions has had disastrous effects, particularly on the exclusion of migrants from human rights. Since migrant labour implies a rupture between 'the land of one's birth and the site of one's labour' this necessarily leads to a disjunction between 'the country of one's citizenship and that of one's residence' (ibid: 50), with the result that human rights are not available to non-citizens who are not members of political community as defined by the state.

Mamdani's points are extremely enlightening in that they correctly recognise the central statist assumptions of liberalism and its exclusion of non-citizens from 'human rights', yet they are also limited for they link xenophobia exclusively to state nationalism. First I want to stress the fact that - as Mamdani indeed recognises in the case of Africa - there have been many struggles over the rights to be afforded to foreigners, including migrants, in various historical and social contexts. In particular during the French Revolution there existed a fundamental universal conception of human emancipation which accompanied the formation of a nation and citizenship (Bensaïd 2005). The 1793 constitution, the most radical of the revolution, authored primarily by Saint-Just, actually distinguished citizenship from nationality, thus:

> Any man born or resident in France for a year, living from his labour, owning property, or having married a French woman, or having adopted a child, or having maintained an elderly person, finally any foreigner who is declared by the legislative body to have earned the recognition of Humanity is entitled to the exercise of French citizenship rights. [Saint-Just had expressed the point as follows in his Draft of the Constitution: 'the motherland of a free people is open to all men of the world', 2004: 551].[55]

Therefore one could be a citizen without being French (Bensaïd 2005: 37-8). This demarcation between citizenship and nationality in fact shows that there was indeed a struggle within liberal thought over the nature of rights and concerning human emancipation. From an emancipatory perspective, it is of course meaningless for the legal system to treat some people differently from others, all must be addressed in the same manner.

Second, and coming back to the South African situation, it is in fact the case that here, the supreme court of the land – the Constitutional Court – has been sensitive to the plight of non-citizens and has made a series of judgements in which it has asserted, for example, the right of foreigners legally resident in the country to claim state benefits, something which gave rise to statements of fear in the press.[56] Although helpful, this does not alter the distinction in law between citizens and foreigners and does not apply to undocumented migrants. It is thus is unlikely to impact much on the hegemonic prevalence of xenophobia, it could indeed even have the opposite effect. Of course this does not amount to the granting of full citizenship rights, as these are impossible for foreigners to acquire under this constitution, yet it suggests that at least some 'human rights' may be applicable to all with documentation in South Africa and not just to citizens. It would be much more democratic however if people could have rights to social benefits on the basis of their working in the country. In this sense social rights could be linked to place of work rather than to a politicised indigeneity which can only encourage essentialist communitarian politics. Thus, a progressive demand on the state would be to regularise all those working in the country, at least until they can show that they are working. Thereafter they could be considered for permanent residence. I shall return to this idea below.

Over and beyond what foreigners may be entitled to in law, it has been my concern to argue that because of the political passivity induced by liberalism, Human Rights Discourse makes xenophobia possible. Ultimately, Human Rights Discourse, which forces people into victim-hood as it has come to constitute a humanism without an emancipatory project, has discarded human agency in favour of appeals to the state. It is precisely this process, the replacing of political agency by appeals to the state, which had made xenophobia possible and is enabling its existence in South Africa today. Wamba-dia-Wamba (1994) has shown how a culture of political passivity in post-colonial Africa – how the absence of democratic politics among the people themselves – is a consequence of the statisation of society, in other words of the dominance of a subjectivity which simply reflects and defers to state discourses.[57] He notes that this:

> has made people become unable to restrain the state in its exclusivist or symmetrized treatment of difference (whether of nationality, gender, intellectual/ manual labour, levels of education, etc). In the face of the maltreatment of refugees, women and national minorities for example, people have been made to watch this passively ... Society has become divided into two: those with guaranteed interests – no matter how insignificant – and those without any interests or even rights. Any state treatment of differences (citizen/ non-citizen, male/female, etc.) has been made socially acceptable and inequality has become accepted as a natural element: the right of the fittest. Even accountability has been redefined as a technical matter, as a performance rather than as a democratic issue. The idea of an Africa of peoples which arose in the late 1950s – leading to the All African Peoples' Conferences – has become impossible and absent in people's forms of consciousness. The state has no difficulty in opposing one group (refugees or university students for example) against society (op cit.: 253).

This is the kind of process I have been concerned to outline here. The process of the naturalisation of differences is a state ideological process, which is made possible by political passivity in society. Xenophobia is never in the interests of the vast majority, but only in those of a tiny minority whose forms of politics and state rule require the division of the working people. Popular prescriptive politics cannot be bypassed without popular identities becoming simply a reflection of state interpellation; this is evidently the case where little or no popular political prescriptions on the state exist. If identities are not to be such a simple reflection of the state power, then politics must exist, in other words an independent and alternative – emancipatory – politics must exist. To put the point somewhat differently, a state subjectivity can only be internalised automatically in the absence of a contestation of the consensual *status quo* occasioned by the existence of politics in society, and expressed through political prescriptions of various kinds which contest state interpellation and propose alternatives to it.

According to Badiou (1998a, 1998b, 2001), there can be no human subject without such politics, and no (contextual) rights without such a subject (activists/ militants/ organisations). Rights then cannot be alienated to a state power without losing their prescriptive character altogether, as they become abstracted form their context which alone had given them popular meaning and political content; they are now no longer to be fought for by people politically, but rather claims must be made to the state to deliver them; the state then becomes the guarantor and defender of human rights. As a result, popular political passivity dominates as rights are to be 'delivered' by the state, and people are to petition the courts for them if such 'delivery' is not forthcoming. In this manner, a struggle by people to defend their rights against the state is transformed and incorporated within the state itself, and simultaneously managed between different state institutions to the exclusion of the people. The consequence can only be the erosion of those very rights. In actual fact only the organised political activity of people can defend and extend these rights. The historical and political process of the state construction of a Discourse of Human Rights first de-contextualises rights and second de-politicises them, with the result that rights, politics and subjects all get lost through their abstraction as they become essentialised (de-historicised) and falsely universalised (through the exercise of power). They thus amount to a justification for retaining the status-quo; i.e. they become conservative, a-contextual and become established parts of state subjectivity (more or less, depending on how contested the state discourse is) under liberalism. From concrete contextual rights, they have now become abstract human rights so that rights and entitlements have to be fought for all over again, now in different contexts of the dominance of political passivity and the dominant conception of people as victims. Broadly speaking, it is this state of affairs which underlies and enables the hegemony of xenophobic discourse, as those deemed to be foreign do not have rights due to their lack of (a state-defined) citizenship – they are not indigenous. Xenophobia then can be said to exist because of the hegemonic character of a particular kind of state politics: liberalism. It follows that in South Africa xenophobia is not antagonistic to human rights discourse but congruent with it.

Xenophobia and the authoritarianism of which it is but an example, are a product of liberalism, liberal democracy and Human Rights Discourse. It is not an irrational aberration brought about from outside the liberal realm (for example from an authoritarian or irrational 'other', from a 'backward tradition') but rather it is made possible/enabled by liberalism itself. It must be understood and can only coherently be understood as a result of a form of politics where the state is seen as the sole definer of citizenship and where, given the absence of prescriptive politics among the people, passivity prevails. It is such a conception of the state and politics, a liberal conception, which makes possible an essentialist and primordialist conception of culture and tradition. State-centred notions of culture and nation are always unequivocally essentialist/primordialist, as power always naturalises both itself and the conditions of its existence, while the character of naturalism is always to refer to the unchanging nature of social relations, unless these are impacted from beyond their limits (Neocosmos 2003). The overcoming of xenophobia then, presupposes the recovery of a prescriptive politics in society, and hence the recovery of an active citizenship which alone, under current conditions in post-colonial Africa, can make such prescriptive politics possible. In the same way as the struggle against racism was and can only be a political struggle, so must the struggle against xenophobia be a political struggle. The problem is that an emancipatory politics has disappeared from post-apartheid society in favour of appeals to the state. Simultaneously, state politics has systematically de-politicised the people with emphasis being exclusively placed on managerialism (to deliver 'human' rights), juridical expertise (to protect 'human' rights) and education (to alter xenophobic attitudes). In all cases, technicism has replaced active politics. People's rights cannot be protected by state institutions, but ultimately only by an active citizenship and popular politics, for it is the state itself which is the main threat to such rights.

The recovery of an emancipatory politics is clearly the crux of the matter. Evidently, this cannot arise out of nothing, so it is imperative for the state to enable the development of organisations of migrants and active citizenship within society in general. Of course it will need to be pressurised to do so, but without extensive politicisation within society, civil or otherwise, the emergence of an emancipatory mode of politics is more difficult. Active citizenship is therefore the first necessary step. What kind of political demands could then be made on the state vis-à-vis undocumented migrants? The main demand should be for everybody to be documented rather than deported, for it is the absence of documentation which criminalises people's attempts to earn a living and to survive in South Africa. It is only if everyone is treated equally by the state that systematic discrimination against some people can be overcome. It should also be clear that the continued xenophobic treatment of foreigners creates the conditions for others to be oppressed as in the obvious case of South Africans of Asian origin; already for many government policies,

'Indian' South Africans are no longer considered to be in the enviable category of 'previously disadvantaged'. It is thus prescriptions along these lines which should be made of state institutions. This is one of the main lessons to be drawn from the struggles of undocumented migrants in other countries such as France.[58]

For example, if temporary residential and social rights were to be granted to all who wish to settle and work in South Africa, then after a period of one or two years, extension or even permanent residence could be provided solely on the basis of gainful employment. In this way migration could be regularised, the police and other state agents would have less power over migrants, and the state would give a lead on democratic anti-xenophobic practices. At the same time any criminals could be more easily controlled as they would be traceable by the state. Moreover such a demand is likely to gather widespread support as research shows, as I have noted, that South Africans are likely to welcome foreigners whose economic impact is demonstrably positive. However, this kind of prescription cannot be made by isolated individuals or human rights NGOs substituting themselves for popular political self-activity. In any case, the concern of human rights NGOs is for immigrants and refugees to be treated fairly within the existing legal system. Only a democratic political organisation and/or self-organised migrants can make such kinds of prescriptions on the state, prescriptions which must be truly political in order to contribute to a process of genuine democratisation. On the other hand, in the present context, such demands would constitute political suicide for any professional politician, so that politicians can be counted upon to do nothing, to remain passive. It seems therefore that it is only a genuine political slogan such as 'documentation for all working people' which ties rights to place of work, which today could hope to fulfil and revive the prescription of the Freedom Charter according to which 'South Africa belongs to all who live in it'!

For the argument developed here, an alternative conception of politics is thus not about attaining state power; politics now refers to popular-democratic prescriptions on the state and to a critique of what exists towards emancipation of the collectivity. Here, rights are entitlements which are no longer attributes of a universal human subject ('Man'), but fought for by people (anyone) in a context of contestation of what exists. Thus this politics does not amount to a psychological account or to a phenomenology, a humanism founded on a transcendental human subject. There is no abstract notion of 'Man' to define what is human or not. In fact it is the argument here that xenophobia cannot be adequately understood without moving away from a 'human' rights discourse altogether so that a radical anti-humanism must be our point of departure in thinking alternatives. Rather, subjects are not given by the state or by nature, but must be understood as made through a process of production of 'a person who thinks', questions and acts (a truly human person) so as to make possible, in the realm of social activity, the existence of emancipatory politics. The existence of such prescriptions means that we are in the presence of people who think and who do not simply 'go with the flow' of the consensus of 'common sense', who do not just react to their narrow interests within the situation which they simply accept as normal or given; anyone and everyone is capable of thought. The prevalence of xenophobia suggests the opposite, in other words the absence of thought, and the weakness of popular prescriptions on the state. Politics properly understood as emancipatory politics reflects a universality which is never bound by interest, an 'interest' which, after all, is given by the political economy of contemporary capitalism with its division of labour and 'market exigencies'.

EPILOGUE

May 2008 and the Politics of Fear

We are the ones who fought for freedom and democracy and now these Somalis are here eating our democracy (NAFCOC – National African Federated Chamber of Commerce and Industry – leader, Khayelitsha, Cape Town, *Mail and Guardian*, September 5-11, 2008)

The police are making as if we are criminals. We don't have firearms. We have babies and kids. Why are they so scared? (African refugee at the Blue Waters safety site in Strandfontein outside Cape Town, *Cape Argus* June 3rd, 2008).

An action can be illegal. A person cannot be illegal. A person is a person wherever they may find themselves (Abahlali baseMjondolo, 'Statement on the Xenophobic Attacks in Johannesburg', 21/05/2008)

The explosion that occurred in South African townships and informal settlements in May 2008 traumatised the country for a while. The fact that sixty-two people died as a result of pogroms in which apparent foreigners, primarily from the rest of Africa, were sought out and killed, were violently expelled from communities, and their belongings looted in an orgy of plunder and mayhem, left the country reeling under a number of questions. How could such a thing happen in the 'rainbow nation'? How could Black South Africans act so callously towards their fellow Africans and brothers? How could people who have been living in the country for as long as 12 to 15 years be attacked by their neighbours? The public soul-searching lasted for a few weeks thereafter as the scale of the disaster sunk in. This phase of xenophobic violence displaced large numbers of people estimated between 80 000 and 200 000 (FMSP, 2009: 20). The number of people staying in shelters at their peak reached 24 000 in Gauteng and 20 000 in the Western Cape (loc. cit.). The government found itself completely outflanked and unable to respond, blaming at times a 'third force', at other times 'criminals' and 'trouble-makers and opportunists' as it hesitated, lost as to what to do. Well known xenophobic politicians appeared on TV crying over the plight of injured Mozambicans, while others, who had been out of the spotlight for a while visited mothers and children to comfort them. Most national politicians appeared on TV condemning the violence and referring to the crisis in Zimbabwe and the lack of border controls, as well as to poverty and living conditions in informal settlements as the underlying causal factors of the violence.

Most victims were sought out by their attackers (men, women and children) because they were deemed to be foreigners and massacred, robbed, raped and their belongings stolen and their houses burned. The violence was sometimes organised and at other times spontaneous. It is therefore valid to talk in terms of 'pogroms' of foreign residents during this period. The humanitarian assistance which followed was also largely both disorganised and coercive, the government deciding to re-integrate people into townships (often against the will of both sides) but also failing to ensure their safety. What most commentators stressed was the underlying eco-nomic causes of the problem, blaming poverty and deprivation, yet it requires little imagination to see that economic factors, however real, cannot possibly account for why it was those deemed to be non-South African who bore the brunt of the vicious attacks. Poverty can be and has historically been the foundation for the whole range of political ideologies from communism to fascism and anything in between. In fact, poverty can only account for the powerlessness, frustration and desperation of the perpetrators, but not for their target. Neither can it account for the violence of their actions. Moreover, blaming xenophobic violence on poverty, relative depriva-tion or uneven development, is to blame the poor. In other contexts, poverty has not lead to xenophobic violence, and we shall see below that in certain instances, even in South Africa it did not do so. Xenophobia as a practice of more or less open form of discrimination and oppression, as this book shows, is widespread in South Africa and not restricted to those living in informal settlements. It is also a widespread phenomenon among the middle-class and particularly among state em-ployees, as is the expression of prejudices towards Africans from the continent.

What needs to be done, I argue, is to explain xenophobia politically. The events of May 2008 were not a sudden unexpected occurrence. Obviously similar events, although not on such a scale, had been occurring since 1994, as this book has already shown. The violence consisted of a series of pogroms. It was about iden-tifying a solution to perceived problems and executing it. It was an issue of politics. As the expulsion of Asians from Uganda by Idi Amin was a political act, as the mutual slaughter and exclusion of ethnic groups in the ex-Yugoslavia were political acts, as the destruction of the European Jews by the Nazis was a political act, and so on. This must be the starting point of any adequate explanation as I have already argued in detail in this book.

In what follows, I will first briefly outline the events as they unfolded, I will then take a look at the few studies which attempt to tell us about the social characteristics, either of the events themselves or of the various actors along with the various accounts offered for the events, and will end with a discussion of what I see as the nature of the politics underlying these events, namely what I have called the 'politics of fear'.

The Events of May 2008

The xenophobic attacks of May 2008 obviously did not fall out of the blue. Enough has been said in this book to make the point that xenophobia has been endemic in South Africa, among all sections of the population since liberation in particular. Yet in their intensity and duration as well as their spread throughout the country, the events of May 2008 were largely unique.

The accounts of xenophobia in this book ended in December 2005. Xenophobic violence against foreigners by the state and by individuals did not stop then. It has been ongoing since that period. Some of the more notorious episodes were in December 2005 at Olievenhoutbosch (Gauteng) where foreign Africans were chased out of the town's informal settlement and from their houses, shops and businesses; in July 2006 in Knysna (Western Cape) where Somali small businessmen were thrown out of the area and at least 30 'Spaza shops' were damaged; in Cape Town during August 2006 where between 20 and 30 Somalis were killed; in Motherwell (Eastern Cape) where the accidental shooting of a young South African man resulted in the looting of over one hundred Somali owned shops in the period of a day in February 2007. Throughout 2007 similar stories were reported in Ipeleleng Township (North West), Delmas (Mpumalanga) and Mooiplaas (Gauteng) where two foreigners were killed, 18 were brutally injured and 111 shops were looted in October. By 2008, according to newspaper reports, the trend of people mainly from informal settlements and other poor areas scapegoating perceived foreigners for their problems seems to have been on the increase (Misago et al., 2009: 22-23). In these cases the role of the police was at best to remain aloof and only to intervene after shops had been looted and property stolen and vandalised, or at worst to be active participants in violent attacks. For example, visiting the Eastern Cape shortly after the Motherwell incidents, Landau and Haithar (2007) remark:

> Police have harassed Somali residents with weekly visits ostensibly to check for drugs and illegal weapons. Each visit is an opportunity to demand – and sometimes confiscate – refugee papers and cash. Those unwilling to fork out protection money risk being arrested just long enough for the locals to clean out their shops....A former [Somali] shopkeeper [stated]: 'Somalis are easy prey they don't have access to the law'.

The fact that foreigner migrants from Africa do not in practice have the right to rights, is evidenced here by the fact that police and community members (sometimes also businessmen, sometimes political leaders, sometimes youth as we shall see in more detail below) are in cahoots in excluding foreigners from access to rights. This is not an isolated example but is, by many accounts of attacks on migrants, a common occurrence.

In 2008, regular incidents of violence against foreign migrants increased. January saw at least two Somalis burnt to death in Duncan Village (Eastern Cape), shops owned by Somalis attacked in Jeffrey's Bay (Eastern Cape), and one 'foreigner' burned to death, three others killed, ten seriously injured and 60 shops looted in Soshanguve outside Pretoria. February saw more incidents in Laudium (Gauteng), Valhalla Park (Western Cape), Kroonstadt (Free State) and Atteridgeville in Pretoria. In the last case at least seven lives were lost in a series of incidents over a week. The deceased included Zimbabwean, Pakistani and Somali nationals as well as a South African mistaken for a foreigner (Misago et al.: 23). March and April saw incidents of looting in Worcester (Western Cape) and Mamelodi outside Pretoria where residents went house to house torching houses and shops abandoned by non-nationals. April also saw an attack by the police on the Central Methodist Church in Johannesburg where many refugees from Zimbabwe had taken refuge. Police went about beating people who had sought sanctuary in the church and who had no other place to live.[59]

In May the country exploded in an orgy of killing, looting and burning. The outcome in Gauteng was 62 people dead of whom 21 were South Africans. There are no officially acknowledged deaths resulting from attacks in Cape Town although reports claim that 2 or 4 people died at the height of the unrest. In addition 342 shops were reported to have been looted and 213 burnt down. There is no available data on the number of shacks and houses looted and burnt. The number of people displaced was estimated to be between 80 000 and 200 000. At the peak of the crisis the number of people estimated to be living in shelters was said to have reached 24 000 in Gauteng and 20 000 in the Western Cape. It was estimated that as many as 30 000 people left Cape Town in the first few days of the violence. The Mozambican authorities estimated that 40 000 of their nationals returned home as a result of the violence (Misago et al., 2009: 20).

The brutality unleashed was extreme and atrocious. Gangs were seen on television marching down the street singing 'struggle songs', and revolting pictures of a man who had been doused with petrol and set alight were broadcast on prime time television. The sequence of events was broadly as follows. The violence erupted in Alexandra outside Johannesburg on May 11th where supposed foreigners were violently attacked and women raped. From there the violence spread to northern Johannesburg, Eastern Gauteng, to central Johannesburg and then to Western Johannesburg and Western Gauteng. By May 17th violence had spread to Durban; between May 20th and May 22nd violence had spread to the Free State, North West and Limpopo provinces. By this time the violence in Johannesburg had started to subside but violence in the Western Cape forced large numbers of foreign nationals to flee from townships in the region. On May 26th the Minister of safety and Security declared that the violence had been brought under control although violence continued sporadically after then and still does (for details see Misago et al.: op.cit: 24-7). As recently as January 2009, mobs in Durban were throwing people out of high rise flats on the suspicion of being 'illegal immigrants' (*Mail*

and Guardian, January 9-15 2009; *Mercury*, Durban, January 14th 2009). Also important to note is that in the initial phases of the violence, people sought refuge in police
stations, churches, mosques and other religious facilities. As these facilities became
overcrowded, authorities made available community halls and other public buildings. By the end of May, the government announced plans to establish central areas
of shelter or camps to house the internally displaced. The experience of people in
these camps also tended to be one of xenophobic attitudes, primarily by state
officials.

Predictably, the language of hatred was directed at those attacked who were
named: 'Makwerekwere' the standard derogatory name for African foreigners,
'Grigambas' (dung beetles), 'Amagundane' (rats) 'Cockroaches', and so on. Most
foreigners were referred to as Shangaan even though they could be Zimbabweans,
while the language of 'cleansing' was used by both perpetrators and newspapers
(*Sunday Independent*, May 26th). These terms were of course similar to those used
during the genocide in Rwanda, ex-Yugoslavia and Nazi Germany. The language is
typical of such ethnic violence and is clearly meant to refer to the extermination of
vermin. Also similar to the Rwandan case was the fact that it was neighbours who
were often perpetrators even though some neighbours were also reported as protecting foreigners who were under attack. It was not usually state actors who were
the direct perpetrators as in other such cases although this statement may have to be
qualified, given police xenophobic activities.

Reactions by state representatives often took the form of denial; this was the
case in particular with the President of the Republic who put the issue down to
criminality. Mbeki made it clear that, to him, the violence was not xenophobic but
purely criminal:

> The dark days of May which have brought us here today were visited on our country
> by people who acted with criminal intent. What happened during these days was not
> inspired by a perverse nationalism, or extreme chauvinism, resulting in our commu-
> nities expressing the hitherto unknown sentiment of mass and mindless hatred of
> foreigners – xenophobia.[60]

Totally unhelpful of course, this kind of statement could only encourage other
politicians to also refuse to address reality. It also could be inferred that the state
would address the issue primarily as one of criminality, i.e. repressively. Moreover,
such sentiments could also be interpreted as appeasement, as was mentioned on a
number of occasions (e.g. *Natal Mercury*, Jan 14th 2009). No one should really be
surprised by this kind of reaction; professional politicians are rarely capable of
recognizing publicly the nefarious consequences of their own political choices and
statements. More seriously perhaps, it was reported that Mbeki had been told about
the regular brutality against foreigners in the country, both by the intelligence services and by the *African Peer Review Mechanism's* report of 2007 which had noted that
'xenophobia against other Africans is currently on the rise and must be nipped in the
bud'. Mbeki apparently ignored the warnings as he disputed the findings of these

reports. If true, such accounts would mean that Mbeki shares a large part of personal responsibility for the government's unpreparedness and lack of response to the xenophobic events (*Business Day*, July 11th 2008; SAMP, 2008: 20).

Declarations and expressions of regret by politicians abounded, some using the occasion to repair their dented image as notorious xenophobes. The ex-minister of Home Affairs Mangosutu Buthelezi, whose xenophobic statements were notorious when he was in power as this book has shown, made sure he was seen on television crying for the plight of the victims, while Winnie Madikizela Mandela who had been out of the media spotlight for some time, consoled the victims and even offered a family the temporary use of her home.[61] The most heart-warming reaction came however from ordinary people, not only those who helped their friends and neighbours hide from the mobs, but also the largely middle-class civil society response which provided food, blankets and other necessities for the displaced.

Early accounts of the violence from government agencies and the press blamed a 'third force' ('agitators' in South African state parlance) conspiracy, organised crime, mob violence, the flooding of migrants due to the lack of border controls, lack of 'service delivery' and finally the supposedly 'deeper' issue of economic conditions such as pervasive poverty. Most of these statements eventually tended to blame poverty and the lack of 'state delivery', hence the poor themselves, an account which became pervasive when filtered through the 'expert' utterances of 'analysts' and academics.

For example, the Congress of South African Trade Unions (COSATU) stressed that the 'underlying cause' of xenophobia was 'intolerable levels of poverty, unemployment and crime, and the shortage of housing in poor communities' (*Business Day* May 14th 2008). At the same time, COSATU rightly stressed of course that:

> Even if they [foreign immigrants] were all to leave tomorrow, the levels of unemployment would remain about the same, and so would the extent of poverty which afflicts at least half our population.
> (http://www.queensu.ca/samp/ migrationresources/xenophobia/#press)

As three well known academics put it: 'South Africa is in a state of emergency because of the failure to address desperate poverty'.[62] However, it is important to stress as I tried to do at the time, that economic factors, however important, cannot possibly account for why it was those deemed to be non-South African who bore the brunt of the vicious attacks. In fact, poverty can only account for the powerlessness, frustration and desperation of the perpetrators, but not for their target. Why were not Whites, or the rich, or white foreigners in South Africa targeted instead? (*Pambazuka News*, June 12th 2008). Was it simply because poor Africans were more easily available as scapegoats? This argument is not really convincing. For this to happen, for non-nationals to be targeted systematically, non-native Africans would have first to be politically and socially constructed as 'the other', as legitimate targets in popular belief. I will make an argument for how this alterity was constructed based on the main theses of this book as I proceed. In what follows, I will first take a critical look at the sociological background to the pogroms from published studies, and will then provide an explanation for the events in terms of what I have called the 'politics of fear'.

The Sociology of the Events and the Poverty of Explanation

From the research which was undertaken between 2006 and the xenophobic explosion of May 2008, a number of studies stand out as being of major importance. By far, the dominant character of these studies is to undertake attitude surveys which I have already commented on in the book. Such surveys are important so long as we do not assume that they measure some kind of inherent psychological attribute of respondents. The most rigorous of these surveys was undertaken by SAMP in 2006 and published in 2008. This report is particularly important for it measures the attitudes of the South African population in a representative sample during the period immediately before the events of May. Moreover, the authors were able to compare the results with those attitude surveys which they had undertaken in the late 1990s and which I have had occasion to discuss in the main part of this book. The results, according to the authors, show 'that South Africa exhibits levels of intolerance and hostility to outsiders, unlike virtually anything seen in other parts of the world' (SAMP, 2008: 1). The litany of xenophobic attitudes in South Africa thus goes like this:

> The proportion of people wanting strict limits or a total prohibition on immigration rose from 65 percent in 1997 to 78 percent in 1999 and the proportion of those favouring immigration, if there were jobs available, fell from 29 percent to 12 percent.

> The proportion of those wanting a total ban on immigration increased from 25 percent in 1999 to 35 percent in 2006... and 84 percent feel that South Africa is allowing 'too many' foreign nationals into the country.

> Nearly 50 percent support or strongly support the deportation of foreign nationals, including those living legally in the country.

> 74 percent support a policy of deporting anyone who is not contributing economically to South Africa.

> If migrants are allowed in, South Africans want them to come alone as they were forced to, under apartheid. Less than 20 percent think that it should be easier for families of migrants to come with them.

> 72 percent think that foreign nationals should carry identification papers with them at all times

> The proportions of South Africans wanting their borders electrified increased from 66 percent in 1999 to 76 percent in 2006 (Ibid.: 2).

I will stop here. Enough has been said to note that there has been, according to the authors, a hardening of xenophobic attitudes in the country since the late 1990s. The proportion stating, for example, that foreign nationals use up resources grew

from 59 percent in 1999 to 67 percent in 2006, those believing that foreign nationals are associated with crime grew from 54 percent in 1999 to 67 percent in 2006
and with diseases 24 percent in 1999 to 49 percent in 2006. Despite the fact that
migrants, from North America and Europe are viewed more favourably, a majority
have an unfavourable impression of migrants, wherever they come from. The idea
then that Africans are more disliked than other foreigners is purely relative. Finally,
South Africans have today more contact with foreigners, leading the authors to
conclude that 'attitudes are still formed independently of personal contacts with
migrants' (ibid.: 4).

I had noted earlier in this book the important point that in 1999 SAMP could
not identify a 'xenophobic profile', thereby making traditional sociological accounts
impossible. In 2006 the authors developed a 'composite xenophobic score' for each
respondent ranging from 0 (very xenophobic) to 10 (not xenophobic at all). The
scores were then grouped by variables such as race, class, income, etc. Some of the
results were that the average score was 3.95, i.e. high general levels of xenophobia;
Whites were more xenophobic than Coloureds and then Africans and then Asians/
Indians were the least xenophobic, although all scored below 5. Afrikaans speakers
were much more xenophobic than other language groups. In terms of self-defini-
tions of class, the 'upper' and the 'lower' were the most xenophobic, while in terms
of income, xenophobia scores were highest among the lowest income groups as
were the same scores among those with lower education, predictably. Interestingly,
DA supporters were slightly more xenophobic than ANC supporters, but given that
they are overwhelmingly White, this makes sense. Finally the most xenophobic
attitudes were displayed by pensioners (ibid. 5, 33- 36).

Overall then, these data are still not very helpful in terms of constructing a
xenophobic profile. Not only do all groups score below 5, in other words they are all
highly xenophobic, but it is clear that all class and income groups are xenophobic
with minor variations, and that the most xenophobic are presumably White DA
supporting pensioners, hardly a group that could be re-educated or isolated for anti-
xenophobic campaigns. As with the case with earlier attitude surveys, we are not left
with much of sociological significance, other than the fact that xenophobic attitudes
seem to have hardened throughout the country. Moreover, the recommendations
of the report are quite staggering, given the findings of the report. The authors ask:
'How can attitudes that are so entrenched, pervasive and negative be changed?' And
then proceed to answer: 'in brief by attacking the disease of xenophobia with the
same commitment that state and civil society have shown towards attacking the
scourge of racism in post-apartheid South Africa'. Leaving aside the contentious
assertion that racism has been attacked with commitment since the 1990s, it would
be useful to ask who is going to lead this attack on xenophobia? The state whose
institutions, employees and politicians overwhelmingly operate politically within a
crudely exclusionary form of nationalism? Particular social forces which cannot be
identified? Which would these be when '76 percent of South Africans want their
borders electrified, 65 percent want all refugees to be corralled in camps near the

borders and 61 percent wish to expel any foreign national with HIV/AIDS'? (ibid.: 39). The authors continue: 'bold political leadership and a broad based public education campaign in the media schools, communities and the workplace would have done much to mitigate and avoid the mayhem [of May]...The events of May 2008 may provide the necessary spur to political action' (ibid.: 40, 42).

But despite proffering their abhorrence at xenophobic violence, few politicians are likely to take the risk of leading a vigorous anti-xenophobic campaign, given their need for re-election by a xenophobic populace. The politics of fear on which xenophobia is founded have deep roots in society. There is more to it than simple ignorance; rather xenophobia must be understood as very much embedded in the politics of interest which govern local politics as we shall see below. This is arguably also why it is so deeply entrenched within social relations in the country. In any case, when the previous President of the Republic was in such obvious denial, who else could be expected to provide leadership? The incoming president is not only facing criminal charges in court (unlike poor foreigners, he has the right to be innocent until proven guilty), but also mobilises his supporters (many of whom come precisely from the poor townships guilty of xenophobic attacks) by singing his trademark militaristic song 'Awuleth' Umshini wami'. When attackers of supposed foreigners sang the same song to galvanise themselves into battle, he meekly condemned its singing (*Pretoria News* May 19th 2008) and later apologised to Mozambicans saying 'we were very surprised by (the xenophobic attacks), because for many years, there had never been any such incident or attack in South Africa' (*Daily News Foreign Service*, July 31st 2008). Indeed the level of commitment to eradicating xenophobia simply shines through these remarks.[63]

In fact sadly, the authors of the SAMP report do not seem to have distinguished between state employees and others in their assessment of xenophobic attitudes, as evidence from migrants themselves has underlined this distinction, as I noted earlier in the book. In this particular context, it is useful to look briefly at a study by the Centre for the Study of Violence and Reconciliation (CSVR) of the attitudes to migrants of the police (a representative sample of 580 uniformed police) in the Johannesburg area. Most of the 'vignettes' cited illustrate in fact what we knew already:

> It is difficult to police foreigners because we do not understand their language or culture. As a result, we sometimes do not believe what they say because most police officials believe that foreigners are lying [in order] to remain in the country...

> [There was a view that the increase in the number of foreigners in the country]... is as a result of the police not being tough [enough] on illegal immigrants. They do what they want and commit crime and when we arrest them they run to human rights groups who then accuse police of being racist.

> We do not want foreigners in this country because they cause a lot of serious crimes, don't pay tax and it is often difficult to solve a crime caused by illegal immigrants because of lack of their fingerprints. We can never solve especially serious crimes

because of these faceless people who do not even have a physical address where we can find them...whenever we suspect that they are illegal we arrest them and in many instances they try to be clever by producing fake papers...we tear those up in front of them to frustrate their efforts and send them to Lindela.

There is pressure on us (police officials) to effect arrests. In the police you are promoted, respected and given accolades if you have many arrests under your name. Often it is less important that an arrest results in a successful prosecution because that is the job of the prosecutor and investigating officer. As a result, we target illegal immigrants for arrest because you cannot afford to have under your name a zero arrest in a month. (Masuku, 2006: 2-3)

These statements speak for themselves; xenophobia is obviously dominant within the Johannesburg force. Of course, policemen did not admit to treating foreign nationals like mobile ATMs, but they did make the point which I had not previously noted, that they have a major incentive to arrest people, and that foreigners being easy targets, they can easily become 'arrest fodder'. Interestingly in this work, evidence from other countries is cited approvingly to suggest that 'forums' (sic) where police and foreigners can be exposed to each other need to be created in order to improve relations. For this to happen, non-nationals would have to be organised into identifiable groups with chosen leaders. The South African idea of the 'forum' is not necessarily effective in ensuring a democratic environment, neither would educating police in the 'multi-cultural sensitivity' be sufficient; foreign nationals often report leaving community meetings when locals started to shout for their expulsion. In order to ascertain the problems with such meetings, it may be useful to briefly discuss the idea of 'community policing' and the effects that it seems to have had within some poor communities. The reference to the importance of 'community policing' is a common and ubiquitous response in South Africa in relation to crime prevention; yet given the prevalence of xenophobia among both police and 'communities' as outlined above, this process can easily have deleterious effects within such a xenophobic social environment.

'Community policing' so-called was thought up in the 1990s as a way of building trust between community and police and in fighting crime after an apartheid period during which relations between urban communities and police had totally broken down. Yet, given the frequent commonality of attitudes (as well as of interests) between community leaders and police in combating the crime of 'illegal immigration', the supposed neutrality of the police towards all community members could easily be compromised. In an important piece in an otherwise pretty mediocre book on the May events, Hornberger (2008: 139) points out the fact that a police station commander, in an unguarded moment, admitted that the presence of fleeing foreign nationals in his compound ran the risk of undermining all the painstaking work in building cooperation with the community. She guardedly states:

Perhaps it is...through the panacea of community policing and the kind of close-up interaction between police and community which it propagates that has produced a practice which demands xenophobic attitudes from the police...When to keep peace and when to enforce the law ... is largely an issue of police discretion. Community policing implies that discretion is applied in such a way as to gain the trust of community. It is the triad of trust-discretion-community which can potentially produce legitimacy for the police and the state on a local level, but it might be exactly that which also produces – with the complicity of the police – brutal forms of local justice and vengeance. (op.cit.: 142-3).

In fact, Hornberger's point dovetails nicely into what is known, i.e. that 'communities' are neither active agents nor politically homogeneous, with the result that 'community leaders' have power not only over other community members but also, it seems, over the police whom they can order to engage in various activities which are in their interests. It is common practice for councilors for example, to order police to engage in actions particularly against the poor (Pithouse, 2008) as it is common for MPs to order councilors around. Such is the hierarchy of power as it has developed in this country and the manner it has impacted on urban communities. In rural areas it is 'traditional leaders' so-called who have and do use the powers to call upon police to maintain order in their interests. For example, there is evidence to suggest that 'community leaders', however understood, were often involved in directing the xenophobic violence and that they further prevailed on the police to let arrested perpetrators out of jail. Already in an incident in 2006 in which criminals had been arrested for xenophobic violence, it was reported by a respondent that:

> The criminals were arrested but released because the Premier and MEC Ramathlakane negotiated with the police. People said that they can't speak to the Premier unless the people arrested are released. The Premier met the Station Commander in Ocean View and they were released, but some were not released. The negotiations started. The South African shop owners did not want the competition with the Somalis – Somalis prices were cheaper – and the community preferred to buy from the Somalis. (Misago et al.: 33).

Again during the May 2008 events another respondent stated:

> When Atteridgeville police arrested comrades, councilor told people that if they can go to police station to demand that people be released, they will be released. So this sends signal that foreigners can be attacked and nothing will happen. (ibid.).

Being caught between their duty to uphold the law, to effect arrests and to respond to community leaders, it is not particularly surprising to see which way police officers would tilt, especially given their own xenophobic proclivities.

The next major study worth discussing was a Human Sciences Research Council (HSRC) attitude survey which questioned community members about their attitudes to foreign nationals during the events themselves in order to 'investigate the causes underlying the outbreak of xenophobic violence' (HSRC, 2008:4). The study used focus groups as its main technique in different locations where reports of xenophobia had been common. It sought primarily to gain an understanding of the views of South African 'community members', on 'foreigners' and xenophobia. Interestingly not only did the study assume that one can ascertain causal relations – in other words the truth, however understood – simply from collecting and reporting the perceptions of people, a staggeringly methodologically inept assertion, it also did not seem fit to attempt an understanding of the world from the point of view of the victims. The study could in fact be said therefore to have been tainted from its inception, precisely by the 'othering' of foreign nationals it was attempting to diagnose in others, by assuming that the views of South African township poor would provide them with the 'causes' of violence against foreigners during a period of high tension. Ultimately then, the study ended up being a collection of popular prejudices, and astonishingly pushed its methodological ineptitude to its logical conclusion by making recommendations to government founded precisely upon these prejudices.

These prejudices make interesting and predictable reading, but give us no inkling as to the real causes of the pogroms.

> They [foreign nationals] bribe officials to issue them with our ID so that they can get jobs... the generation that is supposed to govern us in the future is struggling to get IDs but an illegal alien from Angola has a South African ID, passport and driver's license, that is why I crush government's call for these people to stay here, if they go, South Africa will go back to where it was.

It seems that in many cases 'Community Policing Forums' (CPFs) were expected to act as vigilantes to 'root out' supposed illegal immigrants:

> ...in every township we need CPFs to cooperate with the police to keep our areas on the straight and narrow, a foreigner should be here for a reason; that way we can relax and breathe easily;...we need an effective solution where they leave according to a timeframe and whoever comes back must do so lawfully...

RDP houses which were built to house the poor and distributed to South Africans are then sometimes sold to foreign nationals, giving the impression that South Africans are still waiting for housing while 'foreigners' live in government provided housing:

> Even I don't have a RDP house, but go to Madalakufa you'll find foreigners owning houses which they have bought from South Africans... the community needs to learn that you get a house in order to use it, not to sell it for R20 000 as down payment for a house in the suburbs.

> Government is fighting against us, employers are fighting against us and foreigners are fighting against us, that is we fight against them because they are nearer; they don't support us in our struggle (HSRC 2008: 29, 30, 38, 45)

The last remark makes it clear that especially people in informal settlements feel hemmed in and 'besieged', as the authors put it, by a whole number of pressures. Yet what also seems to be the case is the absence of a form of politics and/or leadership which could unite people around a clear identification of their problems and their enemy. As it stands, leadership is allowed to wander into the hands of unscrupulous leaders.

Not surprisingly then, the HSRC report absurdly recommends the establishment of 'community forums' on migration and follows popular prejudice in stating 'that it is essential that government move urgently and effectively to protect South Africa's borders' and to 'ensure that only South Africans occupy this form of public shelter [RDP houses]' (ibid.: 48-9).   It is then the migrant who is seen as the source of the problem exactly as those interviewed saw it. If only we can keep all 'foreigners' out, there will be no xenophobia. The HSRC simply ended up reproducing the preju-dices of its informants. As the authors of the SAMP report commented, 'what this fails to recognise...is that this is precisely what the South African state has been trying to do since 1994, actually since 1910, without much success. The post-apartheid state could no more seal its borders than the apartheid state before it.' (SAMP, 2008: 14).[64]

The HSRC report was also criticised by Professor John Sharp (2008) from the University of Pretoria who in a thoughtful piece referred to its upholding a notion of 'Fortress South Africa'. Sharp makes three basic points. First the important idea that, contrary to HSRC assumptions, xenophobic violence did not simply emanate from the attitudes of the poor but that as I have argued earlier in this book, a discourse and politics of xenophobia has been endemic in the South African public sphere since liberation at least. In particular, he stresses the fact that price to pay for the supposed miraculous transition from apartheid to democracy was the 'abject capitulation to neo-liberal democracy', a price which is being paid by the poor in both South Africa and the rest of the continent (ibid.: 2). The resulting policing of strictly demarcated compartments between local and foreign poor is intimately con-nected to indigeneity which is seen as the main way in which entitlements can be successfully claimed.

The second point which Sharp stresses is the important one that not all poor South Africans are characterised by the possession of xenophobic attitudes, but that in specific circumstances a xenophilia was in evidence as well an array of positions in between depending on circumstances. (ibid.: 3, Sichone, 2008). I shall have occa-sion to return to this point, but it is apparent that most reports on the violence did precisely that, i.e. reported on those areas where violence had taken place; only one of these which I shall presently assess, also took the trouble to examine areas where violence had not occurred despite people being desperately poor.

Sharp's final point is a methodological one and concerns the importance for him of stressing the 'flexible' approach to citizenship advocated in particular by Nyamnjoh (2006) rather than the rigid 'all or nothing' conception of citizenship which one either possesses or not. Given that the evidence suggests that most foreign nation-als see themselves as only temporarily resident in south Africa, i.e. as migrants rather than immigrants, their desire is not necessarily to compete with fully fledged 'citi-zens'. In any case, given that the ability to access citizenship rights is variable on the basis of one's social status (poor-rich, male-female, young-old, etc), the latter seems a much more appropriate conception of citizenship for understanding differences rather than the 'bounded' one.

These point are worth discussing in some detail and I shall return to them later, but it is important to note at this stage that Sharp reminds us that at the core of the whole process of the development and acting out of xenophobic violence, is not only a question of attitudes, but fundamentally a question of politics, in particular the politics of citizenship. Sharp's arguments therefore enable us to make this shift in our enquiry, from an emphasis on attitudes to an emphasis on politics. The next report to be briefly assessed delves explicitly in to political processes, particularly at local level.

This report was commissioned by the United Nations International Organisation for Migration (IOM) and undertaken by a group of authors from the Forced Migration Studies Programme (FMSP) at the University of the Witwatersrand. The study which was undertaken in seven sites in Gauteng and the Western Cape sought explicitly to go beyond the assessment of attitudes to an outline of 'the political economy of violence against outsiders' (Misago et al., 2008: 1). This makes this report particularly interesting. It is important to mention that the authors show quite clearly that it was not necessarily the poorest areas nor indeed those with the most or the most recent foreign arrivals where violence dominated. It was not then a matter of greater poverty or foreign presence which could have been the most important factors (ibid.:29, 32). Moreover, many of the foreign nationals attacked had been living there for many years and had been integrated into the community; therefore xenophobic violence is not necessarily the result of lack of integration (ibid.: 28).

Importantly, the study addresses specifically the questions as to why the violence occurred in some poor areas and not in others, and why it occurred at the time it did. It concludes:

> This study's findings are that in almost all cases where violence occurred, it was organised and led by local groups and individuals in an effort to claim or consolidate the authority and power needed to further their political and economic interests. It therefore finds that most violence against non-nationals and other 'outsiders' which occurred in May 2008 is rooted in the micro-politics of the country's townships and informal settlements. (ibid.:1-2)

The study establishes a very important shift in the analysis. Given the xenophobic politics and discourses at the level of the national state apparatuses assessed at length in this book, this study consists of an attempt to explain the unfolding of xenophobic violence at the local level. It finds that local power was at the root of the violence. In fact, the study notes that much of the language used during the attacks drew 'directly from political rhetoric espoused by [national] leaders across the political spectrum' (op.c.it.: 16). In many instances, people often saw themselves as doing the government's work based on state induced prejudices:

> South African freedom is poor, how can people enter this country without IDs? ...
> So if government is failing to stop them at the borders, we shall stop them here ...
> We are not the police; we do not ask for passports, they are forged anyway. (ibid.: 18).

Echoing the utterances of his leader Buthelezi, an 'Induna' ['traditional' headman]
and IFP leader at Madala hostel in Alexandra stated:

> The government is now pampering them and taking care of them nicely; as long as
> the foreigners are here, we will always have unemployment and poverty here in South
> Africa ... there was no poverty and unemployment in South Africa before the influx
> of foreigners ... there is too much of them now, if the government does not do
> something, people will see what to do to solve the problem because it means it is not
> the government problem, it is our problem (ibid.: 28)

In fact, the report notes that for many who were involved in the violence, as for
many who were not, 'attacking foreigners was a legitimate means of protecting
South African lives and livelihoods' (ibid.: 22). It further notes that the vigilantism
which dominated either characterised much of the actions of CPFs or was a reaction to perceived failures by CPFs and had its roots in the tradition of township
residents taking the law into their own hands. The pogroms in Alexandra started
after a CPF meeting after which residents as well as hostel dwellers decided to take
the law into their own hands:

> Prior to the attacks (on May 11th) there was a meeting on the 10th of May 2008 and it
> was decided that they will attack around the hostel and the shack area. This was not
> the first meeting, it was a follow-up meeting (ibid.: 43).

In another area, a respondent said that police had actually encouraged people to
take the law into their own hands:

> There was a police who issued a statement that people must decide on how they deal
> with someone who has entered their kraal and took their cattle. This statement, for
> me, started the violence (ibid.: 42).

For another respondent, the attacks in Alexandra were designed to create an IFP
stronghold:

> the violence was not about xenophobia ... it was about politics The violence was
> started by Zulus at the hostel and not the general community; it was started by the
> same group that instigated violence in the early 90s. The cause of the violence was
> the political ploy and the purpose was to create a stronghold for IFP/Zulus in
> preparation for the elections (ibid.: 30).

In other words, ethnic political tensions were often present as dominant ethnic groups
in some areas themselves exclude other South African ethnic groups from entitlements in that area (ibid.: 36). But ethnicity was not at the core of the violence, it
simply enabled it. Far more crucial than any other factor according to the authors
of the report was the character of local leadership and power.

The authors maintain that in all research sites where violence occurred, the most important factor was said to be the nature of local leadership (ibid.: 37). While the authors tend to assume that other power groupings filled the gaps in the absence of 'legitimate elected leadership', they do not show this, and there is evidence to suggest that both formal (e.g. councillors) and informal (e.g. 'comrades', 'izinduna', CPFs, Street Committees, Block Committees, SANCO and so on) operate sometimes independently, sometimes together in exercising power over community members. These different loci of power would mean complex and shifting alliances in different communities, but this was not investigated. What is noted however is that:

> community membership is an attractive alternative for the largely unemployed residents of the informal settlements ... It is common practice that those (sic) supposedly voluntary structures: i) charge for their services; ii) levy protection fees; iii) sell or let shacks/stands and RDP houses and iv) take bribes in exchange for solving or influencing tender projects for development projects (ibid.: 38).

Indeed, much of this exercise of power mirrors the regular plundering of the poor justified by 'traditions' and 'traditional' powers (chiefly, religious leaders, etc) which has been operating for years in rural areas. A CPF chairperson confirmed that 'CPF sub-committee members do not get paid and survive on 'community compassion''; while an informant observed: 'in the townships they have CPFs. Here they wanted R5.00 to pay those patrolling at night. People refused'. (ibid.: 38). It was also reported that in Du Noon, both the local SANCO branch and the local taxi association were requesting fees in order to protect re-integrating foreign businessmen. Apparently the paying of protection money had been going on since 2005. Given that each of the 85 Somali traders had been paying a monthly protection fee of R100.00, the protection racket was a lucrative business. Evidently, all wish to cash in on what have become known as 'mobile ATMs' (*Cape Argus*, June 23rd 2008).

Given this kind of power structure, it is not surprising to hear the authors of the report assert:

> The xenophobic violence in most affected areas was organised by the ... parallel structures or by some self-serving members of formal institutions who capitalised on residents' feelings, fears and negative attitudes towards non-nationals ... the study found that in most affected areas, the attacks on foreigners were organised and led by different local community leadership structures and/or known influential groups (ibid.: 39).

Further, a respondent asserted:

> The leaders ... led the fighting of foreigners. They had no option ... they must do what the community wants. If they don't we shall remove them ... Police know they are the ones who led attacks on foreigners. (ibid.)

While another expressed surprise when asked what leaders did to stop the violence: 'no you are missing the point. Leaders were with us at all times. They directed us on where to go and when.' (ibid.). Religious figures also came to a similar conclusion as

Bishop Paul Verryn for example told the press that: 'based on the testimony of his colleagues working on the ground ... some police and councilors were involved in stoking the attacks' (*Business Day*, May 22nd).

However, what is important to note is that in two areas studied by Misago, violence was prevented from taking place. In the first case, a deal was arrived at between attacking Zulus from hostels and local leaders who, promised to remove foreign residents themselves. It was believed that if they had been attacked, outsiders would not have been able to distinguish foreign nationals from South Africans and many of the latter would have been killed. It is not clear if this means that had 'foreigners' been wearing some kind of distinguishing sign (as the Jews in Nazi Germany), then that would have been fine. In fact, most foreign nationals left and it was reported that when they returned, they found their property intact (ibid.: 44-5). In the second case, it was clear from all respondents that community leaders with police support played a central role in preventing violence. Groups from outside were prevented from attacking by community leaders after it had been agreed that they were opposed to violence. According to the authors, the organised resistance was the result of the good relations between locals and foreign nationals (op.cit.: 45).

> We asked them how will they differentiate between migrants' shacks and South Africans' shacks. We also reminded them that this is an informal settlement and the shacks are close to each other; if they burn one shack, the whole place catches fire ... 'we have struggled with these people for so long, we cannot turn against them'. (ibid.: 46).

The authors of the report note that this outcome reflects the fact that the local leadership represented all who lived there; but this seems a rather tautological argument as the argument presented to show that the leadership represented all, was precisely that they were able to deflect the violence. More than this, it seems rather that the cause has more to do with the politics which local leaders chose to follow. Had leaders capitulated to pressure, however representative they may have been, violence would not have been prevented.

Finally, we now need to wind up the discussion of the literature by covering a few remaining areas. In particular, we need to assess two issues briefly, the first being the experience of migrants who were corralled into government Centres of Safe Shelter, the second being the main reason for the relatively large number of South African victims of violence. Both of these require some assessment, as they show first that xenophobic violence was not exclusively restricted to poor informal settlements, but that victims experienced systematic discrimination by state authorities within the camps. And second, that such prejudice is so extreme as to consider all non-urban residents as in some way 'foreigners'.

The evidence concerning the moving of foreign nationals affected by the violence into reception centres suggests that this was assumed to be a temporary measure, as the government's idea was for them to be re-integrated into their communities.

Reports of this experience are replete with accounts of disorganisation, xeno-phobic attitudes and practices by Home Affairs and Police officials, and general maladministration. The humanitarian response was described variously as 'chaos', mismanaged and without 'a clear and pro-active lead agency' (FMSP, 2009: 8). A detailed assessment of the humanitarian assistance following upon the pogroms is not able to provide a clear picture of the experiences of the victims as it is over-burdened with the technical discourse of disaster management. Yet, one is able here and there to acquire snippets of information which, taken together with other re-ports from eyewitnesses and newspapers, give a basic account of such experiences.

One recurring theme concerns the fact that civil servants were often concerned that IDPs (the bureaucratic designation for Internally Displaced Persons) may be getting and may be seen to be getting more in assistance than citizens. It is not at all clear whether this was a simple result of endemic xenophobia among the civil serv-ice (mainly drawn from the Home Affairs Department) or whether there was a genuine fear of the possibility of resentment. In either case, it shows that the victims of xenophobic violence were not safe from discrimination in their supposed 'havens'. In fact, the evidence overwhelmingly points in this direction. Another reported feature of civil servants was their general xenophobic attitudes which be-came evident as 'they were required to provide services which they may not have personally agreed with' (ibid.: 9). Immigration control practices continued well into the period of the violence and during the period of 'humanitarian response' police continued to arrest and deport people they deemed to be 'illegal immigrants' which led, according to researchers, to 'break-downs in protection' (ibid.). What this meant was that there was clear evidence of dissonance between the police duties to protect people from attack and avail them of their rights, and their supposed duties to deport 'aliens'. In this context is it not surprising that when herded into government camps, foreign nationals regularly demanded to be taken away from government facilities and into the custody of the UNHCR. The latter did not have its own centres and deferred to the state, so there was usually no way out for the displaced victims of violence.

A report in *Pambazuka News* on My 30th illustrates this precisely.[65] It states in detail how police came to a temporary camp outside Pretoria (Rosslyn) and com-manded the refugees to move to a Disaster Management camp run by the South African government. When the refugees requested to be attended to by the UNHCR and moved to a safer country, police forced people to move and fired rubber bullets and a number of people (including children) were injured. All this happened within the camp and the police (both Black and White) were verbally abusing people while they were aggressing them. Of course, after having suffered violence at the hands of their neighbours, people were extremely angry to face the same in supposed areas of safety.

A final recurring theme concerns the question of documentation. This issue was so serious that it led to 'the most significant and at times violent conflicts between government agencies and the displaced' (FMSP, 2009: 9). This problem resulted from the government insisting on providing those displaced in shelters with temporary documents which it was genuinely feared would reduce the rights of those who were already in possession of full refugee or asylum seeker documentation. They did so under the threat of deportation (ibid.: 136). Not surprisingly, given the distrust of Home Affairs, these state decisions were resisted with similar results to those outlined above. The fact that arrest and deportations of foreign nationals continued throughout the violent attacks could only suggest to perpetrators that their actions were legitimate in the eyes of the state.

Finally, very few, if any, of the perpetrators were brought to justice despite pledges by the highest ranking politicians. On the 25th August, the Ministry of Safety and Security reported that 1446 charges had been laid related to the May violence and that a total of 421 cases were pending (ibid.: 137). In the areas where Misago et al. (2009) undertook interviews, respondents reported that none of the perpetrators were brought to justice, confirming a general impression of impunity, and creating the suspicion that the perpetrators were doing illegally what the state had long been wanting to do but had not been able to do legally, namely to get rid of so-called 'foreign immigrants'. One participant in the attack was quoted as stating: 'the government must work hard to secure our borders. Home Affairs must be sorted out. We're helping the government now to send them back.' (cit. Coplan, 2008: 119).

At this stage, a slight digression on the operations of the department of Home Affairs may be pertinent in order to clarify the question of corruption which is held by all, including perpetrators, to be prevalent within this department of the civil service. While some see corruption at Home Affairs as exploitative of powerless foreign nationals, xenophobes see it as advantageous to 'illegal foreigners'. They are both right. The difficulties in obtaining refugee status for example, have been commented on at length, and the queues of people outside the Marabastad offices of Home Affairs in Tshwane are particularly notorious in this regard. An investigation by Lawyers for Human Rights revealed the following picture:

> Rarely does an asylum seeker gain entry to a refugee reception office on their first attempt. The office accepts a limited number of applications per day. Entitlement to one of these positions is controlled by a hazy coalition of security guards, migrant agents, interpreters and officials who solicit bribes and favours in return for favourable treatment and employ oblique force against those who would challenge the integrity of their parallel system. Those who do not have the capacity to pay have a choice; well, a choice that is not really a choice. They can return at a later date and risk being caught by the police without documentation, or they can sleep overnight outside the office and retain their place in the official queue. On the nights when LHR did headcounts they discovered between 80 and 300 people sleeping outside the office. At night armed criminals visit the site. Incidents of theft are common. There have been several reports of rape. There is no shelter in the vicinity of the office and people often endure rain and very cold conditions while waiting outside. Women sleep with babies by their side. On some occasions the police have visited during the

night and arrested asylum seekers or extorted them for bribes. (cit. Vigneswaran, 2008: 4)

Given that people can be in such conditions for several months, it is not surprising that they look for ways to get their papers faster. Vigneswaran argues that far from simply being an obsession with acquiring funds through corruption, there is an institutional culture pertaining to the Home Affairs Department in which:

> DHA officials are embedded in an institution which sanctions its officials engaging in extra-legal practices that prevent foreigners from entering and residing legally in South Africa. This culture, which has its roots in the DHA's Apartheid days, continues to inform how agents of the Department understand their responsibilities to new laws, and plays a considerable role in limiting access to asylum and undermining the integrity of the status determination system (ibid.: 6).

Wigneswaran argues that senior management encourages such a culture, yet at the same time it is arguably also the introduction of a commercial culture into the process which helps to account for the prevalence of corruption. For example, at the Home Affairs Department in central Pretoria there is a private company with offices in the basement which offers, for a fee, to acquire the relevant official papers without the hassle of queuing and filling in forms. This company also advertises in Pretoria its ability to get official papers including drivers' licenses, for anyone willing to pay. Clearly this operation is not illegal, or at least it is tolerated. One simply provides them with the necessary documentation and money and they do the queuing and produce the appropriate papers at the end of the process. It would indeed be surprising if they did not grease a few palms here and there along the way in order to expedite matters. Given the personal relations established with the civil servants, they probably also get preferential treatment in having their papers processed. Presumably having such a company doing this work also saves time as documents are properly completed etc.

It could therefore be argued that given the cumbersome nature of the administrative process of acquiring documentation, an exclusionary culture inherited from apartheid and a gradual commercialisation of operations which are supposed to be free, corruption at Home Affairs is largely inevitable. It has also been noted that such corruption is endemic at border posts, as entry into South Africa has been turned into a lucrative business (Coplan, 2008). The point then is that corruption must be understood in the context of a situation where access to official papers is so cumbersome and difficult (due either to the law itself or to the administrative manner of issuing them) that commercial practices have entered the civil service in a big way. This problem is not restricted to the Home Affairs Department but is also evident at the Department of Transport for example, where the existence of corruption in issuing drivers' licenses is also a well known problem. These commercial practices may simply be tolerated at present, rather than formally being in existence, but the point is simply that a commercial culture has become the accepted if not always the admitted norm. Under these circumstances, corrupt activities are not out of the ordinary especially if top management also feels it should have its cut (Coplan, op.cit.).

On the question of the reasons for as much as a third of all dead in May being South Africans, we need to recall the fact that foreigners' were distinguished simply on the basis of stereotypes such as skin colour, language use, etc. But even more importantly, demographic statistics regarding migration to the large conurbations of Gauteng in particular, show a majority of South Africans migrating from rural areas.

> Because of its economically dominant position within both South and Southern Africa, Gauteng continues to be a major destination for domestic and international migrants. The net migration gain (i.e. the difference between the arrivals and departures from the province) was 418,000 between October 2001 and February 2007. This translates into an annual gain of approximately 78,000 migrants. Although domestic migration accounts for the vast majority of new arrivals in Gauteng, the Province is also a primary destination for international migrants. In 2007, Gauteng Province hosted 46 percent of South Africa's population born outside South Africa. This is up from 42 percent in 2001 and is expected to increase in the years ahead. The trend for new arrivals is visible in the composition of the Province's 'non-native' stock. Of the total number of residents not born in Gauteng but residing within the Province, 16 percent arrived between 2002 and 2007. *Most of the new arrivals are young adults born in other provinces of South Africa* (Landau and Gindrey, 2008:7 *emphasis added*).

Given the large number of rural migrants and the urban-centred culture of discrimination noted already, it is scarcely surprising that many South Africans would be taken to be 'foreigners'. From 'foreign natives', we have clearly arrived at a situation where 'native foreigners' have been systematically produced inside their own country. The failure of the post-apartheid state to take rural development seriously is at the core of the massive influx from rural areas, as is the conflation of freedom with a job and the more general but fundamental urban-bias of South African nationalism. This has been sufficiently discussed in this book not to warrant further comment.

Given all that has been said above, it should be reasonably apparent that explanations for the pogroms of May which stress the economic factors of poverty, inequality and absence of service delivery by the state, cannot fully explain the violence. Even the socio-psychological notion of 'relative deprivation' is unhelpful as its own origins have to be explained. Xenophobia as an attitude is not simply an attribute of the poor but is prevalent among the middle classes, yet these express it in a completely different manner and they do not usually do their own killing. The exclusion of foreign colleagues from jobs, the snide remarks, the ostracising of foreign colleagues and regular exclusionary comments are all common among the professions. During the pogroms, foreign doctors were even considering leaving South Africa (SABC News May 30th 2008). Evidently, recourse to violence to 'solve' political problems has a long history among the urban poor, both under the apartheid state and during the struggle for liberation. The failure of the state has not just been one of 'slow delivery' as many commentators observed, but perhaps more fundamentally a failure to enable the solving of problems other than through violence. The fact that the poor's alienation from the state has continued in the post-apartheid period and the tendency of the local state to resort to violence often as a first resort, has not facilitated the development of conflict resolution structures. The latter require not only a different kind of leadership but the ability to think subjectively a different way of addressing their problems, in other words a different form of politics.

Broadly speaking, the mainstream media condemned xenophobia outright. The only exception was the tabloid press which sees itself as reflecting the views of township residents. Like its British counterpart, the *Daily Sun* newspaper has prided itself in propagating crass sexism and xenophobia justified as a reflection of popular views. It sees itself as reflecting the views of the 'small guy in blue overalls' which basically means often pandering to the crudest prejudices of people in order to sell newspapers. Of course, as is common for such tabloids, the problem is seen as 'big business', 'big government', 'bribery, corruption and neglect in high places', 'crass officialdom'; a position very much along the lines of right wing ideologies everywhere. According to its publisher, 'the *People's Paper* leaves its target audience in no doubt that they – South Africans – come first' (*Mail & Guardian*, June 6th-12th 2008); even if it means referring to the pogroms as a 'war on aliens' (much like a 'war on terror') and presumably wanting the return of the death penalty. Pandering to the crassest of chauvinisms, the paper failed to condemn the violence clearly, but covered it as one of the many expressions of violence in townships (Harber, 2008: 163). Clearly it is the idea of what it means to be a 'South African' which is the real problem here, in particular the construction of an exclusionary, violently aggressive and narrow conception of the citizen.

It is here that a notion of citizenship becomes crucially important as I have argued in this book. If the origins of the widespread and endemic xenophobia in the country are to be sought, then these can be found in state practices and statements, and in the construction of a nationalism which is both urban-centred and exclusionary. If indeed, as I have argued, the source of xenophobia is to be found not just simply in the actions of elites, but fundamentally in a state conception of politics, then the recommendations of various reports such as those by SAMP are problematic, for they are directed to state and civil society, and are not concerned with thinking a different politics based on agency, something which they see as clearly beyond their purview. This process ends up being quite absurd (most apparent in the case of the HSRC report) as the state is required to provide leadership on an issue for which it is the main culprit. In addition, there is no attempt (by the various reports cited) to think about which social forces could provide a basis for enacting their recommendations, given the overwhelming dominance of xenophobia in the country. In fact, the whole idea of recommendations has been reduced to a simple state-directed ritualistic exercise.

It should perhaps be recalled that the citizenship which South Africans fought for was primarily an urban form which demanded, not 'land to the tiller' as in the classical national-democratic revolutions, including that of Zimbabwe across the border. It was a nationalism which equated freedom and democracy primarily with urban citizenship and primarily with the possession of a job and a house. It is in this context that 'foreigners' can be perceived as 'eating our democracy' as one of the quotations heading this chapter notes. And it is here that John Sharp's contrast between a 'bounded' and a 'flexible' notion of citizenship becomes relevant.

There are arguably two simultaneous ways in which citizenship, understood as a set of relations between state and people in which the latter have the right to rights, is regulated in any one society/nation. The first is a formalised state and usually legal conception and practice, the second refers to a set of practices on the ground so to speak, in any social situation. The former is usually fixed, the latter is often variable. Both are subjected to political pressures and operate within very definite political subjectivities. The former is rigid and understood as a 'yes or no' affair. One either possesses rights or one does not; either one is a citizen or not. The latter is eminently flexible and one's rights vary depending on one's location in society and on the political power one can exert. Various degrees of citizenship are possible within this situation. The former is more easily understood as politics codified in law, the latter as politics expressed in unequal social relations. However, both are fundamentally the outcome of politics and its attendant subjectivities. Rather predictably, the former has been studied primarily by political scientists and lawyers, the latter by anthropologists and sociologists.

Although valid, as I have noted already, Sharp's idea seems to assume that these different notions of citizenship are mutually exclusive. Yet, both occur simultaneously at least in popular discourses as well as in experience. The more flexible variety is more readily experienced in practice as different categories of people experience different ranges of rights depending on their power or lack thereof in society. The poor of course would not be able to claim as many rights or entitlements as the rich, women as men, children as adults, etc, while foreigners would be close to being able to claim only few, partly because of their lack of possession of the state papers which express the bonded variety of citizenship. The two versions are then connected, and while it is important to note the existence of flexible citizenship, the reality is one which combines both. Given the various types as well as degrees of exclusion which are produced both by the neo-liberal economic world and by its political counterpart in an imported democracy, citizenship is bound to be a complex and indeed contradictory relationship.

What both political scientists and anthropologists tend to forget however, is the notion of citizenship as agency, the idea that citizenship does not simply refer to a relationship which is given (bounded or fluid), by the state or by social relations, but to one which can also be passive, active or any shade in between, depending on circumstances. In fact, the idea of active citizenship (or its possibility) is usually occluded when this is the case, as it is assumed that the state or society are structured in such a way as to automatically (so to speak) allow for access to (a range of) particular entitlements or rights. In fact, without some form of agency, these rights are rarely forthcoming to the poor, and even then there is no guarantee that they will be.[66] This is why I have insisted that this distinction is a necessary one to make, and that (neo-) liberal politics tend to produce a passive citizenship which thus restricts access to rights to a few only. When such passivity is systematically rejected as in the present case under study, the agency thus expressed is invariably located within the hegemonic, state subjectivity, and offers little in terms of alternative modes of thought.

If citizenship is not only seen as being a result of state injunction, e.g. of whether the state provides the South African poor with subsidised housing, but is rather seen as the outcome of different political forces (including those from the poor who may wish not only to claim but also to struggle for their entitlements as they perceive them), then its character is also understood as determined by popular agency. It is apparent that in May 2008, poor South Africans attempted to assert their own conception of citizenship in opposition to what they saw as the government's (but not the state's) understanding, which they dismissed as far too inclusive of outsiders. Yet they clearly did so from within an overall state subjectivity evidenced by their equating citizenship with indigeneity.

I have argued earlier in this book that state notions of citizenship emphasise indigeneity, simply because such an (essentialised) notion is always in the interest of those in power; while popular conceptions of citizenship can be inclusive and democratic. Clearly the poor South Africans who were asserting their citizenship in May were doing so on the basis of stressing their indigeneity, on the basis of nativism. They were thus doing so within the parameters of state subjectivity, of state politics. Yet there was also evidence of alternative politics at play among the poor. An understanding of citizenship and of politics as agency is particularly important, precisely because it also enables a thinking of subjectivities outside the limits of state thought. In the absence of such a capacity to think politics beyond the parameters of state subjectivity, citizenship can only be understood as indigeneity, as if this were the natural way of doing so.

The absence of an alternative politics to those of the state from within different sites generally means the absence of alternatives to state thinking, to state political subjectivity. Such sites of alternative political thought were few and far between in May 2008, and this clearly pointed to a failure of alternative politics, particularly of Left politics. In the absence of such an alternative, people were abandoned to, and left to think within the parameters of state subjectivity. The pictures on television of gangs in Alexandra wearing Anti-Privatisation Forum T-shirts, were also an indication of a depressing failure of the politics of some social movements.[67] The absence of alternatives was precisely why the xenophobic violence took the form of a seemingly unstoppable 'tsunami' which only petered out when engaging in it started to become too risky for perpetrators. Only in rare cases were such politics challenged.

The Politics of Fear

To end this chapter, I want to argue that the fundamental causes of the May pogroms of 'foreigners' must be sought in what can be called, the 'politics of fear';
basically the widespread fear that foreign nationals would swamp and overwhelm
the country in such a way as to make the hard won gains of the 1990s liberation
irrelevant. It is here then that it makes sense to understand the comment that
foreigners 'are eating our democracy'. The use of a name like 'the politics of fear'
is thus an attempt to stress the etymological roots of the term 'xenophobia' in order
not to understand it simply as a psychological 'attitude', but as a political subjectivity
and practice.

The fear of being swamped by foreigners perceived as stealing one's entitlements has a long history, but is said to prevail in many countries today, given the
effects of 'globalisation' where indigeneity has become the main vehicle for making
claims on the state and where the poor are systematically excluded from partaking in
the increasing wealth of the rich. While there is no space here to assess the fundamental reasons for this apparent shift within a changing political economy and the
decline of political alternatives, recognition of this trend is important. Recent events
in Europe for example have pointed to the fact that, far from being a prerogative of
the fringes of right-wing politics, xenophobia has entered the mainstream. Slavoj
Zizek, for example has noted that:

> *This* is the truth of globalisation: the construction of new walls safeguarding pros-
> perous Europe from the immigrant flood [...] the segregation of the people is the
> reality of economic globalisation. This new racism of the developed is in a way
> much more brutal than the previous ones, its implicit legitimation is [...] unabashed
> economic egotism. The fundamental divide is between those included in the sphere
> of (relative) economic prosperity and those excluded from it [...] The big event of
> 2006 [in Europe - MN] was when anti-immigration politics went mainstream and
> finally cut the umbilical cord that had connected it to far-right fringe parties [...] in the
> new spirit of pride in cultural and historical identity, the main parties now found it
> acceptable to stress that immigrants are guests who must accommodate themselves
> to the cultural values that define the host society – It is our country, love it or leave it
> – (Slavoj Zizek, 2008: 87, 35).

And Alain Badiou adds:

> There existed, up to around the nineties of the previous century, an ideological wall,
> a political iron curtain; there is now a wall which separates the pleasures (*jouissance*) of
> the rich from the desires of the poor. Everything takes place as though, in order for
> the unique world of objects and monetary signs to exist, one is required to harshly
> separate living bodies according to their origins and resources [...] Many people
> animated by fear and organised in this fear by the state, anxiously ask themselves
> how many are there here, how many of these people who come from another
> world? Tens of thousands? Millions? A horrible question when one thinks about
> it, a question which necessarily prepares the ground for persecution, for prohibition,

for mass expulsion, a question, which in other circumstances laid the foundations
for extermination (Alain Badiou, 2007: 75-6, 78 author's translation).

Of course, to refer to such changes in Europe is in no way to seek to justify those
in South Africa; it is rather to argue that a politics of fear has been developing there
also and that we should therefore not be surprised, given our common position as a
destination for poor migrants, that a similar political fear may exist here. In fact, it is
uncanny how these remarks speak to our situation here, as if in fact they had been
written with South Africa in mind. In fact, they are common to what has been
termed 'globalisation'.

It should be apparent then that xenophobia and its attendant violence is a political issue. The criminalisation of migrancy, the xenophobic public culture among
politicians since the early 1990s, the failure to develop genuinely democratic legislation and the hiding behind notions of 'Fortress South Africa' in devising existing
legislation, the widespread xenophobic culture among the civil service and the police, the exploitation of the vulnerable in the country, the appalling practices at the
Lindela detention centre, the xenophobic opportunism of local politicians and the
absence of alternatives, have all contributed to the creation of a hegemonic xenophobic political subjectivity. The first characteristic of the politics of fear is then
the hegemonic state discourse and politics of xenophobic exclusion which I have
assessed at length in this book. It is from this political discourse and practice that it
can be deduced that to be a foreigner, particularly a poor Black foreigner, is in itself
a crime; very much as being a Jew in Nazi Germany was considered to be a crime.
By the time May 2008 arrived, it was no longer a question of the possession of
adequate official documents; in any case the transition from legality to illegality
could easily result from the police tearing up perfectly valid documents. Legality of
illegality was no longer the issue. Anyone could be attacked simply because they
were supposedly 'foreign'.

The second characteristic of the politics of fear is a discourse of South African
exceptionalism. The construction of a South African nationalism around an urban
culture and a pro-Western ideology of unabashed neo-liberalism, has helped to entrench a continuity with the apartheid ideology according to which South Africa is
understood as existing apart from, and superior to, the rest of the African continent.
The prevalent idea here is that the country is not really a part of Africa and that its
intellectual and cultural frame of reference is in the United States and Europe.
Given that South Africa is industrialised, democratic, advanced in relation to other
countries of the continent and also a paragon of reconciliation and political liberalism, Africa is seen as the place of the other. It was thought until recently that what
happened in Rwanda in 1994 and more recently in Kenya could not possibly happen
here. According to this perception, South Africa is somehow more akin to a Southern European or Latin American country, given its relatively high levels of industrialisation and now (increasingly) of liberal democracy.

To this must be added the view that South Africa must be celebrated as it is
the envy of the world for having managed a reconciliation process successfully.

A corollary of this view is one that sees Africa as some kind of strange backward continent characterised by primitivism, corruption, authoritarianism, poverty and failed states; so that apparently its inhabitants wish only to partake of South African resources and wealth at the expense of its citizens. Africa is thus a continent to be guided, advised, developed and visited by tourists in search of authentic primitivism and wild animals. It is not a continent to which we really belong, only a place to be acted upon. This view is regularly upheld by the press, which simply takes its cue from its European largely neo-colonial sources (which are reproduced totally uncritically). The rhetoric of an African Renaissance, upheld by ex-President Mbeki is one which maintains that such a renewal can take place as an effect of neo-liberal policies such as NEPAD (the New Economic Partnership for African Development) within which South African capital and expertise has a prominent role in securing a continental resurgence. While such views combine a commitment to liberalism and to the continent's development, they regularly come up against the narrow arrogant nationalism which sustains the idea of South African 'leadership' of the continent. NEPAD, the internationally sponsored programme for continental development, launched with much fanfare in South Africa a few years ago, is simply the neo-liberal Western entry into the continent. Neither the ideas of the *African Renaissance* nor those of *Ubuntu* have been taken beyond the stage of being simply state slogans with little in terms of roots in the population at large.

While such views are not universal, they are indeed dominant within the state apparatuses and beyond. This dominance can be connected to a schizophrenia characteristic of the new Black ruling elite which, on the one hand, wishes to assert its Africanness vis-à-vis the old ruling elite of Whites, but which concurrently and stridently asserts its adherence to a Western culture of neo-liberal economics and politics. Presumably, its ability to become super-rich is predicated precisely on its acceptance of the globalised world of the new capitalist world order. Africa seems to be an embarrassment to the new elite as it reminds them of those they would rather forget, their poorer relatives; although simultaneously it is seen as a place where fortunes can be made in extractive industries for example. The dominant South African discourse on Africa is thus undoubtedly neo-colonial in its essence. Blackness is only stressed vis-à-vis Whites, not in relation to other Africans. In fact, there has been a complete failure by the post-apartheid state to construct a nationalism which is firmly rooted in Africa. Even within South African academia, an Africanisation of the curriculum has, with few exceptions, not been forthcoming as in the Social Sciences and Humanities in particular, it is the West which provides the main intellectual reference point for cultural and intellectual discourse.

The third characteristic of the politics of fear is an ideology of indigeneity and nativism. The idea that South Africans are not quite Africans is complimented by the dominant perception that indigeneity is the only way to acquire resources, jobs, and all the other goodies and entitlements which should be reserved for native peoples only. This necessarily leads to a debate on who is more indigenous, and hence to nativism, the view that there is an essence of South Africanness which is to be found in 'natives'. Hence what follows from this conception is a stress on the native (e.g. as in the *Native Club*)[68] which itself leads to privileging the twin ideas of birth and phenotype ('race') as the essence of the indigenous, and hence as the basis for accumulation and legitimate private acquisition in the general interest. Nativism is an extremely dangerous ideology which legitimises the exclusion of minorities, differently conceived at different times, from access to whichever rights and entitlements happen to be of relevance. A letter to a weekly newspaper at the height of the pogroms (*Mail & Guardian*, May 16-22, 2008) argued that *Black Economic Empowerment* (BEE) deals should be restricted to the indigenous, by which the author meant that 'Indians' and 'Coloureds', being somehow less indigenous should be excluded. This stress on indigeneity, when it comes to access subsidised accumulation, is unfortunately a common way of arguing in the public sphere. In fact, historically, the only truly indigenous people in Southern Africa would be San speakers, all other groups having migrated from somewhere else at one time or another in history. Indigeneity, then, is never a historical fact or a natural one. It is always politically defined by those with power. The previous apartheid regime spent much intellectual time and effort trying to prove that there were no people living in South Africa before the White colonisers arrived, precisely in order to stress their autochthony and, hence, to exclude Africans from its conception of the nation. Most states on the African continent and elsewhere have done the same as they organised citizenship rights around political indigeneity after independence as Fanon acutely observed.

The post-apartheid state has continued to classify people according to apartheid groupings, ostensibly to measure the social progress of the 'previously disadvantaged' in the new post-apartheid society. This is a fundamental problem, as it contributes to the thinking of politics through the lenses of racial and national stereotypes which thus become 'naturalised'. In actual fact however, the way indigeneity is understood by power can change quite rapidly. Under apartheid, indigeneity was defined in racial terms and White immigrants were given citizenship rights soon after their arrival. In the 1990s, Basotho mineworkers were given temporary citizenship rights to vote in the 1994 elections and were later given the opportunity to apply for full permanent citizenship. Here, the rules of indigeneity were bent in order to provide citizenship rights on the basis of the place of labour. A strong case can thus be made that it is labour, rather than indigeneity which must constitute the basis for rights in Africa (Mamdani, 1991). Only in this way, it seems, will migrants, who change their place of residence in order to work, have equal rights with everyone else. Citizenship must thus be prised away from statist conceptions of indigeneity for it to acquire a democratic content.

It is thus important to end this discussion through an assessment, however brief, of the alternative anti-xenophobic politics evidenced during and soon after the events. It would be a major mistake not to submit them to a level of critical scrutiny, for it may be possible to ascertain therein, possible alternatives to state understandings of citizenship rights and democracy on the one hand and to nativist nationalism on the other.

In a thoughtful piece, Landau (2008) has tried to make sense of the middle class civil society response to the xenophobic pogroms of May which took the form of the charitable provision of basic living resources (foodstuff, blankets, baby food, etc) for the displaced in large amounts, and culminated in a demonstration of condemnation of xenophobia in Johannesburg on May 24th. This was taking place while government and ANC officials were telling people in townships that 'the ANC's message was for everyone to work with the police' and to 'form street committees and organise themselves' (*Business Day*, May 26th 2008). Given what we now know about the reasons for the pogroms, these statements were at best useless, and at worst were adding fuel to the fire. Landau's assessment of the middle class response is that while murder and forced removals are daily occurrences in the country, it requires sustained political engagement and critique to develop political alternatives. Many middle class people do not have the time to engage in politics or fear the reactions of the state. But furthermore he asserts, given the minority character of the White and Indian middle classes in particular, who feel excluded from the new South African nation in many ways, nativism:

> while it may not immediately threaten middle class lives, ... threatens their position in a future South African society. Coupled with anxieties over Zuma, and Zimbabwe just up the road, few need to be reminded of what can happen if xenophobic nativism migrates from the streets into mainstream policy. For many, condemning the violence is one way that an economically powerful political minority can protest that possibility, defending tolerance to migrants already in the country becomes a proxy claim for themselves in a diverse South Africa (Landau 2008: 4)

There is no doubt that these comments make sense, yet it should perhaps be stated that the daily passivity of people turning a blind eye to the multiple expressions of exceptionalism and xenophobic culture in South Africa can understandably be greeted with cynicism. It has been precisely the 'doing nothing' of the middle classes until it was too late, which has enabled the rise to power of historically various forms of nativism from Nazism in inter-war Germany to Hindu fundamentalism in present day India (See Arundathi Roy, 2008). Clearly, the horrific pictures on TV including that of a man set alight by the mob, galvanised humanitarian sensibilities. However, such images depicting suffering 'do not function as a conduit for reasoned understanding, but rather act empathetically as channels for heightened emotion and pathos' (Millar, 2009). The resulting humanitarian outburst could assuage the middle class conscience, but politically it could only treat people as victims. Thus, it could not form the basis of an alternative to state political subjectivity.[69]

Much more interesting and potentially more important is the experience of anti-xenophobic activity within urban poor communities themselves. Two qualitatively different responses were observable here. The first was a reaction along the lines of that already noted when common interests between those deemed to be local and outside migrants enabled communities to challenge successfully attempts to divide them along indigenous/non-indigenous lines. One such incident was reported in the *Natal Witness* on October 29th 2008. The paper reported that in Howick West, near Pietermaritzburg in Kwazulu-Natal, local men and women vented their anger at the police for arresting more than 30 foreign migrants whose immigration documents had apparently expired. Apparently most of the migrants worked for a local shoe factory and for local residents, meaning that they had successfully shown that they were engaging in labour along with other community members for the benefit of the community. One of the locals was heard to shout at the police:

> Howick is full of crime committed by South Africans, but you are wasting your energy and government resources arresting people who do honest jobs to support their children.

We have here the assertion that rights must be based on the place of labour, a point which I have already made at some length. It is this simple observation which provides the basis for a completely new conception of citizenship in a country which after all, is made up of people who migrated over many years in different waves, precisely to work and in doing so built a nation, as in fact used to be recognised during the struggle for liberation itself. Without in some way or other recognizing this contribution and re-assessing the whole basis of citizenship, there seems little way of providing a politically valid alternative to indigeneity and nativist ideologies.

Perhaps, the most sophisticated response to the xenophobic pogroms came in a statement from Abahlali baseMjondolo, an organisation of shack-dwellers located principally in Durban. Not only was this statement politically sophisticated, it did not tell people simply to 'first help the police root out criminals' as did the trade union NUMSA,[70] but it also emanated from an independent organisation of the poor themselves, thus having even more legitimacy. Here, the statement showed the development of a democratic alternative politics to those of the state founded on one simple axiom: 'An action can be illegal. A person cannot be illegal. A person is a person where ever they may find themselves' (AbM 2008: 1). The statement argued that while xenophobia was widespread throughout the country, the violence occurred in Alexandra because of a poverty which has been induced by the state which threatened people's hold on the land. They continued by pointing out how their members who happened to be foreigners have been coerced and oppressed by police, Home Affairs and the employees of Lindela; how politicians, police and the media have constantly talked about 'illegal immigrants' as if migrants were all criminals. They also stressed, what few have done, that South African companies and often the government have been treating the rest of Africa with contempt, and that 'they must also be held responsible' (ibid.: 2). The statement throughout tried to make people understand that they could not blame foreign nationals for their plight but that the culprits are to be found elsewhere. In doing so, it developed a truly democratic conception of citizenship. They then ended with an assertion of their capacity to think for themselves which is worth quoting in full:

> We hear that the political analysts are saying that the poor must be educated about xenophobia. Always the solution is to 'educate the poor'. When we get cholera we must be educated about washing our hands when in fact we need clean water. When we get burnt we must be educated about fire when in fact we need electricity. This is just a way of blaming the poor for our suffering. We want land and housing in the cities, we want to go to university, we want water and electricity – we don't want to be educated to be good at surviving poverty on our own … it is time to ask serious questions about why it is that money and rich people can move freely around the world while everywhere the poor must confront razor wire, corrupt and violent police, queues and relocation or deportation … Some of us are taken to transit camps and some of us are taken to Lindela. The destinations might be different but it is the same kind of oppression. Let us all educate ourselves on these questions so that we can all take action. (ibid.: 3-4).

This statement speaks for itself and its level of sophistication is such that it can teach most intellectuals, let alone those in government how to think through the issue of xenophobia.   The issue here is not one of condemning or recommending but a straightforward statement is produced regarding the kind of subjectivity necessary to begin to understand and confront the problem.   Together with an understanding of an insistence that rights should be founded on place of labour, this statement can provide the basis of a politics of peace if this can acquire a broad organisation form.   It should also be stated that AbM did not restrict themselves to issuing a statement, but that their practice of treating everyone the same in their communities and their systematic involvement in patrolling communities at night during the pogroms were able to ensure that there were no xenophobic attacks in areas where they had an organisational presence in Durban.

Concluding Remarks

We are now in a position to conclude.   There is already a name for the kind of political activity which we witnessed during a few weeks in May: *the politics of (ethnic) cleansing*, made infamous in the ex-Yugoslavia of the 1990s and then repeated in several parts of the African continent (Rwanda and, more recently, Kenya being the most infamous).   The notion of 'cleansing' with all its dehumanising connotations of dirt and purification is a common *leitmotif* of all these politics irrespective of their historical specificities. The term was also invoked in the recent South African pogroms by perpetrators.   It should be clear that this violent 'cleansing' is the consequence of a politics of fear, which can easily tip over into a politics of war against those who are seen to be different for whatever reason.   To counter these politics, an active politics of peace is necessary, but for this to develop, we need first to understand the politics of fear which prevails in South Africa today.   I have argued that this politics of fear has at least three major components: a state discourse of xenophobia, a discourse of South African exceptionalism and a conception of citizenship founded on indigeneity. All three of these components need to be confronted and to be confronted politically. It is not enough to make statements deploring violence and to make recommendations to state agencies. It is certainly totally inopportune to call for more controls of the border.

South African politics has been characterised since liberation by a contradiction between democracy and rights on the one hand and the redressing of national grievances on the other. While a human rights culture has been introduced to which the state is being held to more or less successfully by the media and organisations of civil society, there is on the other hand a strong justifiable belief, that the majority has been cheated of the promises of liberation. In particular, the new Black elite is clamouring for greater access to the capital of their White counterparts, and for an end to the dominance of White capital. The Black urban poor on the other hand feel cheated because of the continued and even increased levels of poverty and unemployment which they daily have to face. It would be a total catastrophe for the country if these two classes were to find common cause around a nativist conception of nationalism expressed by (a series of) populist politicians. The outcome would not only be a threat to democratic gains but to the whole fabric of society, very much along the lines of what has been happening in Zimbabwe. There is already evidence that this is happening to some extent in the nationalist threats to the judiciary. A way has to be found to construct an alternative to both the state 'democratic' and state 'nationalist' manner of addressing this problem. The national demands for jobs and housing (not to forget land which has not been seriously addressed at all) are legitimate demands by the poor. Not to take the poor seriously not only undermines their rights, but also fails to satisfy their national concerns. In this context it makes sense to re-think Black Economic Empowerment to be directed primarily towards the eradication of poverty through the encouragement and funding of co-operatives for example. The old co-operativist traditions of the continent (the example of Tanzania in the late 1960s comes particularly to mind) have to be urgently re-discovered.

Indeed, the state could begin to provide conditions for addressing democratically the problem of populist nativism and it could do this by taking a few drastic steps such as first providing reparations to the frontline states (in the form of untied development aid for example) for their sacrifices during the struggle against apartheid a proposal first put forward it seems on June 3rd (Cape Times June 18th, 2008); it could then begin by providing papers for all in the country, to begin with on a temporary basis until all can be regularised according to their employment. It should close down the Lindela detention centre and enforce both a rational processing of applications and a decriminalisation of migration; along with this it could change the law where necessary, and take seriously the SADC protocol on the free movement of persons. Yet to force the state to do this requires major changes in society itself. The struggle against nativism requires a re-thinking of an inclusive South African nationalism and a greater focus on the fact that we are part of Africa in all ways. The arrogance of exceptionalism must be shed before any of this stands the chance of success. Of course all of this is a tall order and cannot take place overnight. It requires patient and long term political work over a long period. Yet, this is not a reason for not starting now. While the state and the middle class can provide a shift in public discourse, this cannot be effected without a systematically new politics in urban (and rural) communities.

Two types of responses to the xenophobic violence of May 2008 from within poor communities have been briefly examined here. In both cases, it was a political subjective difference which avoided and actually stood up against xenophobic violence. There was a conscious decision to resist hegemonic ideologies and practices. Here we find the alternative to both democracy/rights and to state nationalism/nativism. Since the 1990s, an independent popular politics, independent that is from state subjectivity, political parties, corporatist unions, etc. has struggled to manifest itself. It is gradually emerging at the margins of 'civil society' among some shack-dwellers organisations which have kept themselves apart from the politics of civil society and the thinking of NGOs and movements which see their existence simply in relation to the state, as so-called 'watchdogs' or whatever (Neocosmos, 2007). For this new politics, it is not a matter of constructing people as victims, of raising awareness about their suffering as NGOs do, but of confronting directly, of addressing clearly through political activity, the currently oppressive relations between state institutions and the poor. It is not therefore a matter of appealing to the state to provide comfort in whatever form, nor of calling for the formation yet again of a 'vanguard party of the working class' whose main concern is precisely to engage in state politics, but of asserting a new politics which the state must be forced to recognise. By asserting themselves outside state political thinking and by outlining the problems so clearly, the poor of AbM are thus attempting to restructure relations between state and people, reconfiguring democracy so as to give the nation a new content. A nation worthy of the name – a truly *political* community - can only be imagined and constructed on the basis of respect for the other; social justice cannot be bought at the expense of the oppression of others (foreigners, ethnic groups, women, children or whoever).

This constitutes the beginnings of a new conception of politics, one which takes seriously the axiom of the *Freedom Charter* that: 'South Africa belongs to *all* who live in it' (*emphasis added*). There is no guarantee that such a politics will be sustained over time, but it does seem as though, for the moment, it enables us to think a way forward. This is clearly a long term project, yet, however fragile, it is the only one in existence at present which makes an attempt to provide a viable answer to both state democratic-liberalism and state nativist-nationalism. It is worth taking seriously. What is abundantly clear is that in the absence of a concerted attempt to develop a politics of peace based on an axiom of equality along the lines of the one outlined by AbM according to which all count the same and all must be treated the same, then the likelihood is that more communal violence, more inter-ethnic violence and more incidents of xenophobic violence will be experienced. This is quite predictable. It is up to all thinking people to begin to act now to stop it.

Notes

1. The best source of empirical data on xenophobia by far is the Southern African Migration Project (SAMP) under Jonathan Crush at Queens University Canada (http://www.queensu.ca/samp/).

2. Another developing ideology of exceptionalism is the one propagated in religious terms by Desmond Tutu *inter alia* according to which the world is praising South Africa for its successful reconciliation between 'races'(which in fact was primarily a reconciliation among elites). This argument fits well within a constant celebration of South African democracy and its constitution, and not only contributes to a national sense of superiority, but also undermines a critical and objective assessment of this 'democracy' which is structurally limited by its liberalism. Of course it may be useful to recall the Christian basis of Human Rights Discourse as for both all men are equal before the Law/State/God.

3. A more apt title would have been: The Sociology of the Algerian Revolution, the original French title is *L'an V de la Revolution Algerienne*.

4. Commenting on post-colonial Africa, Mamdani (1991: 244) asks rhetorically: 'What is the connection between cross-border migrants and refugees? That while both are either an actual or a potential source of cheap labour, both share that status of "non-citizens", a status tantamount to being without rights under the law'.

5. Mamdani's argument regarding the political identities in Africa is not without its problems. I have argued at some length elsewhere (Neocosmos 2003) that it is in fact overwhelmingly state-centred.

6. These were the so-called TBVC (Transkei, Bophutatswana, Venda and Ciskei) states. The BLS countries refer to Botswana, Lesotho and Swaziland.

7. On the attempts by the apartheid state to regulate urbanisation through legislation see Hindson (1987).

8. 'Section 10 rights' referred to the appropriate section of the Urban Areas Act of 1952 which conferred urban residence on its holder. It was enacted by the state under pressure due to shortage of skilled labour, to enable the urbanisation of skilled labour primarily for the manufacturing sector of the economy. For details see Hindson 1987.

9. Resistance took many different forms and combinations of forms and not just trade unionism. So-called 'millenarian' movements, the setting up of African churches, women's movements were all different forms of resistance to local and colonial state coercion. See Beinart and Bundy (1980:276-98) for examples of these movements in the Transkei. For peasant movements in other parts of South Africa see in particular Hirson (1989: chapter 10), Delius (1990), Chaskalson (1987), Beinart and Bundy (1987). For a review of the literature on peasant movements in Africa as a whole (including Southern Africa) see Isaacman (1990).

10. See Lacey (1981: chapter 3) and Mamdani (1996:chapter 3) in particular. It is important to stress the absolutely fundamentally different conceptions on the 'native problem' held by

the colonial state in Southern Africa during the 1920s and 30s, from the views it held during an earlier period. For the 1932 Native Economic Commission for example, the basic idea was to strengthen an authoritarian form of 'tradition'; for the South African Native Affairs Commission Report of 1903-1905 on the other hand, the idea was to let tradition gradually fade away (even to help it in that direction), thus: 'the abolition of the tribal system and chieftainship is being left to time and evolution towards civilisation, assisted by legislation where necessary and administrative methods' (p.42).

11. This statement should not be read as an idealisation of the ICU. The organisation was dominated by populist rhetoric and was riven with internal contradictions under the weight of which it eventually collapsed (Bradford 1987). Nevertheless, for the first time in South Africa, it succeeded in giving expression to the widespread nation-wide griev-ances of the rural oppressed (in particular) throughout the country, thus enabling the development of a mass country-wide social movement. By the 1930s, after segregation was firmly entrenched, such a 'pan-ethnic' social movement became no longer possible in rural areas.

12. Evidence shows that in Natal as elsewhere, the bourgeoisie's conception of tradition was challenged; see McClendon (1992) for example.

13. In 1984 South Africa sent home tens of thousands of Mozambican miners as punish-ment for Samora Machel's support for the ANC. The exception to the migrant-depend-ency rule is Malawi which deliberately embarked on migrant reduction policy in the late 1970s.

14. Lesotho Bureau of Statistics Household Budget Survey (1987). This does not rule out a possibility of rapid accumulation by some sections of the worker-peasantry on the basis of migrant remittances and other means of resource mobilisation, as noted by Pae (1992) in the highlands of Lesotho.

15. The single major exception to this trend was the work of First (1983) on Mozambique. First's analysis of the peasantry in Southern Mozambique recognised differentiation between poor and middle peasants and understood that the proceeds of migrant la-bour contributed to the reproduction of middle peasant production. However the economic and political consequences of this insight did not find their way into the literature in any major way. For a detailed analysis of this literature see Neocosmos, 1993a.

16. Although Wolpe's work was by far the most sophisticated theoretically, a whole body of literature developed around this mode of thinking. In actual fact the economic reductionism of this perspective was one which was also held by the liberal theorists which it opposed. See for example Lipton (1986). In fact debates between liberals and Marxist perspectives were undertaken on the basis of the common assumption that apartheid was in fact primarily about labour control and the restriction of the move-ment of labour. It was only with Mamdani's work as noted that apartheid could begin to be thought of in political terms.

17. The exceptions here were Marxist analyses of the apartheid state by O'Meara (1983) and Wolpe (1988) as well as the recent work of Evans (2003).

18. This position was adhered to by the NUM in particular, an organisation which organises mineworkers – i.e. overwhelmingly migrant labour – and which has still to confront periodic 'ethnic clashes' on the mines.

19. The following section relies on the work presented in Neocosmoc, 1998.

20. For greater detail see Lodge op cit.: 135-139, Seekings 1989; and also UDF 1986: 35-41. See also Marx 1992, Seekings 2000, Van Kessel, 2000.

21. It is interesting to note here the distance between these popular methods to hold leaders accountable and those contained in the utterances of returning exiles such as 'leadership codes'; see for example the interview with Joe Slovo in *New Era* (vol. 5, no. 1, March 1990: 35-40). The Chinese wall between popular practices and the isolated exiles is here clearly exposed. There is also evidence that at the first ANC national consultative conference inside the country, there was 'tension between the patrician style of the previously jailed and exiled leaders of the 1950s and the activists who [had] developed constituencies during the 1980s; the former were accused of ignoring the principles of mandate and accountability which had developed inside the country' (Friedman 1992: 85).

22. A similar process was debated at length in relation to the 'Indian community' and the formation of the Transvaal Indian Congress, but interestingly enough not in relation to 'Coloureds', although the UDF's non-racialism was criticised as phoney by various coloured organisations such as the Unity Movement and the Cape Action League for example.

23. At the other end of the continent, see also Rachik 2000:37 on the case of Morocco.

24. The expression Black (n.b., not 'African') Economic Empowerment is itself significant as it shows that national distinctions are equated with racial ones. Of course official statistics are still gathered in racial categories enabling the reproduction of racial distinctions as well as making it possible for a racial language to continue, although now this is justified in terms of 'redressing the inequalities of the past'.

25. A 1996 article which reviewed the progress of corporatism with reference to NEDLAC (the National Economic, Development and Labour Council - the successor to the National Economic Forum) in particular, correctly predicted that 'there is a strong danger that the incorporation of "community groups" into Nedlac or other forums will serve not to empower civil society but to bureaucratise it' (Friedman and Reitzes 1996:66).

26. Incidentally it may be important to point out that Davies and Head's linear speculations were not borne out by facts in subsequent years. Between 1990 and 2000 there has been consistent downsizing in the mine workforce but this has affected South African miners more than foreign workers (Crush et al., 2001, SAMP, Migration Policy Brief No 10, p.7).

27. For Davies and Head, 'the migrant labour system has long been criticised as both exploitative and an impediment to growth and development in "labour reserve" areas' (op cit.: 448). While the first assertion is arguably true (although the original formulation from the 1970s that migrant labour was 'super-exploited' was more accurate as it was paid below value), the latter is certainly not so. The wages which peasants earn from migrating enable them not only to survive but also to reproduce themselves as petty commodity producers as well as to accumulate (see First 1983, Neocosmos 1987, 1993a, 1993b, Johnston, 1996). It seems sad to have to repeat what has been established over

ten years ago now, but the migrant peasantry in the 'labour reserve areas' is not uniformly impoverished but rather differentiated.

28. The available evidence regarding the investments in which such deferred pay was put shows that these were mainly unproductive (for example, real estate and merchant activity) while it is reputed to have fuelled corruption among state officials. The Lesotho state has made no effort to control the emigration of skilled professionals from the country to South Africa. Although detailed figures are not available, circumstantial evidence suggests that numbers must be relatively high among teachers, professionals and high ranking civil servants in the country. Dual citizenship is in theory illegal in Lesotho, yet it is common among members of the elite.

29. This a translation of the French concept 'les gens de partout' advocated by the political journal *La Distance Politique*. See Wamba-dia-Wamba (1994) for an explication of this idea.

30. Although the Bill of Rights (Chapter 2 of the South African Constitution) [s20] states says that 'no citizen may be deprived of citizenship', the citizenship act of 1995 (Chapter 3 s8-10) details a number of instances under which such deprivation may occur including, for naturalised citizens, when 'the Minister [of Home Affairs] is satisfied that it is in the public interest that such a citizen shall cease to be a South Africa citizen'. The Citizenship Amendment Act of 2004 did not repeal the section cited above. This section could be unconstitutional.

31. http://wwwserver.law.wits.ac.za/listserv/archives/saimmigold/msg00657.html p.2.

32. See http://www.oneworld.org/ips2/mar98/21_05_093.html p.1.

33. http://www.dispatch.co.za/1999/08/14/southafrica/parly2.HTM.

34. One of the most notorious was that by Joe Modise, at the time Defence Minister in the first post-apartheid government who said: 'if we are not coping with the influx of illegal immigrants and our people are being threatened, there will come a time when we will switch on the fence (the electric fence on the Mozambican border) to lethal mode' (The Star, 6 May 1997).

35. http://www.queensu.ca/samp/migrationresources/xenophobia/responses/anc.htm.

36. See http://www.queensu.ca/samp/migrationnews/2000/mar.htm, p.2.

37. In fact a number of Human Rights NGOs were 'criticised by government officials, ministers, the police and various political parties for this stand, which was represented as "interfering" with legal processes, supportive of crime and unpatriotic' (Harris 2001: 55).

38. See http://www.vukaplan.co.za/project2.htm.

39. The following account is taken from the *Mail and Guardian*, 29 October 2000.

40. See *Business Day* 29 October 2000 article by Vincent Williams of SAMP.

41. See http://mail.unwembi.co.za/pipermail/anctoday/2001/00020.html.

42. Without wishing to stretch the analogy too far, it could indeed be argued that this particular episode is not all that different from the case of Radio Milles Collines which incited (often in coded language) the murder of Tutsi by Hutu in Rwanda in 1994.

43. Interviews were carried out in March-April 2003 and again in July-August 2003 with respondents, usually from West Africa (both Anglophone and Francophone) in Sunnyside, Pretoria and Braamfontein, Johannesburg. In total, thirty four in-depth interviews were conducted; the evidence gathered corroborated the narratives gathered by other more detailed projects by the CSVR, HRW and SAHRC. *inter alia.*

44. Presumably this means that the whiter one is the more likely one is to be South African; the essence of South Africanness then being 'whiteness'. This corresponds in all respects to the idea of South African exceptionalism pointed out by Mamdani, according to which the essence of South Africa in hegemonic discourse is the world the settlers made. I am grateful to Jonathan Mafukidze for reminding me of this point.

45. In fact this is an underestimate as the 30 day detention refers to continuous detention not necessarily at the same facility and many people have already been detained in prisons and police stations for considerable amounts of time before arriving at Lindela.

46. In fact the terms are constantly used jointly despite the fact that the overwhelming majority of migrants in the country enter legally - see McDonald et al., (1998: 14).

47. I mean this in the sense of the 'making of tradition' along the lines argued by Ranger (1985) and Vail (1989) on ethnicity in Southern Africa.

48. Wallerstein (1995) shows that both conservative and socialist strategies in nineteenth century Europe gradually came close, from different starting points, 'to the liberal notion of ongoing, [state-] managed, rational normal change' (p.96). He also notes that between 1848 and 1914, 'the practitioners of all three ideologies turned from a theoretical anti-state position to one of seeking to strengthen and reinforce in practice the state structures in multiple ways'. Later, conservatives were transformed into liberal-conservatives, while Leninists were transformed into liberal-socialists; he argues that the first break in the liberal consensus at the global level occurred in 1968 (pp. 97, 103).

49. For a brilliant critique of human rights and the conception of ethics which underpins them see Badiou (2001).

50. The reasons for this 'oversight' were both theoretical and political, as inclusion of the working class into politics and civil society was generally equated with the attainment of legal status by socialist and later by communist parties - politics tended to be equated with state politics, and institution substituted for class. Such legalisation, of course, went along with the acceptance of the 'rules of the liberal game' by such parties, from which it was only a short step to turning fully into state institutions. It is in this sense of an absence of working class political representation that one must understand Marx's reference to the working class as 'a class in civil society that is not a class of civil society' (Marx 1844: 127). As is well known, the main working class struggles in nineteenth century Europe were largely concerned with the establishment of independent working class representation in politics.

51. This is why the much publicised anti-corruption drive of the Director General of Home Affairs Barry Gilder was not straightforwardly progressive. His main effort seems to have been directed towards stopping the provision of passports for organised crime syndicates rather than the petty corruption affecting migrants anyway (see for example *Pretoria News*, 6 November, 2003); appointed in July 2003, by early 2005 he was no longer in his job.

52. The General Assembly of the United Nations adopted resolution 3068 on 30 November 1973 which was the culmination of a series of resolutions declaring apartheid to be a 'crime against humanity' (Coleman 1998: 2).

53. 'The public' as an entity to which state institutions constantly refer to justify their actions and practices, is a product of state politics, and exists in a 'public sphere' as an outcome of state-society relations. It would be important to study the formation of 'the public' in depth, as its production differs in different contexts.

54. The main slogan of the United Democratic Front, the main popular organisation in the 1980s was: 'UDF Unites, Apartheid Divides'.

55. It is worth noting Saint-Just's remark that: 'the origins of the subjugation of peoples is to be found in the complex power of governments', evidently very little has changed since (op cit.: 537). It is also interesting to note Saint-Just's speculations that governments were able to do this when people 'lost their taste' for assemblies and meetings, i.e. for politics.

56. See the judgement of the Constitutional Court Khosa and Others v Minister of Social Development, CCT 12/03 in which the Court held that the 'constitution vests the right to social security in "everyone" and that permanent residents are bearers of this right' (Media Summary, 2004). It should perhaps also be noted that this was not a unanimous judgment and that two judges dissented from the majority view.

57. One of the aspects of this absence of politics outside state politics is precisely the replacement of the banning of books by self-censorship rightly noted by Es'kia Mphahlele above. The net result of each kind of restriction on thought is similar, although the latter is a much more subtle process of censorship as it gives the impression of 'freedom', of not being oppressive (the 'choice' to simply do nothing as all is being taken care of by power); it is this latter process which is typical of liberalism and Human Rights Discourse.

58. In France, it is the political organisation of Alain Badiou, L'Organisation Politique which has provided the most important political thinking on the 'sans papiers' (undocumented immigrants) from Africa. See the website of the organisation http://www.organisationpolitique.com as well as its publications such as *La Distance politique* and *Le Journal politique*.

59. During the raid, police told refugees that they were holding invalid 'Mbeki papers' as Zuma was now heading the ANC (Misago et al. 2009: 29). As recently as March 14th 2009, the *Citizen* newspaper reported that the MEC for Local Government in Gauteng was publicly stating that Zimbabwean refugees should not be permitted to stay in the church (a haven for them over the past 2 years) which is filled to capacity, with an additional 2000 Zimbabweans living on the streets in its vicinity. Of course such statements if not tempered contribute to providing a picture of illegality which then legitimise police attacks.

60. Address of the President of South Africa, Thabo Mbeki, at the National tribute in Remembrance of the Victims of Attacks on Foreign nationals, Tshwane July 3rd 2008.

    http://www.queensu.ca/samp/migrationresources/xenophobia/#press

61. See for example *Pretoria News* May 15th, *Mail & Guardian* May 30th- June 5th 2008, *Sapa* 28th May, *Mail & Guardian* May 31st.

62. Drucilla Cornell, Mahmood Mamdani and Sampie Terreblanche, *CapeTtimes*, May 28th 2008, see also *Pambazuka News* June 3rd 2008. See www.pambazuka.org/en

63. According to Misago et al, (2008: 29), some respondents expressed the hope that unlike the Mbeki leadership, the new ANC leadership would help to rid the community of foreigners.

64. According to the authors of SAMP (2008: 17), the HSRC has a history of providing scientific legitimacy to the idea that South Africa was being "swamped" by the poor and desperate of Africa.

65. http://www.pambazuka.org/en/category/refugees/48467

66. This is the case even though for example these rights may be perfectly legitimate in law, such as the right to housing or the right to work, or the right to land, or the right to safety, or even the right to life, etc.

67. See the comment in Hassim et al. 2008: 17. Apparently two months before the pogroms, women in the Anti-Privatisation Forum had protested against foreigners whom they saw as bribing themselves into government housing.

68. In its own words: "The Native Club was established three years ago with the primary objective to provide a platform for dialogue on ideas, philosophies, values and knowledge that reflect the indigenous identity of the South African nation". Ex-president Mbeki was instrumental in the establishment of this organisation which is particularly supported by the new Black middle class.

69. The setting up of a *Coalition Against Xenophobia* (CAX) was also part of the civil society reaction to the events. The coalition of civil society groups has found it difficult to sustain a campaign against xenophobia and has so far only organized a 'picket' of the Lindela detention centre rightly demanding its closure. It is not at all clear however, that the language and politics of protest groups derived from politics at the point of production are always appropriate in the present context. NGOs are very adept at raising awareness, they have very little capacity to confront oppression and force the state to make concessions. This rather requires the thinking of a different kind of politics.

70. The National Union of Metalworkers of South Africa. See Numsa leaflet on Xenophobia issued by NUMSA PO Box 260483 Excom 2023; May 20, 2008.

Bibliography

Abahlali baseMjondolo 2008, 'Statement on the Xenophobic Attacks in Johannesburg' Wednesday May 21st. http://abahlali.org

Abrahamsson, H. and Nilsson, A., 1995, *Mozambique, the Troubled Transition: from Socialist Construction to Free-market Capitalism*, London: Zed Books.

Adelzadeh, A. and Padayashee, V., 1994, 'The RDP White Paper: Reconstruction of a Development Vision', *Transformation*, no. 25.

African National Congress (ANC), 1969, Strategy and Tactics of the African National Congress, adopted at the 1969 Morogoro Conference, Tanzania.

African National Congress, 1994, *The Reconstruction and Development Programme*, Johannesburg: Umanyano Publications.

African National Congress, 2001a, 'ANC Policy on Xenophobia, Xenophobia: Intolerance Towards Fellow Africans must be Tackled', *ANC Today*, Vol. 1, No. 31 August.

African National Congress, 2001b, 'Zandspruit Attacks', ANC Today, Vol. 1, No. 40, 26 October.

Amisi, B. and Ballard, R., 2005, 'In the Absence of Citizenship: Congolese Refugee Struggle and Organisation in South Africa', A case study for the UKZN Project entitled: Globalisation, Marginalisation and New Social Movements in post-Apartheid South Africa, University of Kwazulu-Natal.

Alexander, J., 1993, 'Things Fall Apart, The Centre Can Hold: Processes of Postwar Political Change in Zimbabwe's Rural Areas' in Lauridsen, L. S., ed., *Bringing Institutions Back In - The Role of Institutions in Civil Society, State and Economy*, Roskilde University, International Development Studies, Occasional Paper No.8.

Althusser, L., 1971, 'Ideology and Ideological State Apparatuses' in L. Althusser, *Lenin and Philosophy and Other Essays*, London: New Left Books.

Arrighi, G. and J. Saul, 1973, Nationalism and Revolution in Sub-Saharan Africa', in Arrighi, G. and J. Saul, eds., *Essays in the Political Economy of Africa*, New York: Monthly Review Press.

Badiou, A., 1985, *Peut-on penser la politique?* Paris: Seuil.

Badiou, A., 1998a, *Abrégé de métapolitique*, Paris: Seuil.

Badiou, A., 1998b, *D'un désastre obscur: sur la fin de la vérité d'état*, Paris: éditions de l'aube.

Badiou, A., 2007, De Quoi Sarkozy est-il Nom?, lignes.

Baskin, J., 1982, 'Growth of a New Worker Organ: The Germiston Shop Stewards' Council', *South African Labour Bulletin*, Vol. 7, No. 6, April.

Baskin, J., ed., 1996, Against the Current: Labour and Economic Policy in South Africa, Johannesburg: Ravan Press.

Beinart, W. and C. Bundy, 1980, 'State Intervention and Rural Resistance: the Transkei, 1900-1965', in M. A. Klein, ed., Peasants in Africa, Beverly Hills: Sage.

Beinart, W. and C. Bundy, 1987, Hidden Struggles in Rural South Africa, London: James Currey.

Bensaïd, D., 2005, 'La Revolution Francaise Refoulée', Manière de Voir, 82, August-September.

Bond, P., 2000, Elite Transition: from apartheid to neoliberalism in South Africa, London: Pluto Press, Pietermaritzburg: University of Natal Press.

Bradford, H., 1987, A Taste of Freedom, the ICU in Rural South Africa, 1924-1930, New Haven: Yale University Press.

Bundy, C., 1988, The Rise and Fall of the South African Peasantry, London: James Currey.

Canguilhem, G., 1991, The Normal and the Pathological, New York: Zone Books.

Central Bank of Lesotho, 1993, Annual Report 1992, Maseru: Central Bank of Lesotho.

Central Bank of Lesotho, 1995, Survey of Migrant Workers Attitudes to Permanent Residence in RSA, Maseru: September.

Chaskalson, M., 1987, 'Rural Resistance in the 1940s and 1950s', Africa Perspective, New Series Vol. 5 & 6 December.

Chatterjee, P., 2004, The Politics of the Governed: Reflections on Popular Politics in Most of the World, New York: Columbia University Press.

Cohen, S., 2001, States of Denial, Cambridge: Polity Press.

Coleman, M., 1998, A Crime Against Humanity: Analysing the Repression of the Apartheid State, Cape Town: David Philip.

Collins, D., 1994, 'Worker Control', South African Labour Bulletin, vol. 18, No. 3, July.

Comaroff, J. and Comaroff, J., 2001, 'Naturing the Nation: Aliens, Apocalypse and the Postcolonial State', Journal of Southern African Studies, Vol. 27, No. 3, September.

Constitutional Assembly, 1996, Constitution of the Republic of South Africa as adopted by the Constitutional Assembly on 8 May 1996.

Constitutional Court (of South Africa), 2004, Khosa and Others v Minister of Social Development, Media Summary, CCT 12/03.

Coplan, D., 1994, In the Time of Cannibals: the word music of South Africa's Basotho migrants, Chicago: University Press.

Coplan, D. 2008, 'Crossing Borders' in S. Hassim et al. (eds.) Go Home or die Here: Violence, Xenophobia and the Reinvention of Difference in South Africa, Johannesburg: Wits University Press.

Coplan, D. and T. Thoahlane, 1995, 'Motherless Households, Landless Farms: employment patterns among Lesotho migrants', in Crush, J. and W. James, eds., 1995, Crossing Boundaries: mine migrancy in a democratic South Africa, IDASA/IDRC.

Cowen, M. and B. Shenton, 1996, Doctrines of Development, London: Routledge.

Crush, J., ed., 1998, *Beyond Control: Immigration and Human Rights in a Democratic South Africa*, Cape Town: IDASA/SAMP.

Crush, J., 1999, 'Fortress South Africa and the Deconstruction of Apartheid's Migration Regime', Geoforum, 30.

Crush et al., 2001, 'Undermining Labour: the Social Implications of Sub-contracting on the South African Gold Mines', *Journal of Southern African Studies*, Vol. 27, No. 1, March.

Crush, J. and James, W., 1991, 'Depopulating the Compounds: Migrant Labour and Mine Housing in South Africa', *World Development*, Vol. 19, No. 4.

Crush, J. and James, W., eds., 1995, *Crossing Boundaries: Mine Migrancy in a Democratic South Africa*, IDASA/IDRC.

Crush, J. and Pendleton, 2004, 'Regionalizing Xenophobia? Citizen Attitudes to Immigration and Refugee Policy in Southern Africa', *SAMP: Migration Policy Series* No. 30, http://www.queensu.ca/samp.

Crush, J. and Peberdy, S., n.d., 'Criminal Tendencies: Immigrants and Illegality in South Africa', *Migration Policy Brief*, No. 10, SAMP.

Danso, R. and McDonald, D., 2000, 'Writing Xenophobia: Immigration and the Press in Post-apartheid South Africa', *Migration Policy Series* No. 17, SAMP.

Davies, R. and Head, J., 1995, 'The Future of Mine Migrancy in the Context of Broader Trends in Migration in Southern Africa', *Journal of Southern African Studies*, vol. 21, No. 3.

Delius, P., 1990, 'Migrants, Comrades and Rural Revolt: Sekhukhuneland 1950-1987', *Transformation* No. 13.

De Vletter, F., 1985, 'Recent Trends and Prospects of Black Migration to South Africa', *Journal of Modern African Studies*, vol. 23, No. 4.

Edgar, Robert, 1983, *Prophets with Honour: A Documentary History of the Lekhotla la Bafo*, Johannesburg: Ravan Press.

Englund, H., 2004, 'Transnational Governance and the Pacification of Youth: The Contribution of Civic Education to Disempowerment in Malawi', *CCS Research Report* No. 13, Durban.

Erasmus, Z., 2005, 'Race and Identity in the Nation' in J. Daniel, R. Southall and J. Lutchman, eds, *State of the Nation, South Africa: 2004-2005*, Cape Town: HSRC.

Evans, I., 2003, 'Native Administration and the Transition from Segregation to Apartheid', in C. Crais, ed., *The Culture of Power in Southern Africa: Essays on State Formation and the Political Imagination*, Portsmouth: Heinemann.

Fanon, F., 1989, *Studies in a Dying Colonialism*, London: Earthscan.

Fanon, F, 1990, *The Wretched of the Earth*, London: Penguin.

First, R., 1983, *Black Gold*, Brighton: Harvester Press.

Forced Migration Studies Programme (FMSP) 2009, *Humanitarian Assistance to Internally Displaced Persons in South Africa: Lessons Learned Following Attacks on Foreign Nationals in May 2008*, FMSP, University of the Witwatersrand http://migration.org.za

Foucault, M., 2000, *Power: Essential Works of Foucault 1954-1984*, vol. 3, London: Penguin.

Friedman, S., 1992, 'Bonaparte at the Barricades: The Colonisation of Civil Society', Special Issue of *Theoria*, No 79, May, Atkinson, D., ed.

Friedman, S. and Reitzes, M., 1996, 'Democratisation or Bureaucratisation? Civil Society, the Public Sphere and the State in Post-apartheid South Africa', *Transformation* No. 29.

Fullard, M. and Rousseau, N., 2003, 'An Imperfect Past: the Truth and Reconciliation Commission in Transition', in J. Daniel, A. Habib, and R. Southall, eds., *State of the Nation, South Africa 2003-2004*, Cape Town: HSRC.

Gay, J., 1997, 'Riding the Tiger: Lesotho Miners and Attitudes to Permanent Residence in South Africa', SAMP *Policy Studies* No. 2, IDRC, Canada.

Geschiere P. and F. Nyamnjoh, 2000, 'Capitalism and Autochthony: The Seesaw of Mobility and Belonging', *Public Culture*, Vol. 12, No. 2.

Glaser, D., 2008, '(Dis)connections : Elite and Popular "Common Sense" on the Matter of Foreigners'" in S. Hassim et al. (op.cit.).

Gourevitch, P., 1998, *We Wish to Inform You That Tomorrow We Will be Killed with Our Families: Stories from Rwanda*, London: Picador.

Harber, A. 2008, 'Two Newspapers, Two Nations? The Media and the Xenophobic Violence' in S. Hassim et al., (op.cit.).

Harris, B., 2001, 'A Foreign Experience: Violence, Crime and Xenophobia During South Africa's Transition', Centre for the Study of Violence and Reconciliation, Violence and Transition Series, Vol. 5, August, http://www.csvr.org.za/papers/papvtp5.htm.

Hassim, S., 1999, 'From Presence to Power: Women's Citizenship in a New Democracy', *Agenda*, No. 40.

Hassim, S. et al. (eds.) 2008, *Go Home or Die Here: Violence, Xenophobia and the Reinvention of Difference in South Africa*, Johannesburg: Wits University Press.

Hindson, D, 1987, *Pass Controls and the Urban African Proletariat*, Johannesburg: Ravan.

Hirson, B., 1989, *Yours for the Union: Class and Community Struggles in South Africa, 1930-1947*, Johannesburg: University of the Witwatersrand Press.

Hornberger, J. 2008, "Policing Xenophobia – Xenophobic Policing: A Clash of Legitimacy" in S. Hassim et al., (op.cit.).

Human Rights Watch, 1998, '"Prohibited Persons": Abuse of Undocumented Migrants, Asylum Seekers, and Refugees in South Africa', New York: Human Rights Watch.

Human Sciences Research Council (HSRC) 2008, *Citizenship, Violence and Xenophobia in South Africa: Perceptions from South African Communities*, Democracy and Governance Research Programme, HSRC June.

Isaacman, A., 1990, 'Peasants and Rural Social Protest in Africa', *African Studies Review*, Vol. 33, No. 2.

James, W., 1997, Draft Green Paper on International Migration, Presented to the South African Minister of Home affairs, 13 May.

Johnston, D., 1996, 'The State and Development: An Analysis of Agricultural Policies in Lesotho, 1970-1993', *Journal of Southern African Studies*, Vol. 22, No. 1, March.

Keegan, T., 1988, *Facing the Storm: Portraits of Black Lives in Rural South Africa*, Cape Town and Johannesburg: David Philip.

Kimble, J., 1982, 'Labour Migration in Basutoland, c.1870-1885', in S. Marks and R. Rathbone, eds., *Industrialisation and Social Change in South Africa*, London: Longman Publishers.

Krenshaw, K., 2000, 'Were the Critics Right about Rights? Reassessing the American Debate About Rights in the Post-reform Era', in M. Mamdani, ed., *Beyond Rights Talk and Culture Talk*, Cape Town: David Philip.

Kriger, N., 1991, 'Popular Struggles in Zimbabwe's War of National Liberation', in P. Kaarsholm, ed., *Cultural Struggles and Development in Southern Africa*, London: James Currey.

Kriger, N., 1992, *Zimbabwe's Guerrilla War: Peasant Voices*, Cambridge: CUP.

Lacey, M., 1981, *Working for Boroko*, Johannesburg: Ravan.

Lambert, R., and Webster, E., 1988, 'The Re-emergence of Political Unionism in Contemporary South Africa', in Cobbett, W. and R. Cohen, eds., 1988.

Lan, D., 1985, *Guns and Rain: Guerillas and Spirit Mediums in Zimbabwe*, Harare: Zimbabwe Publishing House.

Landau. L. 2008, 'The Meaning of Living in South Africa: Violence, Condemnation and Community After 5-11' Migration Studies Working Paper Series # 39, FMSP, University of the Witwatersrand http://migration.org.za

Landau, L. and H. Haithar 2007, 'Somalis Are Easy Prey' *Mail and Guardian*, March 6th, 2007.

Landau, L. and V. Gindrey 2008, *Migration and Population Trends in Gauteng Province, 1996-2055*, Migration Studies Working Paper Series #42 Forced Migration Studies Program University of the Witwatersrand http://migration.org.za

Lawyers for Human Rights, 2004, Seminar on Regional Integration, Migration and Poverty, http://www.lhr.org.za/refugee/publics/sem0204.

Lazarus, S., 1996, *Anthropologie du Nom*, Paris: Seuil.

Legassick, M. and H. Wolpe, 1976, 'The Bantustans and Capital Accumulation in South Africa', *Review of African Political Economy*, no. 7.

Lesotho Bureau of Statistics, 1987, *Household Budget Survey 1987*, Maseru: Bureau of Statistics.

Levin, R. and M. Neocosmos, 1989, 'The Agrarian Question and Class Contradictions in South Africa: Some Theoretical Considerations', *Journal of Peasant Studies*, 16, 2 January.

Levin, R. and D. Weiner, 1994, 'Community Perspectives on Land and Agrarian Reform in South Africa', Final project report prepared for MacArthur Foundation, Chicago, Illinois.

Lipton, M., 1986, *Capitalism and Apartheid*, Cape Town: David Philip.

Lodge, T. et al., 1991, *All Here and Now: Black Politics in South Africa in the 1980s*, Cape Town: Ford Foundation, David Phillip.

Mamdani, M., 1987, 'Contradictory Class Perspectives on the Question of Democracy: the case of Uganda' in P. Anyang' Nyong'o, ed., *Popular Struggles for Democracy in Africa*, London: Zed Books.

Mamdani, M., 1991, 'Social Movements and Constitutionalism in the African Context', in I. Shivji, ed., *State and Constitutionalism: an African Debate on Democracy*, Harare: SAPES.

Mamdani, M., 1995, 'Democratic Theory and Democratic Struggles', in Chole, E. and Ibrahim, J., *Democratisation Processes in Africa: Problems and Prospects*, Dakar: CODESRIA.

Mamdani, M, 1996, *Citizen and Subject: Contemporary Africa and the Legacy of Late Colonialism*, London: James Currey.

Mamdani, M., 1998a, 'When Does a Settler Become a Native? Reflections on the Colonial Roots of Citizenship in Equatorial and South Africa', Text of Inaugural Lecture as A. C. Jordan Professor of African Studies, University of Cape Town, 13 May, New Series No. 208.

Mamdani, M., 1998b, 'Truth Seen Only Through Narrow Lenses', *The Star*, 16 December.

Mamdani, M., ed., 2000, *Beyond Rights Talk and Culture Talk,: Comparative Essays on the Politics of Rights and Culture*, Cape Town: David Philip.

Mamdani, M., 2001, *When Victims Become Killers: Colonialism, Nativism and the Genocide in Rwanda*, London: James Currey.

Mamdani, M., 2002, 'African States, Citizenship and War: a Case Study', *International Affairs*, Vol. 78, No. 3, July.

Marais, H., 1998, *South Africa, Limits to Change: the Political Economy of Transformation*, London: Zed Books, Cape Town: University of Cape Town Press.

Maré, G., 1983, 'Africans Under Apartheid in the 1980s', *South African Review*, 1, Johannesburg: Ravan.

Marks, S., 1986, *The Ambiguities of Dependence in South Africa: Class, Nationalism and the State in Twentieth Century Natal*, Johannesburg: Ravan.

Marks, S., 1989, 'Patriotism, Patriarchy and Purity: Natal and the Politics of Zulu Ethnic Consciousness', in *Vail*, L., ed., 1989.

Marshall, T. S., 1964, *Class, Citizenship and Social Development*, Chicago: The University of Chicago Press.

Mathiane, N., 1986, 'The Strange Feeling of Taking Control', *Frontline*, Vol. 6, No. 7.

Marx, A. W., 1992, *Lessons of Struggle: South African Internal Opposition, 1960-1990*, Cape Town: Oxford.

Marx, K., 1844, 'On the Jewish Question', *Marx and Engels Collected Works*, Vol. 3, London: Lawrence and Wishart.

Masuku, T., 2006, 'Targetting Foreigners: Xenophobia Among Johannesburg's Police' *Crime Quarterly*, Number 15.

Mattes, R. et al., 1999, 'Still Waiting for the Barbarians: SA Attitudes to Immigrants and Immigration', *Migration Policy* Series No. 14, SAMP.

Maxwell, D. J., 1993, 'Local Politics and the War of Liberation in North-east Zimbabwe', *Journal of Southern African Studies*, Vol.19, No. 3, September.

Mbeki, G., 1996, *Sunset at Midday*, Braamfontein: Nolwazi Educational Publishers.

Mbeki, T., 2001, 'Statement on Xenophobia', Letter from the President, *ANC Today*, Vol. 1, No. 18, 25 May.

McClendon, T. V., 1992, 'From Aboriginal to Zulu: Ethnicities, 'Customary Law' and the Natal Code in the Segregation Era', Paper presented to the conference on Ethnicity, Society and Conflict in Natal, University of Natal, Pietermaritzburg, 14-16 September.

McDonald, D., et al., 1998, 'Challenging Xenophobia: Myths and Realities About Cross-border Migration in Southern Africa', *Migration Policy* Series No.7, SAMP.

Millar, J. B. 2009, 'The Atrocity Exhibition' http://www.metamute.org/en/content/the_atrocity_exhibition

Misago, J. P. et al. 2009, *Towards Tolerance, Law and Dignity: Addressing Violence Against Foreign Nationals in South Africa*, IOM, DFID, FMSP, University of the Witwatersrand, February.

Morobe, M., 1987, 'Towards a People's Democracy: the UDF View', *Review of African Political Economy*, No. 40, December.

Morris, A., 1999, 'Race Relations and Racism in a Racially Diverse Inner City Neighbourhood: A Case Study of Hillbrow, Johannesburg', *Journal of Southern African Studies*, Vol. 25, No. 4, December.

Morris, M., 1979, 'The Development of Capitalism in South Africa', in M. Murray, ed., *South African Capitalism and Black Political Opposition*, Cambridge, Mass: Schenkman.

Murray, C., 1981, *Families Divided: The Impact of Migrant Labour in Lesotho*, Johannesburg: Ravan Press.

Naidoo, J., 1986, 'Building People's Power: A Working Class Perspective', Speech at Grassroots Conference, 5 April.

Neocosmos, M., 1987, 'Homogeneity and Differences on Swazi Nation Land', in Neocosmos, M., ed., *Social Relations in Rural Swaziland: Critical Analyses*, SSRU: UNISWA.

Neocosmos, M., 1993a, 'The Agrarian Question in Southern Africa and "Accumulation from Below": Economics and Politics in the Struggle for Democracy', Uppsala: Scandinavian Institute of African Studies.

Neocosmos, M., 1993b, 'Towards a Political Economy of Adjustment in a Labour Reserve Economy: The Case of Lesotho', in P. Gibbon, ed., *Social Change and Political Reform in Africa*, Uppsala: Nordic Africa Institute.

Neocosmos, M., 1995, 'Towards a History of Nationalities in Southern Africa', Working Paper 95. 6, Centre for Development Research, Copenhagen.

Neocosmos, M. and Selinyane, N., 1996, 'Labour Migration and Citizenship in Southern Africa: An Analytical Review' Paper presented at the seminar on Constitutionalism and Citizenship in Africa, NAI, Uppsala, Sweden and Institute of Diplomacy and International Studies, University of Nairobi, 13-16 December.

Neocosmos, M., 1998, 'From People's Politics to State Politics: Aspects of National Liberation in South Africa', in A. Olukoshi, ed., *The Politics of Opposition in Contemporary Africa*, Uppsala: NAI.

Neocosmos, M., 1999a, 'Intellectual Debates and Popular Struggles in Transitional South Africa: Political Discourse and the Origins of Statism', Seminar, Centre for African Studies, University of Cape Town, 21 April.

Neocosmos, M., 1999b, 'Strangers at the Cattle Post: State Nationalism and Migrant Identity in Post-apartheid South Africa', in Palmberg, M., ed., *National Identity and Democracy in Africa*, Cape Town: HSRC, Uppsala: NAI.

Neocosmos, M., 2003, 'The Contradictory Position of "Tradition" in African Nationalist Discourse: Some Analytical and Political Reflections', *Africa Development*, Vol. 28, Nos. 1 & 2.

Neocosmos, M., 2005, 'Re-thinking Politics in Southern Africa Today: Elements of A Critique of Political Liberalism', in N. Gibson, ed., *Social Movements in South Africa and the Quest for a New Humanity*, New York: Africa World Press, Forthcoming.

Neocosmos, M. 2007, *Civil Society, Citizenship and the Politics of the (Im)possible: Rethinking militancy in Africa today*, Report for the CODESRIA MWG on Citizenship (forthcoming CODESRIA, 2009). http://abahlali.org/node/1429

Neocosmos, M. 2008, "The Politics of Fear and the Fear of Politics: reflections on xenophobic violence in South Africa" *Journal of Asian and African Studies*, Volume 43, Number 6, December.

Nyamnjoh, F., 2006, *Insiders and Outsiders: Citizenship and Xenophobia in Contemporary Southern Africa*, London: Zed Press, Dakar: CODESRIA.

Olukoshi, A. O. and Laakso, L., eds., 1996, *Challenges to the Nation State in Africa*, Nordic African Institute and IDS, University of Helsinki.

O'Meara, D., 1983, *Volkskapitalisme: Class, Capital and Ideology in the Development of Afrikaner Nationalism 1934-1948*, Johannesburg: Ravan.

Orkin, M., 1995, 'Building Democracy in the New South Africa: Civil Society, Citizenship and Political Ideology', *Review of African Political Economy*, No. 66.

Quinlan, T., 1986, 'The Tribal Paradigm and Ethnic Nationalism: A Case Study of Political Structures in Qwaqwa', *Transformation* No. 2.

Pae, Tüsetso, 1992, 'Labour Migration and the Differentiation of the Peasantry in a Lesotho Village', B.Ed. Dissertation, National University of Lesotho.

Peberdy, S. A. and Crush, J., 1998, 'Rooted in Racism: The Origins of the Aliens Control Act', in J. Crush, ed., *Beyond Control: Immigration and Human Rights in a Democratic South Africa*, Cape Town: IDASA.

Pithouse, R., 2008, 'Elections: A Dangerous Time for Poor People's Movements in South Africa', *The South African Civil Society Information Service*, http://sacsis.org.za/site/article/245.1

Rachik, H., 2000, 'Les Usages politiques des notions de tribu et de nation au Maroc', *Identity, Culture and Politics: An Afro-Asian Dialogue*, Vol. 1, No. 1.

Ramphele, M., 1993, *A Bed Called Home*, Cape Town: David Philip.

Ranger, T., 1985a, *Peasant Consciousness and Guerrilla War in Zimbabwe*, Harare: Zimbabwe Publishing House.

Ranger, T., 1985b, *The Invention of Tribalism in Zimbabwe,* Gweru: Mambo Press.

Reitzes, M., 1997a, 'Undocumented Migration: Dimensions and Dilemmas', SAMP, www.queensu.ca/samp/transform/Reitzes1.htm.

Reitzes, M., 1997b, 'Speaking with Many Voices: South African Immigration Policy, April 1994-December 1995', University of Cambridge, Global Security Fellows Initiative, Occasional Paper No. 7.

Republic of South Africa, 1995, President's Office: South African Citizenship Act, 1995.

Republic of South Africa, Department of Home Affairs, Circular Number 9, 1995.

Republic of South Africa, 1996, *Restructuring the Labour Market: Report of the Presidential Commission to Investigate Labour Market Policy* (South African Labour Market Commission Report).

Republic of South Africa, 1999, Draft White Paper on International Migration.

Roy, A., 2008, 'The Monster in the Mirror' *The Guardian,* December 13th, http:// guardian.co.uk/world/2008/dec/12/mumbai-arundhati-roy

Saint-Just, A. L., 2004, 'Essai de Constitution', in *Oeuvres Complètes,* Paris: Gallimard.

SADC (Southern African Development Community), 1995, Draft Protocol on the Free Movement of Persons in the SADC Region, June.

SAMP (Southern African Migration Project), 2001a, 'The South African White Paper on International Migration: An Analysis and Critique', *Migration Policy Brief,* No. 1, SAMP.

SAMP, 2001b, 'The New South African Immigration Bill: A Legal Analysis', Migration Policy Brief No. 2, SAMP.

SAMP, 2001c, 'Making Up the Numbers: Measuring "Illegal Immigration" to South Africa', Migration Policy Brief No. 3, SAMP.

SAMP, 2002, 'Transnationalism and African Immigration to South Africa, Migration Policy', Brief No. 9, SAMP.

SAMP, n.d., 'Criminal Tendencies: Immigrants and Illegality in South Africa', Migration Policy Brief No. 10, SAMP.

SAMP, 2004, 'Policing Migration: Immigration Enforcement and Human Rights in South Africa', Migration Policy Brief No.14, SAMP.

SAMP, 2008 *The Perfect Storm: The Realities of Xenophobia in Contemporary South Africa,* SAMP: Migration Policy Series No. 50.

Saul, J. and Gelb, S., 1986, *The Crisis in South Africa,* London: Zed Books.

Schmidt, E., 1990, 'Negotiated Spaces and Contested Terrain: Men, Women, and the Law in Colonial Zimbabwe, 1890-1939', *Journal of Southern African Studies,* Vol. 16, No. 4, December.

Sechaba Consultants, 1996, Interviews with Miners in Welkom, 27 August 1996.

Seekings, J., 1989, 'People's Courts and Popular Politics', in Moss, G. and I. Obery , eds, *South African Review 5,* Johannesburg: Ravan.

Seekings, J., 2000, *The UDF: A History of the United Democratic Front of South Africa 1983-1991,* London: James Currey.

Selinyane, N. P., 1995, 'Structural Change and Social Welfare in the Economy of Lesotho: 1966-1993', Research Report, International Development Centre of Japan, March.

Selinyane, N. P., 1996a, 'Continuity and Change in State-Society Relations in Rural Lesotho: A Critical Historical Analysis', Faculty of Humanities Seminar, 28 November.

Selinyane, N. P., 1996b, 'Civil Society, Adjustment and Democracy in Lesotho: some perspectives', CASSAS Seminar NUL, April.

Selinyane, N. P., 1996c, 'Defending Fragile Democracy in the Post-Cold War: Lessons from Lesotho', *Mimeo*, January.

Sharp, J. 2008, '"Fortress SA': Xenophobic Violence in South Africa" *Anthropology Today* Volume 24, number 4, August, Guest Editorial.

Sichone, O., 2001, 'The Making of Makwerekwere: East Africans in Cape Town', Paper for the workshop Interrogating the New Political Culture in Southern Africa: Ideas and Institutions, Harare, Sheraton Hotel, 13-15 June.

Sichone, O. 2008, 'Xenophobia and Xenophilia in South Africa: African Migrants in Cape Town' in P. Werbner (ed.) *Anthropology and the New Cosmopolitanism: Rooted, Feminist and Vernacular Perspectives*, Oxford: Berg Publishers.

Sisulu, Z., 1986, 'People's Education for People's Power', *Transformation*, No. 1.

Slovo, J., 1976, 'South Africa: no middle road', in Davidson, B. et al., *Southern Africa: The New Politics of Revolution*, Harmondsworth: Penguin.

South African Human Rights Commission, 1999, 'Report into the Arrest and Detention of Persons in Terms of the Aliens Control Act', Johannesburg: South African Human Rights Commission.

South African Human Rights Commission, 2000, 'Lindela at the Crossroads for Detention and Repatriation: An Assessment of the Conditions of Detention by the South African Human Rights Commission', Johannesburg: December.

South African Institute of Race Relations, 1986, *Race Relations Survey*, 1985, Johannesburg: SAIRR.

Suttner, R. and Cronin, J., 1986, *Thirty Years of the Freedom Charter*, Johannesburg: Ravan.

Swilling, M., 1984, 'Workers Divided: a critical assessment of the split in MAWU on the East Rand', *South African Labour Bulletin*, Vol. 10, No. 1, August/September.

Swilling, M., 1988, 'The United Democratic Front and Township Revolt', in Cobbett, W. and Cohen, R., eds, *Popular Struggles in South Africa*, London: James Currey.

Tshitereke, C., 1999, 'Xenophobia and Relative Deprivation', *Crossings*, Vol.3, No. 2.

United Democratic Front, 1985, *Isizwe, the Nation*, Vol. 1, No. 1.

United Democratic Front, 1986, *Isizwe, the Nation*, Vol. 1, No. 2.

United Democratic Front, Cape Town Area Committee, 1986, 'Broadening the Base', Discussion Document.

Union Government of South Africa, (UGSA), 1932, *Report of the Native Economic Commission, 1930-1932*, Pretoria, UG 22 1932.

Vail, L. and White, L., 1980, *Capitalism and Colonialism in Mozambique*, London.

Vail, L., ed., 1989a, *The Creation of Tribalism in Southern Africa*, London: James Currey.

Vail, L., 1989b, 'Introduction: Ethnicity in Southern African History', in Vail, L., ed., *The Creation of Tribalism in Southern Africa*, London: James Currey.

Valji, N., 2003, 'Creating the Nation: The Rise of Violent Xenophobia in the New South Africa', CSVR, Centre for the Study of Violence and Reconciliation, July.

Van der Wiel, A., 1977, *Migratory Wage Labour: Its Role in the Economy of Lesotho*, Mazenod: Mazenod Book Centre.

Van Kessel, I., *'Beyond Our Wildest Dreams': The United Democratic Front and the Transformation of South Africa*, Charlottesville: University of Virginia Press.

Vigneswaran, D. 2008, *A Foot in the Door: Access to Asylum in South Africa*, Migration Studies Working Paper Series #40 Forced Migration Studies Program University of the Witwatersrand http://migration.org.za

Wamba-dia-Wamba, E., 1994, 'Africa in Search of a New Mode of Politics', in H. Himmelstrand, ed., *African Perspectives on Development*, London: James Currey.

Webster, E., 1988, 'The Rise of Social Movement Unionism: The Two Faces of the Black Trade Union Movement in South Africa', in P. Frankel et al., State, *Resistance and Change in South Africa*, Johannesburg: Southern Book Publishers.

Welsh, D., 1968, 'The State President's Powers Under the Bantu Administration Act', *Acta Juridica*.

Williams, V., 1997, 'Green Paper Signals Break With Racist Past', *Crossings*, Vol. 1, No.1., http://www.queensu.ca/samp/.

Williams, V., 2002, 'Draft Submission by Vincent Williams', Immigration Bill: Public Hearings, Home Affairs Portfolio Committee; Social Services Select Committee: Joint Meeting, 18 April; South African Parliament.

Wilson, F., 1972, *Migrant Labour in South Africa*, Johannesburg: South African Council of Churches.

Wilson, F. and Ramphele, M., 1989, *Uprooting Poverty: the South African Challenge*, Cape Town: David Philip.

Wilson, R. A., 2001, *The Politics of Truth and Reconciliation in South Africa*, Cambridge: Cambridge University Press.

Winai-Strom, G., 1984, 'Migration and Dependency', Uppsala: Nordic Institute for Africa.

Wolpe, H., 1972, 'Capitalism and Cheap Labour Power in South Africa: From Segregation to Apartheid', *Economy and Society*, 1, 4.

Wolpe, H., 1988, *Race, Class and the Apartheid State*, London: James Currey.

Yuval-Davies, N., and Werbner, P., eds., 1999, *Women, Citizenship and Difference*, London: Zed Books.

Zizek, S. 2008, *Violence*, London: Profile Books.

List of Interviews

1. Senegalese migrant, Sunnyside, 20 March 2003.
2. Senegalese businessman, Pretoria, Sammy Marks Square, 25 March 2003.
3. Cameroonian entrepreneur, Constantia Building, Pretoria, 26 March 2003.
4. Cameroonian traditional doctor, Sunnyside, 30 March 2003.
5. Ghanaian immigrant, Esselen Street, Sunnyside Pretoria, 30 March 2003.
6. Cameroonian businesswoman, Pretoria City Centre, Prinsloo Street, 3 April 2003.
7. Cameroonian hairdresser, Sunnyside, Pretoria, 5 April 2003.
8. Ivorian barber, Sunnyside, Pretoria, 5 April 2003.
9. Cameroonian hairdresser, Sunnyside, Pretoria, 7 April, 2003.
10. Ghanaian woman hairdresser, Sunnyside, Pretoria, 7 April 2003.
11. Ghanaian immigrant, Sunnyside, Pretoria, 8 April 2003.
12. Cameroonian salesperson, Sunnyside, Pretoria, 8 April 2003.
13. Cameroonian businessman, Pretoria West, 11 April 2003.
14. Young Nigerian businessman, Pretoria West, 9 April 2003.
15. Ghanaian businesswoman, Sunnyside, Pretoria, 12 April 2003.
16. Nigerian consultant, Sunnyside, Pretoria, 15 April 2003.
17. Cameroonian businessman, Sunnyside, Pretoria, 20 April 2003.
18. Shop-owner from Sierra Leone, Biccard Street, Braamfontein, Johannesburg, 21-24 April 2003.
20. Nigerian salesperson, Biccard Street, Braamfontein, Johannesburg, 23 April 2003.
21. Cameroonian immigrant, Biccard Street, Braamfontein, Johannesburg, 23 April 2003.
22. Cameroonian businesswoman, Biccard Street, Braamfontein, Johannesburg, 24 April 2003.
23. Nigerian artist, Braamfontein, Johannesburg, 24 April 2003.
24. Nigerian woman, Esselen Street, Sunnyside, Pretoria. 24 April 2003.
25. Cameroonian female migrant, Esselen Street, Sunnyside, Pretoria, 24 April 2003.
26. Cameroonian male migrant, Pretoria, Central Town, 28 April 2003.
27. Malian immigrant, Johannesburg inner city, 24 July 2003.
28. Two Senegalese designers, Johannesburg City, 26 August 2003.
29. Three Eritrean students, Hatfield, Pretoria, 6 August 2003.

30. Kenyan student, Hatfield, Pretoria, 10 August 2003.

31. Zambian immigrant, Braamfontein, Johannesburg, 12 August 2003.

32. Kenyan immigrant, Braamfontein, Johannesburg, 12 August 2003.

33. Zimbabwean lady, Braamfontein, Johannesburg, 13 August 2003.

34. Tanzanian businessman, Braamfontein, Johannesburg, 13 August 2003.